American women dramatists
of the twentieth century:
a bibliography

by Brenda Coven

THE SCARECROW PRESS, INC.
Metuchen, N.J., & London 1982

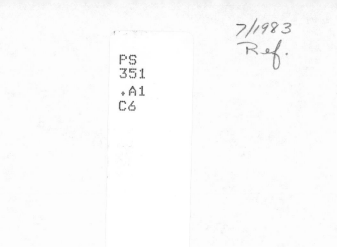
Library of Congress Cataloging in Publication Data

Coven, Brenda, 1940-
   American women dramatists of the twentieth
century.

   Includes index.
   1. American drama--Women authors--Bibliography.
2. American drama--20th century--Bibliography.
I. Title.
Z1231.D7C68   1982   016.812'5'099287   82-5942
[PS351]   AACR2
ISBN 0-8108-1562-1

CONTENTS

INTRODUCTION

This is a bibliography of one hundred and thirty-three of the most
important twentieth-century American women dramatists. All of
the playwrights have had at least one play successfully produced on
the New York stage, either on or off Broadway. They were selected for inclusion as being representative of other women playwrights writing at the same time.

The book is divided into two sections. The first is a selected bibliography of journal, magazine, and newspaper articles;
chapters in books; and dissertations on the general subject of American women dramatists. This listing is meant to serve as an introduction to the main part of this book, which consists of the one
hundred and thirty-three individual bibliographies. For each playwright the following information is provided:

1. Playwright's name and dates.

2. Play titles. Plays are listed alphabetically. Publication
   information for the earliest published edition is cited. If
   the play has been included in a journal or an anthology, full
   bibliographic information is provided. The place and year
   of the play's first professional production is given if known.

3. Biographical information. Material has been selected for its
   comprehensive treatment of the playwright. Consequently,
   books and journal articles have been favored over biographical directories. Biographical directories and other literary
   handbooks are cited only when no other material exists.

4. Criticism and reviews. Selected general criticism is provided whenever possible. For the majority of playwrights,
   however, there is no published criticism other than the original theater critics' reviews. Play reviews are usually for
   the play's first professional production.

AMERICAN WOMEN DRAMATISTS
OF THE TWENTIETH CENTURY:
A Bibliography

SELECTED BIBLIOGRAPHY

Barlow, Judith E. Plays by American Women: The Early Years.
New York: Avon, 1981.

"Black Women Star Behind Scenes in New York Drama." Ebony,
28 (April 1973), 106-8+.

Brown, Janet. Feminist Drama; Definition and Critical Analysis.
Metuchen, N. J.: Scarecrow, 1979.

Burns, S. "Sketches of Several Women Dramatists." Green Book
Album, 4 (September 1910), 632-9.

→ Convocation: Women in Writing. Valerie Harms, ed. Tampa, Fla.:
United Sisters, 1975. (This account of the 1974 Writers Confer-
ence sponsored by NOW includes comments by Megan Terry on
women playwrights.)

Dale, A. "Women Playwrights: Their Contribution Has Enriched
the Stage." Delineator, 90 (February 1917), 7.

Deak, Norma J., and Frantisek Deak. "Anna Halprin's Theater
and Therapy Workshop." Drama Review, 20 (1976), 50-4.

"Earth Onion Scrapbook." Off Our Backs, 2 (October 1971), 2-5.
(Women's improvisational theater.)

⇒ Edmunds, Lynne. "Why Aren't There More Women Writing for the
Stage?" Daily Telegraph, June 12, 1974, p. 17.

Ferguson, Phyllis Marschall. "Women Dramatists in the American
Theatre, 1901-1940." Ph.D. dissertation, University of Pittsburgh, 1957.

"Five Important Playwrights Talk About Theatre Without Compromise
and Sexism." Mademoiselle, 75 (August 1972), 288-9+.

Frame, Virginia. "Successful Women Dramatists." Theatre, 6
(October 1906), 265-6+.

France, Rachel, ed. A Century of Plays by American Women. New York: Richards Rosen, 1979.

Fratti, Mario. "Interview with Ellen Stewart." Drama and Theatre, 8 (1970), 87-9. (Stewart is the founder of LaMama.)

Funke, Lewis. "Broadway Husband-and-Wife Teams." New York Times Magazine, Jan. 12, 1947, pp. 18-9.

Funke, Lewis. Playwrights Talk About Writing. Chicago: Dramatic Publishing, 1975, pp. 89-110, 285-307. (Interviews with Lillian Hellman and Jean Kerr.)

Gelderman, Carol W. "The Male Nature of Tragedy." Prairie Schooner, 49 (Fall 1975), 220-226.

Gillespie, Patti. "A Listing of Feminist Theatres." Theatre News, 10 (November 1977), 22-24.

Gottlieb, Lois C. "Double Standard Debate in Early Twentieth Century American Drama." Michigan Academician, 7 (Spring 1975), 441-51.

Goulianos, Joan. "Women and the Avant-Garde Theater: Interviews with Rochelle Owens, Crystal Field, Rosalyn Drexler." Massachusetts Review, 13 (1972), 257-67.

Gussow, Mel. "Stage: 'Choices,' Women's Anthology." New York Times, Dec. 11, 1978, sec. C, 17:3. (A project of the American Place Theater to encourage the development of women playwrights and directors.)

Gussow, Mel. "Women Playwrights Show New Strength." New York Times, Feb. 15, 1981, Sec. II, 4:3.

Gussow, Mel. "Women Write New Chapter in the Theater." New York Times, June 8, 1979, sec. C, 3:3.

Hewes, H. "LaMama Complex." Saturday Review, 52 (April 19, 1969), 53-4.

Hewes, H. "Spirit Power: Women Theatrical Directors." Saturday Review, 52 (Feb. 8, 1969), 41.

Hoffman, E. "Women's Theatre." Ann Arbor (The Sun), 2, 16 (Aug. 9, 1974), 6.

Houghton, Norris. "It's a Woman's World." Theatre Arts, 31 (January 1947), 31.

Hughes, Charlotte. "Women Playmakers." New York Times Magazine, May 4, 1941, p. 10.

Kalson, H. "Women/Theatre." Herself, 3, (August 1974), 13.

Killian, Linda. "Feminist Theatre." Feminist Art Journal, 3 (Spring 1974), 23-4.

Kriegel, Harriet, ed. Women in Drama: An Anthology. New York: New American Library, 1975.

Kroll, J. "Life with LaMama: First Four Productions in Its New House." Newsweek, 73 (April 28, 1969), 109.

Lamb, Margaret. "Feminist Criticism." Drama Review, 18 (September 1974), 46-50.

Lask, Thomas. "Echoes of American Women Dramatists." New York Times, March 10, 1978, sec. C, 2:3.

LaTempa, Susan, ed. New Plays by Women. Berkeley, Calif.: Shameless Hussy, 1979.

Lewis, Barbara. "What's $80,000 Split 35 Ways?" Ms., 7 (May 1979), 71. (Discusses a grant to women playwrights and directors.)

Little, Stuart W. Off-Broadway: Prophetic Theater. New York: Coward, McCann, & Geoghegan, 1972, pp. 184-98. (Discusses LaMama.)

Longergan, Elizabeth. "Women Who Write Plays." Strand (New York), 41 (June 1911), 594-601.

Lowell, Sandra. "New Feminist Theater." Ms., 1 (August 1972), 17-23.

MacKay, Barbara. "Women on the Rocks." Saturday Review World, April 6, 1974, pp. 48-9.

McKown, R. "Where Are the Women Dramatists?" Theatre World, 17 (June 1932), 280.

Mantle, Robert B. Contemporary American Playwrights. New York: Dodd, Mead, 1938, pp. 227-40. (Discusses the works of collaborating playwrights including husband-and-wife teams.)

Matthews, Brander. A Book About the Theater. New York: Scribner, 1916, pp. 111-25. (Chapter on women dramatists.)

"Men Fading Out of the Play." Literary Digest, 114 (Dec. 24, 1932), 14-5.

Mersand, Joseph. "When Ladies Write Plays." American Drama, 1930-1940; Essays on Playwrights and Plays. New York: Modern Chapbooks, 1941, pp. 145-61.

Mersand, Joseph. "Woman's Contribution to American Drama." Players Magazine, 14 (September/October 1937), 7-8+.

Molette, Barbara. "They Speak. Who Listens? Black Women Playwrights." Black World, 25, 6 (1976), 28-34.

Moore, Honor. "Theater Will Never Be the Same." Ms., 6 (December 1977), 36-9.

Moore, Honor, ed. The New Women's Theatre: Ten Plays by Contemporary American Women. New York: Random House, 1977.

Nathan, George Jean. Entertainment of a Nation; or, Three Sheets in the Wind. New York: Knopf, 1942, pp. 34-41. (Chapter on the status of women playwrights.)

Nathan, George Jean. "Playwrights in Petticoats." American Mercury, 52 (June 1941), 750-5.

Olauson, Judith. The American Women Playwright: A View of Criticism and Characterization. Troy, N.Y.: Whitston, 1981.

Perinciolo, L. "Feminist Theater: They're Playing in Peoria." Ms., 4 (October 1975), 101-4.

Pierce, Lucy F. "Women Dramatists." Green Book Album, 7 (May 1912), 1058-64.

Pierce, Lucy F. "Women Who Write Plays." World Today, 15 (July 1908), 725-31.

Pocock, L. "New York Feminist Theatre." Majority Report, 4, 12 (Oct. 3, 1974), 10.

Rea, Charlotte. "New York Feminist Theatre Troupe." Drama Review, 18 (September 1974), 132-3.

Rea, Charlotte. "Women for Women." Drama Review, 18 (December 1974), 77-87.

Rea, Charlotte. "Women's Theatre Groups." Drama Review, 16 (June 1972), 79-89.

Regelson, Rosalyn. "Is Motherhood Holy? Not Any More." New York Times, May 18, 1969, sec. II, 1:4. (Article on the new feminist repertory.)

Richardson, Anna S. "Rise of the Woman Playwright." McClure, 49 (December 1917), 13+.

Richardson, Anna S. "Woman-Made Season." McClure, 46 (April 1916), 22-3.

Schroeder, Robert. "Symposium: the Woman Playwright." Dramatists Guild Quarterly, 9 (Spring 1972), 45-7.

Stasio, Marilyn. "The Night the Critics Lost Their Cool." Ms.,
4 (September 1975), 37-41. (The reviewing of women playwrights.)

Sullivan, Victoria, and James Hatch, eds. Plays By and About
Women: An Anthology. New York: Random House, 1973.

Suntree, Susan. "Women's Theatre: Creating the Dream Now."
In Women's Culture: The Women's Renaissance of the Seventies.
Metuchen, N.J.: Scarecrow, 1981.

Sutherland, C. "American Women Playwrights as Mediators of the
'Woman Problem.'" Modern Drama, 21 (September 1978), 319-
36.

"Symposium: Women and Tragedy." Prairie Schooner, 49 (Fall
1975), 227-36.

Von Wien, F. "Playwrights Who Are Women." Independent Woman,
25 (January 1946), 12-4.

Weissberg, K. "Earth Onion." Off Our Backs, 1, 23 (June 24,
1971), 22. (Women's improvisational theater.)

"Women and the American Theatre." Nation, 106 (June 1, 1918),
665.

"Women Playwrights." Living Age, 320 (March 1, 1924), 430-1.

"Women Playwrights--A Symposium." Books Abroad, 22, 1 (1948),
16-21.

Zastrow, Sylvia V. H. "The Structure of Selected Plays of American Women Playwrights: 1920-1970." Ph.D. dissertation.
Northwestern University, 1975.

LIST OF DRAMATISTS

Zoë Akins

Maya Angelou

Bernadine Angus

Mary Austin

Marjorie Barkentin

Anna Marie Barlow

Djuna Barnes

Margaret Ayer Barnes

Marie Baumer

Dorothy Bennett

Sally Benson

Gertrude Berg

Julie Bovasso

Jane Bowles

Lillian T. Bradley

Alice Brown

Anne Burr

Anne Caldwell

Vinette Carroll

Rosemary Casey

Vera Caspary

Mary Chase

Alice Childress

Betty Comden

Rachel Crothers

Gretchen Cryer

Catherine C. Cushing

Katharine Dayton

Dorothy Donnelly

Rosalyn Drexler

Shirley DuBois

Edith Ellis

Phoebe Ephron

Mary Helen Fay

Edna Ferber

Dorothy Fields

Eva K. Flint

Harriet Ford

Nancy Ford

Maria Irene Fornes

Rose Franken

Jennie Elizabeth Franklin

Ketti Frings

Zona Gale

Barbara Garson

Eleanor Gates

Alice Gerstenberg

Susan Glaspell

Ruth G. Goetz

Frances Goodrich

Ruth Gordon

Micki Grant

9

Nancy Hamilton

Lorraine Hansberry

Fanny L. Hatton

Theresa Helburn

Lillian Hellman

Beth Henley

Dorothy H. Heyward

Jane Hinton

Tina Howe

Gladys Hurlbut

Fannie Hurst

Corinne L. Jacker

Elsie Janis

Elinor Jones

Fay Kanin

Beatrice Kaufman

Molly Kazan

Adrienne Kennedy

Jean Kerr

Clare Kummer

Myrna Lamb

Isobel Lennart

Anita Loos

Clare Boothe Luce

Carson McCullers

Elizabeth A. McFadden

Kate L. McLaurin

Martha Madison

Marya Mannes

Armina Marshall

Adelaide Matthews

Elaine May

Margaret Mayo

Abby Merchant

Eva Merriam

Annie Nathan Meyer

Elizabeth Miele

Edna St. Vincent Millay

Alice D. Miller

Fanny T. Mitchell

Norma Mitchell

Honor Moore

Anne Morrison

Susan Nanus

Anne Nichols

Frances Nordstrom

Marsha Norman

Joyce Carol Oates

Mary Orr

Rochelle Owens

Dorothy Parker

Josephine Peabody

Olga Printzlau

Gertrude Purcell

Sylvia Regan

Muriel Resnik

Molly Ricardel

Mary Roberts Rinehart

Amelie Rives

Aurania Rouverol

Florence Ryerson

Zelda Sears

Ntozake Shange

Elsa Shelley

Viola B. Shores

Cornelia Otis Skinner

Bella Spewack

Martha Stanley

Gertrude Stein

Elizabeth Swados

Renée Taylor

Megan Terry

Gertrude Tonkonogy

Sophie Treadwell

Gladys B. Unger

Lula Vollmer

Wendy Wasserstein

Maurine Dallas Watkins

Mae West

Susan Yankowitz

Rida J. Young

AKINS, ZOË (1886-1958)

Plays

Another Darling, A Comedy. New York, 1950. Typescript carbon
copy at the library at Ohio State University.

Crown Prince. Unpublished. Produced Broadway, 1927.

Daddy's Gone a-Hunting. First published in: Everybody's Magazine,
45 (December 1921), 93-100. Also in: Akins, Zoë. Déclassée:
Daddy's Gone a-Hunting: and Greatness--A Comedy. New York:
Boni & Liveright, 1923. Produced Broadway, 1921.

Déclassée. In: Akins, Zoë. Déclassée: Daddy's Gone a-Hunting:
and Greatness--A Comedy. New York: Boni & Liveright, 1923.
Also in: Mantle, Robert B., ed. Best Plays of 1919-1920.
Boston: Small, 1920. (Condensation.) Produced Broadway, 1919.

Did It Really Happen? Published in: Smart Set, 52 (May 1917),
343-52. Never produced on the professional stage.

First Love. Unpublished. Produced Broadway, 1926.

Foot-Loose. Unpublished. Produced Broadway, 1919.

The Furies. Unpublished. Produced Broadway, 1928.

Greatness. Variant title of Texas Nightingale. In: Akins, Zoë.
Déclassée: Daddy's Gone a-Hunting: and Greatness--A Comedy.
New York: Boni & Liveright, 1923.

The Greeks Had a Word for It. Unpublished. Produced Broadway,
1930.

The Happy Days. Adapted from a play by Claude-Andre Puget. New York: French, 1942. Produced Broadway, 1941.

The Human Element, A Play in Three Acts. Adapted from a short story by Somerset Maugham. New York, 1933. Typewritten carbon copy at the Library of Congress and several other academic libraries.

I Am Different. Unpublished. Produced Hollywood, 1938.

Little Miracles. New York: Harper, 1936. Also in: Ladies Home Journal, 53 (April 1936), 30-1+. Never produced on the professional stage.

The Love Duel. Unpublished. Produced Broadway, 1929.

Magical City (Broadway Legend), A One Act Play in Free Verse. In: Forum, 55 (May 1916), 507-50. Never produced on the professional stage.

Moon-Flower. n. p., 1924 (?). Only copy at the Library of Congress. Produced Broadway, 1924.

Mrs. January and Mr. Ex, A Comedy in Three Acts. New York: French, 1948. Produced Broadway, 1944.

O Evening Star. Unpublished. Produced Broadway, 1936.

Old Maid. New York: Appleton-Century, 1935. Also in: Mantle, Robert B., ed. Best Plays of 1934-1935. New York: Dodd, Mead, 1935. (Condensation.) Produced Broadway, 1935.

Papa, An Amorality in Three Acts. New York: Kennerley, 1913. Produced Broadway, 1919.

Pardon My Glove. Unpublished. Produced Rochester, N. Y., 1926.

The Portrait of Tiero, A Drama in One Act. First published in: Theatre Arts Magazine, 4 (October 1920), 316-37. Also in: Isaacs, Edith J., ed. Plays of American Life and Fantasy. New York: Coward, McCann, 1929. Never produced on the professional stage.

A Royal Fandango. Unpublished. Produced Broadway, 1923.

Starvation on Red River; A Play in Three Acts. New York: Rialto Service Bureau, 19-. Unfinished typescript at the New York Public Library. Never produced on the professional stage.

Such a Charming Young Man, A Comedy in One Act. First published in: Smart Set, 48 (1916), 67-78. Also in: Thomas, Augustus, ed. One-Act Plays for Stage and Study. Series 1. New York: French, 1924. Never produced on the professional stage.

The Swallows Nest. Unpublished.

The Texas Nightingale. Variant title of Greatness. Produced
  Broadway, 1922.

Thou Desperate Pilot. Unpublished. Produced Broadway, 1927.

The Varying Shore. Unpublished. Produced Broadway, 1921.

Biography

Cranmer, Catherine. "Little Visits with Literary Missourians."
  Missouri Historical Review, 20 (January 1926), 253-61.

Kunitz, Stanley J., and Howard Haycraft, eds. Twentieth Century
  Authors; A Biographical Dictionary of Modern Literature. New
  York: H. W. Wilson, 1942.

New York Times, Oct. 30, 1958, p. 31. (Obituary.)

Criticism

Dickinson, Thomas H. Playwrights of the New American Theater.
  New York: Macmillan, 1925, pp. 208-18.

Quinn, Arthur H. A History of the American Drama from the Civil
  War to the Present Day. Vol. 1: From William Vaughan Moody
  to the Present Day. New York: Harper, 1927, pp. 141-4.

Reviews

New York Times, March 24, 1927, 23:2. [Crown Prince.]

Nation, 113 (Sept. 21, 1921), 324-5. [Daddy's Gone a-Hunting.]

New York Times, Sept. 1, 1921, 18:3. [Daddy's Gone a-Hunting.]

New Republic, 22 (March 17, 1920), 95. [Déclassée.]

New York Times, Oct. 7, 1919, 22:1. [Déclassée.]

New York Times, Nov. 9, 1926, 31:2. [First Love.]

New York Times, May 11, 1920, 12:1. [Foot-Loose.]

New Republic, 54 (March 21, 1928), 155-6. [The Furies.]

New York Times, March 8, 1928, 23:1. [The Furies.]

New York Times, Sept. 26, 1930, 16:5. [The Greeks Had a
  Word for It.]

New York Times, May 14, 1941, 24:2. [The Happy Days.]

New York Times, Aug. 28, 1938, sec. IX, 2:5. [I Am Different.]

New York Times, April 16, 1929, 32:3. [The Love Duel.]

Current Opinion, 60 (May 1916), 331. [Magical City.]

Independent, 112 (April 26, 1924), 231-2. [Moon-Flower.]

New York Times, Feb. 26, 1924, 15:1. [Moon-Flower.]

New Republic, 110 (April 17, 1944), 532. [Mrs. January....]

New York Times, April 1, 1944, 10:2. [Mrs. January....]

Commonweal, 23 (Jan. 24, 1936), 356. [O Evening Star.]

New York Times, Jan. 9, 1936, 24:6. [O Evening Star.]

New Republic, 82 (March 20, 1935), 162. [Old Maid.]

New York Times, April 11, 1919, 9:5. [Papa.]

New York Times, May 23, 1926, sec. VIII, 1:1. [Pardon My Glove.]

Independent, 111 (Nov. 24, 1923), 257. [A Royal Fandango.]

New York Times, Nov. 13, 1923, 25:1. [A Royal Fandango.]

Life, 80 (Dec. 14, 1922), 18. [The Texas Nightingale.]

New York Times, Nov. 21, 1922, 15:2. [The Texas Nightingale.]

New York Times, March 8, 1927, 23:1. [Thou Desperate Pilot.]

Life, 78 (Dec. 22, 1921), 18. [The Varying Shore.]

New York Times, Dec. 6, 1921, 24:1. [The Varying Shore.]

ANGELOU, MAYA (1928-   )

Plays

Adoja Amissah. Written 1967. Unpublished. Never produced.

Ajax. Unpublished. Produced in Los Angeles, 1974.

And Still I Rise! Unpublished. Produced in Oakland, Calif., 1976.

The Best of These. Unpublished. Produced in Los Angeles, 1966.

Cabaret for Freedom. Written with Godfrey Cambridge. Unpublished.
   Produced off-Broadway, 1960.

The Clawing Within. Written 1966-67. Unpublished. Never produced.

Biography

Angelou, Maya. Gather Together in My Name. New York: Random
   House, 1974. (Autobiography.)

Angelou, Maya. I Know Why the Caged Bird Sings. New York:
   Random House, 1970. (Autobiography.)

Current Biography Yearbook 1974. New York: H.W. Wilson, 1974.

Elliot, J. M. "Maya Angelou: In Search of Self." Negro History
   Bulletin, 40 (May 1977), 694-5.

Review

"Cabaret for Freedom ... Smash Hit at Village Gate." Jet, Nov. 17,
   1960, p. 61.

ANGUS, BERNADINE

Plays

Angel Island. ©1937. Unpublished. Produced Broadway, 1937.

Brown Sugar. ©1937. Unpublished. Produced Broadway, 1937.

Pie in the Sky. Unpublished. Produced Broadway, 1941.

Reviews

Nation, 145 (Oct. 30, 1937), 484. [Angel Island.]

New York Times, Oct. 21, 1937, 26:2. [Angel Island.]

Time, 30 (Nov. 1, 1937), 30. [Angel Island.]

New York Times, Dec. 3, 1937, 29:2. [Brown Sugar.]

New York Times, Dec. 23, 1941, 26:5. [Pie in the Sky.]

AUSTIN, MARY (HUNTER) (1868-1934)

Plays

Arrow Maker; A Drama in Three Acts. New York: Duffield, 1911.
Produced Broadway, 1911.

Fire; A Drama in Three Acts. In: Play Book, 2 (October 1914),
1-25. Never produced on the professional stage.

The Man Who Didn't Believe in Christmas. In: St. Nicholas, 45,
2 (December 1917), 156+. Also published in 1969 by Ford Press
in Hong Kong. Never produced on the professional stage.

Merry Christmas, Daddy. Unpublished. Produced Broadway, 1916.

Sekala Ka'ajma. In: Theatre Arts Monthly, 13 (April 1929), 265-
78. Never produced on the professional stage.

Biography

Austin, Mary. Earth Horizon. Boston: Houghton Mifflin, 1932.
(Autobiography.)

Kunitz, Stanley J., and Howard Haycraft, eds. Twentieth Century
Authors; A Biographical Dictionary of Modern Literature. New
York: H.W. Wilson, 1942.

Pearce, T. M. "Mary Austin and the Pattern of New Mexico."
Southwest Review, 22 (Winter 1937), 140-8.

Criticism

Berry, J. Wilkes. "Characterization in Mary Austin's Southwest
Works." Southwestern American Literature, 2 (1972), 119-24.

Lyday, Jo W. Mary Austin: the Southwest Works. Austin, Texas:
Steck-Vaughan, 1968.

Wynn, Dudley. "Mary Austin, Woman Alone." Virginia Quarterly
Review, 13 (Spring 1937), 243-56.

Reviews

Bellman, 11 (July 22, 1911), 114. [Arrow Maker.]

Life, 57 (March 16, 1911), 536. [Arrow Maker.]

New York Times, March 5, 1911, sec. VII, 2:1. [Arrow Maker.]

New York Dramatic Mirror, 77 (Jan. 6, 1917), 7. [Merry Christmas, Daddy.]

BARKENTIN, MARJORIE (1891?-1974)

Plays

Ulysses in Nighttown. James Joyce's Ulysses in Nighttown; Dramatized and Transposed. New York: Random House, 1958. Also
in: Cordell, Richard A. , and Lowell Matson. The Off-Broadway
Theatre; Seven Plays. New York: Random House, 1959. Produced off-Broadway, 1958; Broadway, 1974.

Biography

New York Times, Feb. 28, 1974, p. 40. (Obituary.)

Reviews

Commentary, 57 (June 1974), 78-9. [Ulysses in Nighttown.]

New Republic, 170 (April 6, 1974), 22+. [Ulysses in Nighttown.]

New York Times, June 6, 1958, 30:1. [Ulysses in Nighttown.]

Theatre Arts, 42 (January 1959), 57-61+. [Ulysses in Nighttown.]

Time, 103 (March 25, 1974), 75. [Ulysses in Nighttown.]

BARLOW, ANNA MARIE

Plays

Ambassador. Musical comedy. Book by Anna M. Barlow and Don
Ettlinger. Music by Don Gohman. Lyrics by Hal Hackady.
Based on the novel by Henry James. Unpublished. Produced
Broadway, 1972.

The Artists. Unpublished. Never produced on the professional
stage.

The Bicycle Riders. Unpublished. Never produced on the professional stage.

Cold Christmas. Unpublished. Never produced on the professional
stage.

Cruising Speed 600 MPH. Unpublished. Produced off-Broadway,
1970.

Ferryboat; A One Act Play. New York: Dramatists Play Service,
1971. Produced off-Broadway.

The Frizzly Hen. Unpublished. Produced off-Broadway.

Glory! Hallelujah! Unpublished. Produced San Francisco, 1969.

Half-Past Wednesday. Unpublished. Produced off-Broadway, 1962.

A Limb of Snow. In: Barlow, Anna M. A Limb of Snow, and The
Meeting. New York: Dramatists Play Service, 1969. Produced
off-Broadway, 1967.

The Meeting. In: Barlow, Anna M. A Limb of Snow, and The
Meeting. New York: Dramatists Play Service, 1969. Produced
off-Broadway, 1969.

Mr. Biggs. In: Corrigan, Robert W., ed. New American Plays.
Vol. 1. New York: Hill & Wang, 1965.

On Cobweb Twine. Unpublished. Produced Sea Cliff, Long Island.

Other Voices, Other Rooms. Dramatization of Truman Capote's
novel. Unpublished. Never produced on the professional stage.

Out of Track. Unpublished. Never produced on the professional
stage.

Spit in the Ocean. Unpublished. Never produced on the professional
  stage.

Taffy. Unpublished. Never produced on the professional stage.

Biography

National Playwrights Directory. Phyllis J. Kaye, ed. Waterford,
  Conn.: O'Neill Theater Center, 1977.

Reviews

New York Theatre Critics' Reviews, 33, 25 (1972), 177-8. [Am-
  bassador.]

New York Times, Nov. 20, 1972, 46:1. [Ambassador.]

New York Times, Jan. 6, 1970, 48:3. [Cruising Speed 600 MPH.]

Newsweek, 73 (June 9, 1969), 123. [Glory! Hallelujah!]

New York Times, April 17, 1962, 16:2. [Half-Past Wednesday.]

New York Times, Dec. 13, 1967, 55:1. [A Limb of Snow and The
  Meeting.]

BARNES, DJUNA (1892-)

Plays

The Antiphon; A Play. London: Faber & Faber, 1958. Also in:
  Barnes, Djuna. Selected Works: Spillway; The Antiphon; Night-
  wood. New York: Farrar, Straus, & Cudahy, 1962. Produced
  London, 1958.

The Dove. Unpublished. Produced off-Broadway, 1926.

An Irish Triangle. In: Playboy, 7 (1921), 3-5. Never produced.

Kurzy of the Sea. Carbon copy of typescript at the Library of Congress. Produced Provincetown, R.I., 1920.

A Passion Play. In: Others, 4 (February 1918), 5-17. Never produced.

She Tells Her Daughter. In: Smart Set, 72 (November 1923), 77-
  80. Never produced.

Three from the Earth. In: Little Review, 6 (November 1919), 3-
   15. Produced off-Broadway, 1920.

Biography

Contemporary Authors; A Bio-bibliographical Guide to Current Authors and Their Works. Clare D. Kinsman, ed. Vol. 9-12,
   first revision. Detroit: Gale, 1974.

Kunitz, Stanley J., and Howard Haycraft, eds. Twentieth Century
   Authors; A Biographical Dictionary of Modern Literature. New
   York: H. W. Wilson, 1942.

Scott, James B. Djuna Barnes. Boston: Twayne, 1976.

Criticism

Gerstenberger, Donna. "Three Verse Playwrights and the American
   Fifties." In: Taylor, William E., ed. Modern American Drama:
   Essays in Criticism. Deland, Fla.: Everett Edwards, 1968.

Kannenstine, Louis F. Art of Djuna Barnes: Duality and Damnation.
   New York: New York University Press, 1977.

Scott, James B. Djuna Barnes. Boston: Twayne, 1976.

Reviews

Times (London) Literary Supplement, April 4, 1958, p. 182. [The
   Antiphon.]

New York Times, May 7, 1926, 12:2. [The Dove.]

New York Times, April 4, 1920, sec. VI, 6:1. [Kurzy of the Sea.]

Freeman, 1 (June 1920), 283. [Three from the Earth.]

BARNES, MARGARET AYER (1886-1967)

Plays

Age of Innocence. Dramatization of the novel by Edith Wharton.
   Unpublished. Produced Broadway, 1928.

Dishonored Lady, A Play in Three Acts. Written with Edward Sheldon. New York, 1930. Microfilm copy of the typed manuscript
at the library at the University of California, Berkeley. Produced Broadway, 1930.

Jenny, A Play in Three Acts. Written with Edward Sheldon. New
York, 1929. Microfilm copy of the typed manuscript at the library at the University of California, Berkeley. Produced Broadway, 1929.

Biography

Kunitz, Stanley J., and Howard Haycraft, eds. Twentieth Century
Authors; A Biographical Dictionary of Modern Literature. New
York: H.W. Wilson, 1942.

Taylor, Lloyd C., Jr. Margaret Ayer Barnes. New York: Twayne,
1974.

Criticism

Taylor, Lloyd C., Jr. Margaret Ayer Barnes. New York: Twayne,
1974.

Reviews

Dial, 86 (February 1929), 172-3. [Age of Innocence.]

New Republic, 57 (Dec. 12, 1928), 96-7. [Age of Innocence.]

New Republic, 62 (Feb. 19, 1930), 20-1. [Dishonored Lady.]

New York Times, Feb. 5, 1930, 27:1. [Dishonored Lady.]

Catholic World, 130 (December 1929), 332-3. [Jenny.]

New York Times, Oct. 9, 1929, 34:4. [Jenny.]

BAUMER, MARIE (1905-   )

Plays

Creeping Fire; A Melodrama, in Three Acts and Six Scenes.   New

York, 1934. Xerox copy from a typewritten copy at the New York Public Library. Produced Broadway, 1935.

For Lack of a Nail; A Play for Victory, in One Act. In: Plays, 2 (October 1942), 63-68+. Never produced on the professional stage.

House of Remsen. Unpublished. Produced Broadway, 1934.

It's an Ill Wind; A Play in One Act. In: Rice, Elmer L. One Act Plays for Stage and Study. Fifth Series. New York: French, 1929. Never produced on the professional stage.

Jobyna Steps Out, A Comedy in Three Acts. New York: French, 1932. Never produced on the professional stage.

Little Brown Jug, A Drama in Three Acts. New York: French, 1946. Produced Broadway, 1946.

Penny Arcade. Unpublished. Produced Broadway, 1930.

Seen but Not Heard, A New Play. Written with Martin Berkeley. New York: Dramatists Play Service, 1937. Produced Broadway, 1936.

"Town Boy," A Play in Three Acts. New York: Co-national Plays, 1930. Produced Broadway, 1929.

Biography

Current Biography Yearbook 1958. New York: H.W. Wilson, 1958.

Reviews

New York Times, Jan. 17, 1935, 22:3. [Creeping Fire.]

New York Times, April 3, 1934, 26:4. [House of Remsen.]

New York Times, March 7, 1946, 32:2. [Little Brown Jug.]

New Yorker, 22 (March 16, 1946), 46. [Little Brown Jug.]

New York Times, March 11, 1930, 24:5. [Penny Arcade.]

Catholic World, 144 (November 1936), 214. [Seen but Not Heard.]

New York Times, July 22, 1936, 23:4. [Seen but Not Heard.]

New York Times, Oct. 5, 1929, 22:4. [Town Boy.]

BENNETT, DOROTHY (1906-)

Plays

Best Sellers. Based on Vient de Paraître, by E. Bourdet. Unpublished. Produced Broadway, 1933.

Fly Away Home; A Three Act Comedy. Written with Irving White. New York: French, 1935. Produced Broadway, 1935.

I'd Rather Be Young; A Three Act Comedy for All-Female Cast. Written with Link Hannah. New York: French, 1943. Never produced on the professional stage.

Janey's One-Track Mind; A Three Act Comedy. Written with Link Hannah. New York: French, 1939. Never produced on the professional stage.

The Lovely Duckling; A Three Act Comedy. Written with Link Hannah. New York: French, 1939. Never produced on the professional stage.

Sixteen in August; A Three Act Comedy. Written with Link Hannah. New York: French, 1941. Never produced on the professional stage.

A Woman's a Fool to Be Clever; A Three Act Comedy. Written with Link Hannah. New York: French, 1939. Produced Broadway, 1938.

Reviews

Nation, 136 (May 24, 1933), 594. [Best Sellers.]

New York Times, May 4, 1933, 20:2. [Best Sellers.]

Stage, 10 (June 1933), 11-2. [Best Sellers.]

Literary Digest, 119 (Jan. 26, 1935), 20. [Fly Away Home.]

New York Times, Jan. 16, 1935, 20:4. [Fly Away Home.]

New York Times, Oct. 19, 1938, 18:6. [A Woman's a Fool....]

BENSON, SALLY (1900-1972)

Plays

Memphis Bound! Based on HMS Pinafore, by Gilbert and Sullivan. Book by Sally Benson and Albert Barker. Unpublished. Produced Broadway, 1945.

Seventeen; A Musical Comedy. New York: French, 1954. Adapted from the novel by Booth Tarkington. Produced Broadway, 1951.

The Young and Beautiful, A Play in Three Acts. New York: French, 1956. Based on the Saturday Evening Post Josephine short stories by F. Scott Fitzgerald. Produced Broadway, 1955.

Biography

Contemporary Authors; A Bio-bibliographical Guide to Current Authors and Their Works. Clare D. Kinsman, ed. Vol. 1, perm. series. Detroit: Gale, 1975.

Current Biography Yearbook 1941. New York: H. W. Wilson, 1941.

Kunitz, Stanley J. , and Howard Haycraft, eds. Twentieth Century Authors; A Biographical Dictionary of Modern Literature. New York: H. W. Wilson, 1942.

Reviews

New York Times, June 10, 1945, sec. II, 1:1. [Memphis Bound!]

New Yorker, 21 (June 2, 1945), 36+. [Memphis Bound!]

New York Times, (June 22, 1951), 16:6. [Seventeen.]

New Yorker, 27 (June 30, 1951), 39. [Seventeen.]

New York Times, Oct. 3, 1955, 23:2. [The Young and Beautiful.]

Saturday Review, 38 (Oct. 15, 1955), 26. [The Young and Beautiful.]

BERG, GERTRUDE (1899-1966)

Plays

Me and Molly; A Play in Three Acts. New York: Dramatists Play
Service, 1948. Also in: Chapman, John, ed. Best Plays of
1947-48, and the Year Book of the Drama in America. New
York: Dodd, Mead, 1948. (Condensation.) Produced Broadway,
1948.

Biography

Current Biography Yearbook 1960. New York: H. W. Wilson, 1960.

Freedman, M. "The Real Molly Goldberg." Commentary, 21 (April
1956), 359-64.

Long, J. "Her Family Is Her Fortune." American Magazine, 154
(Dec. 19, 1952), 108-13.

Reviews

New York Times, March 7, 1948, sec. II, 1:1. [Me and Molly.]

New Yorker, 24 (March 8, 1948), 52. [Me and Molly.]

Time, 51 (March 8, 1948), 50. [Me and Molly.]

BOVASSO, JULIE (1930-)

Plays

Down by the River Where Water Lilies Are Disfigured Every Day.
Unpublished. Produced Providence, R. I., 1971; off-Broadway,
1975.

The Final Analysis. Unpublished. Produced off-Broadway, 1975.

Gloria and Esperanza; A Play in Two Acts. New York: French,

1969. Also in: Poland, Albert, and Bruce Mailman, eds. The
Off-Off Broadway Book. Indianapolis: Bobbs-Merrill, 1972.
Produced at LaMama, New York, 1969.

Monday on the Way to Mercury Island. Unpublished. Produced off-
Broadway, 1971.

The Moon Dreamers; A Play in Two Acts with Music. New York:
French, 1969. Produced off-Broadway, 1969.

The Nothing Kid. Unpublished. Produced off-Broadway, 1975.

Shubert's Last Serenade. New York: French, 1972. Also in:
Owens, Rochelle, ed. Spontaneous Combustion. New York:
Winter House, 1972. Never produced on the professional stage.

Standard Safety. New York: French, 1976. Produced off-Broadway,
1975.

Super Lover. Unpublished. Produced off-Broadway, 1975.

Biography

Contemporary Authors; A Bio-bibliographical Guide to Current Authors and Their Works. Clare D. Kinsman, ed. Vol. 25-28,
first revision. Detroit: Gale, 1977.

Who's Who in the Theatre; A Biographical Record of the Contemporary Stage. Ian Herbert, ed. 16th ed. Detroit: Gale, 1977.

Reviews

New York Times, March 25, 1975, 23:1. [Down by the River....]

New York Times, Feb. 5, 1970, 32:1. [Gloria and Esperanza.]

New Yorker, 45 (Feb. 14, 1970), 57. [Gloria and Esperanza.]

Saturday Review, 52 (April 19, 1969), 54. [Gloria and Esperanza.]

New York Times, Dec. 21, 1969, sec. II, 3:1. [The Moon Dreamers.]

New Yorker, 45 (Dec. 20, 1969), 58. [The Moon Dreamers.]

New York Times, Jan. 3, 1975, 14:1. [The Nothing Kid.]

New Yorker, 50 (Jan. 13, 1975), 66. [The Nothing Kid.]

New York Times, Jan. 3, 1975, 14:1. [Standard Safety.]

BOWLES, JANE (AUER) (1917-1973)

Plays

In the Summer House. New York: Random House, 1954. Also in: Kronenberger, ed. Best Plays of 1953-1954. New York: Dodd, Mead, 1954. (Condensation.) Produced Broadway, 1954.

Quarreling Pair. A puppet play published in: Mademoiselle, 64 (December 1966), 116-7. Never produced on the professional stage.

Biography

Contemporary Authors; A Bio-bibliographical Guide to Current Authors and Their Works. Clare D. Kinsman, ed. Vol. 2, perm. series. Detroit: Gale, 1978.

Wakeman, John, ed. World Authors, 1950-1970. New York: H. W. Wilson, 1975.

Reviews

Commonweal, 59 (Feb. 5, 1954), 449-59. [In the Summer House.]

New Republic, 130 (Jan. 11, 1954), 20-1. [In the Summer House.]

New York Times, Jan. 10, 1954, sec. II, 1:1. [In the Summer House.]

BRADLEY, LILLIAN TRIMBLE (1875-)

Plays

As Others See Us. Unpublished. Produced New York, 1917(?).

Beating Back. Unpublished. Produced New York, 1916(?).

Izzy. Written with G. Broadhurst. Unpublished. Produced Broadway, 1924.

Mr. Myd's Mystery. Unpublished. Produced Broadway, 1915.

Out Goes She. Unpublished. Produced London, 1928.

Red Falcon. Unpublished. Produced Broadway, 1924.

Red Hawk. Variant title of Red Falcon.

Virtue for Sale; A Play. Typescript at the New York Public Library.

... What Happened Then? A Melodrama in Three Acts. London:
   Gollancz, 1934. Produced London, 1933.

Woman on the Index. Unpublished. Produced Broadway, 1918.

The Wonderful Thing; A Play in Four Acts. New York, 1920.
   Typescript at the New York Public Library. Produced Broadway,
   1920.

Biography

"Lillian Bradley, Her Career as a Playwright." New York Times,
   Oct. 6, 1918, sec. IV, 4:4.

Mantle, Robert B. American Playwrights of Today. New York:
   Dodd, Mead, 1929, pp. 274-5.

Reviews

New York Times, Sept. 17, 1924, 16:2. [Izzy.]

Theatre, 39 (November 1924), 70. [Izzy.]

New York Dramatic Mirror, 74 (Aug. 18, 1915), 8-9. [Mr. Myd's
   Mystery.]

London News, 173 (Dec. 29, 1928), 1238. [Out Goes She.]

New York Times, Dec. 30, 1928, sec. VIII, 4:1. [Out Goes She.]

New York Times, Dec. 2, 1923, sec. VIII, 2:1. [Red Falcon.]

New York Times, Oct. 8, 1924, 22:1. [Red Falcon.]

Saturday Review, 156 (Sept. 16, 1933), 305. [... What Happened Then?]

Independent, 95 (Sept. 21, 1918), 370. [Woman on the Index.]

Life, 72 (Sept. 12, 1918), 380. [Woman on the Index.]

New York Times, Aug. 30, 1918, 9:1. [Woman on the Index.]

Life, 75 (March 11, 1920), 462-3. [The Wonderful Thing.]

New York Times, Feb. 22, 1920, sec. III, 6:1. [The Wonderful Thing.]

BROWN, ALICE (1857-1948)

Plays

Charles Lamb; A Play. New York: Macmillan, 1924.

Children of Earth; A Play of New England. New York: Macmillan, 1915. Produced Broadway, 1915.

The Crimson Lake. In: Brown, Alice. One Act Plays. New York: Macmillan, 1921. Never produced on the professional stage.

Doctor Auntie. In: Brown, Alice. One Act Plays. New York: Macmillan, 1921. Never produced on the professional stage.

The Golden Ball. In: Brown, Alice. One Act Plays. New York: Macmillan, 1921. Never produced on the professional stage.

The Hero. In: Brown, Alice. One Act Plays. New York: Macmillan, 1921. Never produced on the professional stage.

Joint Owners in Spain; A Comedy in One Act. Boston: W. H. Baker, 1914. Also in: Martin, Constance M., ed. Fifty One-Act Plays. London: Gollancz, 1934. Produced off-Broadway, 1929.

The Loving Cup, A Play in One Act. Boston: W. H. Baker, 1918. In: Woman's Home Companion, 40 (May 1913), 11-2+. Never produced on the professional stage.

A March Wind. In: Brown, Alice. One Act Plays. New York: Macmillan, 1921. Never produced on the professional stage.

The Marriage Feast, A Fantasy. New York: Macmillan, 1931. Never produced on the professional stage.

Milly Dear. In: Brown, Alice. One Act Plays. New York: Macmillan, 1921. Never produced on the professional stage.

Pilgrim's Progress, A Play. Boston: privately printed (Thomas Todd Co.), 1944. Never produced on the professional stage.

The Sugar House. In: Brown, Alice. One Act Plays. New York: Macmillan, 1921. Never produced on the professional stage.

The Web. In: Brown, Alice. One Act Plays. New York: Macmillan, 1921. Never produced on the professional stage.

Biography

"Author of $10,000 Prize Play." Current Opinion, 57 (July 1914), 28-9.

Kunitz, Stanley J., and Howard Haycraft, eds. Twentieth Century Authors; A Biographical Dictionary of Modern Literature. New York: H.W. Wilson, 1942.

Moses, M. J. "Alice Brown." Book News, 36 (October 1917), 36-8.

Reviews

Commonweal, 1 (Feb. 4, 1925), 358-9. [Charles Lamb.]

Drama, 15 (March, 1925), 130. [Charles Lamb.]

Life, 65 (Jan. 28, 1915), 154. [Children of Earth.]

New York Times, Jan. 13, 1915, 9:3. [Children of Earth.]

North American Review, 201 (February 1915), 271-2. [Children of Earth.]

New York Times, May 7, 1929, 28:1. [Joint Owners in Spain.]

Theatre Arts, 6 (January 1922), 80. [Review of book One Act Plays, 1922. Includes the following: The Hero, Doctor Auntie, The Crimson Lake, Milly Dear, The Web, The Loving Cup, Joint Owners in Spain, The Sugar House, The March Wind.]

BURR, ANNE (1937-)

Plays

Better Times. Unpublished. Never produced.

Brothers. Unpublished. Produced Southern Illinois University, 1972.

Chimp Play. Unpublished. Produced High Falls, N.Y., 1970.

Every Man for Himself. Written 1967. Unpublished. Never produced.

Family Communications. Unpublished. Produced Mt. Pleasant, Iowa, 1969.

Huui Huui. New York: French, 1968. Produced off-Broadway, 1968.

Mert and Phil. Unpublished. Produced New York Shakespeare Festival, 1974.

Once I Had a Downy Swan. Written 1965. Unpublished. Never produced.

Stay with Me. Unpublished. Never produced.

Those Things Happen. Unpublished. Produced Washington State College, 1964.

Biography

Contemporary Authors; A Bio-bibliographical Guide to Current Authors and Their Works. Clare D. Kinsman, ed. Vol. 25-28, first revision. Detroit: Gale, 1977.

Reviews

New York Times, Nov. 25, 1968, 58:1. [Huui Huui.]

New Yorker, 44 (Dec. 7, 1968), 142. [Huui Huui.]

Newsweek, 72 (Dec. 16, 1968), 115. [Huui Huui.]

New Yorker, 50 (Nov. 11, 1974), 105. [Mert & Phil.]

Time, 104 (Nov. 18, 1974), 98. [Mert & Phil.]

Yale Theatre, 6 (Winter 1975), 73-80. [Mert & Phil.]

CALDWELL, ANNE (1867-1936)

Plays

The Bunch and Judy. Written with Hugh Ford and Jerome Kern. Unpublished. Produced Broadway, 1922.

Chin-Chin. Written with R. H. Burnside, J. O'Dea, and I. Caryll. Unpublished. Produced Broadway, 1914.

The City Chap. Unpublished. Produced Broadway, 1925.

Criss Cross. Written with O. Harbach. Unpublished. Produced Broadway, 1926.

Go to It. Written with J. L. Golden and J. E. Hazzard. Unpublished. Produced Broadway, 1916.

Good Morning, Dearie. Written with Jerome Kern. Typewritten lyrics at the New York Public Library. Produced on Broadway, 1921.

Hitchy-Koo. Written with G. MacDonough and Jerome Kern. Unpublished. Produced Broadway, 1920.

A Husband by Proxy. Typescript at the New York Public Library.

Jack o'Lantern. Written with R. H. Burnside and I. Caryll. Unpublished. Produced Broadway, 1917.

The Lady in Red. Unpublished. Produced Broadway, 1919.

The Lady of the Slipper. Written with L. McCarty, J. O'Dea, and V. Herbert. Unpublished. Produced Broadway, 1912.

The Magnolia Lady. Unpublished. Written with A. D. Miller and H. Levey. Produced Broadway, 1924.

A Model Girl. Unpublished. Produced Broadway, 1912.

The Nest Egg. Typescript at the New York Public Library. Produced Broadway, 1910.

New Girl. Unpublished. Never produced on the professional stage.

The Night Boat. Written with Jerome Kern. Unpublished. Produced Broadway, 1920.

Oh, Please! Written with O. Harbach. Unpublished. Produced Broadway, 1926.

Once Upon a Time; A Musical Play in Three Acts. Written with L. McCarty and J. O'Dea. New York: Rosenfield, 1921. Typescript at the New York Public Library.

Peg o' My Dreams. Unpublished. Produced Broadway, 1924.

Pom Pom. Written with H. Felix. Unpublished. Produced Broadway, 1916.

She's a Good Fellow. Written with Jerome Kern. Unpublished. Produced Broadway, 1919.

Stepping Stones. Written with R. H. Burnside. Unpublished. Produced Broadway, 1923.

The Sweetheart Shop. Written with H. Felix. Unpublished. Produced Broadway, 1920.

Take the Air. Written with G. Buck. Unpublished. Produced Broadway, 1927.

Three Cheers. Written with R. H. Burnside and R. Hubbell. Unpublished. Produced Broadway, 1928.

Tip-Top. Written with R. H. Burnside and I. Caryll. Unpublished. Produced Broadway, 1920.

Uncle Sam. Written with J. O'Dea. Typescript at the New York Public Library. Produced Broadway, 1911.

When Claudia Smiles. Unpublished. Produced Broadway, 1914.

Yours Truly. Written with C. North. Unpublished. Produced Broadway, 1927.

Biography

Patterson, Ada. "The Only Woman Librettist in America." Theatre, 21 (June 1915), 305-6.

New York Times, Oct. 24, 1936, 17:5. (Obituary.)

"Successful Woman Playwright." Theatre, 13 (March 1911), 90.

Reviews

New York Times, Nov. 12, 1922, sec. VIII, 1:6. [The Bunch and Judy.]

New York Times, Oct. 21, 1914, 11:3. [Chin-Chin.]

New York Times, Oct. 27, 1925, 21:1. [The City Chap.]

New York Times, Oct. 13, 1926, 20:2. [Criss Cross.]

New York Times, Oct. 25, 1916, 9:1. [Go to It.]

Life, 78 (Nov. 17, 1921), 18. [Good Morning, Dearie.]

New York Times, Nov. 2, 1921, 20:2. [Good Morning, Dearie.]

New York Times, Oct. 20, 1920, 11:3. [Hitchy-Koo.]

Green Book, 19 (January 1918), 8+. [Jack o'Lantern.]

New York Times, Oct. 17, 1917, 13:1. [Jack o'Lantern.]

Forum, 61 (June 1919), 755-6. [The Lady in Red.]

New York Times, May 13, 1919, 18:2. [The Lady in Red.]

New York Times, Oct. 29, 1912, 13:1. [The Lady of the Slipper.]

Red Book, 20 (February 1913), 702-4. [The Lady of the Slipper.]

New York Times, Nov. 26, 1924, 17:2. [The Magnolia Lady.]

Dramatist, 3 (October 1911), 199-200. [The Nest Egg.]

New York Times, Nov. 23, 1910, 9:1. [The Nest Egg.]

New York Times, Feb. 3, 1920, 18:1. [The Night Boat.]

Life, 89 (Jan. 13, 1927), 21. [Oh, Please.]

New York Times, Dec. 22, 1926, 24:3. [Oh, Please.]

New York Times, May 6, 1924, 25:3. [Peg o' My Dreams.]

Green Book, 15 (May 1916), 799+. [Pom Pom]

New York Times, Feb. 29, 1916, 9:1. [Pom Pom.]

Forum, 61 (June 1919), 755. [She's a Good Fellow.]

New York Times, May 6, 1919. 16:4. [She's a Good Fellow.]

New York Times, Nov. 7, 1923, 14:3. [Stepping Stones.]

New York Times, Sept. 1, 1920, 13:4. [The Sweetheart Shop.]

New York Times, Nov. 23, 1927, 28:2. [Take the Air.]

New York Times, Oct. 16, 1928, 28:1. [Three Cheers.]

Theatre, 48 (December 1928), 46. [Three Cheers.]

New York Times, Oct. 6, 1920, 13:2. [Tip-Top.]

Life, 63 (Feb. 19, 1914), 13:2. [When Claudia Smiles.]

Life, 89 (Feb. 24, 1927), 318-9. [Yours Truly.]

New York Times, Jan 26, 1927, 16:5. [Yours Truly.]

CARROLL, VINNETTE (1922-   )

Plays

But Never Jam Today. Unpublished. Produced off-Broadway, 1969.

Croesus and the Witch. Written with Micki Grant. Unpublished. Produced off-Broadway, 1971.

Don't Bother Me, I Can't Cope. Written with Micki Grant. New York: French, 1972. Produced off-Broadway, 1970; Broadway, 1971.

Old Judge Mose Is Dead. Written with Micki Grant. Unpublished. Produced off-Broadway, 1969.

Step Lively, Boy. Written with Micki Grant. Unpublished. Produced off-Broadway, 1973.

Trumpets of the Lord. Based on the poetry of James Weldon Johnson. Unpublished. Produced off-Broadway, 1963; Broadway, 1969.

The Ups and Downs of Theophilus Maitland. Written with Micki Grant. Unpublished. Produced off-Broadway, 1975.

Your Arms Too Short to Box with God. Book by Vinnette Carroll. Music and lyrics by Alex Bradford and Micki Grant. Unpublished. Produced Italy, 1975; Broadway, 1976.

Biography

Harris, Jessica. "Broadway's New Breed: Black Producers on the Great White Way." Essence, 8 (December 1977), 72+.

Hepburn, D. "Vinnette Carroll, Woman on the Run." Sepia, 10 (October 1961), 57-60.

Mitchell, Loften. Voices of the Black Theatre. Clifton, N.J.: James T. White, 1975, pp. 189-207.

Who's Who in the Theatre. Ian Herbert, ed. 16th ed. Detroit: Gale, 1977.

Reviews

New York Times, April 24, 1969, 40:1. [But Never Jam Today.]

New York Times, Aug. 27, 1971, p. 18. [Croesus and the Witch.]

New Yorker, 47 (Sept. 4, 1971), 54. [Croesus and the Witch.]

Ebony, 28 (February 1973), 100-2+. [Don't Bother Me....]

Nation, 214 (May 8, 1972), 604. [Don't Bother Me....]

New York Times, April 20, 1972, 51:1. [Don't Bother Me....]

New Yorker, 48 (April 29, 1972), 104. [Don't Bother Me....]

New York Times, April 29, 1969, 25:1. [Old Judge Mose Is Dead.]

New York Times, Dec. 23, 1963, 22:3. [Trumpets of the Lord.]

New York Times, April 30, 1969, 37:1. [Trumpets of the Lord.]

New York, 10 (Jan. 10, 1977), 63. [Your Arms....]

New York Times, Dec. 23, 1976, 20:1. [Your Arms....]

Newsweek, 89 (Jan. 10, 1977), 66. [Your Arms....]

Time, 109 (Jan. 24, 1977), 55. [Your Arms....]

CASEY, ROSEMARY (1904-1976)

Plays

Agatha Calling. Unpublished. Produced Philadelphia, 1935.

All the News. Unpublished. Never produced on the professional
stage.

Glass Houses. Unpublished. Never produced on the professional
stage.

Late Love, A Comedy in Three Acts. New York: French, 1954.
Produced Broadway, 1953.

Love Is Not Important. Unpublished. Never produced on the professional stage.

Mary Goes to See. Written with I. Payne. Unpublished. Produced
London, 1938.

Once an Actor. Unpublished. Produced Stockbridge, Mass., 1950.

Saint's Husband. Unpublished. Never produced on the professional
stage.

The Velvet Glove, A Comedy in Three Acts. New York: French,
1950. Produced Broadway, 1950.

Biography

New York Times Biographical Services, 7, 3 (March 1976), 335.

Notable Names in the American Theatre. Clifton, N. J.: James T.
White, 1976.

Reviews

New York Times, Oct. 1, 1935, 27:5. [Agatha Calling.]

New York Times, Oct. 14, 1953, 35:2. [Late Love.]

New Yorker, 29 (Oct. 24, 1953), 69-70. [Late Love.]

Saturday Review, 36 (Oct. 31, 1953), 30-1. [Late Love.]

New Statesman, 15 (Feb. 26, 1938), 328. [Mary Goes to See.]

New York Times, March 6, 1938, sec. IX, 3:6. [Mary Goes to See.]

Theatre World, 29 (March 1938), 116. [Mary Goes to See.]

New York Times, Aug. 1, 1950, 19:8. [Once an Actor.]

New Republic, 122 (Jan. 16, 1950), 31. [The Velvet Glove.]

New Yorker, 25 (Jan. 7, 1950), 44. [The Velvet Glove.]

Theatre Arts, 34 (March 1950), 10. [The Velvet Glove.]

CASPARY, VERA (1904-)

Plays

Blind Mice. Written with Winifred Lenihan. Unpublished. Produced
    Broadway, 1930.

Geraniums in My Window. Unpublished. Produced Broadway, 1934.

Laura: A Play in Three Acts. Written with George Sklar. New
    York: Dramatists Play Service, 1945. Produced Broadway, 1947.

Wedding in Paris. Unpublished. Produced London, 1954.

Biography

Contemporary Authors; A Bio-bibliographical Guide to Current Au-
    thors and Their Works. Clare D. Kinsman, ed. Vol. 13-16,
    first revision. Detroit: Gale, 1975.

Current Biography 1947. New York: H. W. Wilson, 1947.

Kunitz, Stanley J. , ed. Twentieth Century Authors; A Biographical
    Dictionary of Modern Literature. 1st supplement. New York:
    H. W. Wilson, 1955.

Reviews

New York Times, Oct. 16, 1930, 28:2. [Blind Mice.]

New York Times. Oct. 27, 1934, 20:6. [Geraniums in My Window.]

New York Times, June 27, 1947, 16:1. [Laura.]

Newsweek, 30 (July 7, 1947), 82. [Laura.]

Time, 50 (July 7, 1947), 56. [Laura.]

The Times (London), April 5, 1954, p. 5, col. F. [Wedding in
    Paris.]

CHASE, MARY (COYLE) (1907-1981)

Plays

The Banshee. Variant title of The Next Half Hour.

Bernadine, A Comedy in Two Acts. New York: Oxford University
Press, 1953. Also in: Chapman, John, ed. Theatre '53. New York:
Random House, 1953. Produced Broadway, 1952.

Cocktails with Mimi. New York: Dramatists Play Service, 1974.

Dog Sitters, A Comedy in Three Acts. New York: Dramatists Play
Service, 1963.

Harvey, A Comedy in Three Acts. New York: Dramatists Play
Service, 1944. Also in: Corbin, Richard K. , and Miriam Balf,
eds. Twelve American Plays 1920-1960. New York: Scribner,
1969. Produced Broadway, 1944.

Lolita. Unpublished. Produced Abingdon, Va. , 1954.

Me, Third. Variant title of Now You've Done It.

Mickey. New York: Dramatists Play Service, 1969. Produced
Denver, 1969.

Midgie Purvis; A Comedy in Two Acts and Seven Scenes. New York:
Dramatists Play Service, 1963.

Mr. Thing. Variant title of Mrs. McThing.

Mrs. McThing, A Play. New York: Oxford University Press, 1952.
Also in: Chapman, John, ed. Best Plays of 1951-1952. New
York: Dodd, Mead, 1952. (Condensation.) Produced Broadway,
1952.

The Next Half Hour. Unpublished. Produced Broadway, 1945.

Now You've Done It. Denver, 1936. Copy of typescript at the
Library of Congress. Produced Broadway, 1937.

The Prize Play, A Skit. New York: Dramatists Play Service,
1961. Never produced on the professional stage.

A Slip of a Girl. Unpublished. Produced Camp Hall, Col. , 1941.

Sorority House; A Comedy in Three Acts. New York: French, 1939.

Too Much Business, A Comedy in One Act. New York: French, 1940. Never produced on the professional stage.

The White Rabbit. Variant title of Harvey.

Biography

Contemporary Dramatists. James Vinson, ed. 2nd ed. New York: St. Martin, 1977.

Current Biography 1945. New York: H. W. Wilson, 1945.

Harris, E. "Mary Chase, Success Almost Ruined Her." Cosmopolitan, 136 (February 1954), 98-104.

Kunitz, Stanley J. , ed. Twentieth Century Authors; A Biographical Dictionary of Modern Literature. 1st supplement. New York: H. W. Wilson, 1955.

Reef, W. M. "She Didn't Write It for Money, She Says." Saturday Evening Post, 218 (Sept. 1, 1945), 17+.

Reviews

Life, 33 (Nov. 24, 1952), 83-4+. [Bernardine.]

New York Times, Nov. 9, 1952, sec. II, 1:1. [Bernardine.]

Saturday Review, 35 (Nov. 1, 1952), 26. [Bernardine.]

New Statesman and Nation, 37 (Jan. 15, 1949), 55. [Harvey.]

New York Times, Nov. 12, 1944, sec. II, 1:1. [Harvey.]

Saturday Review of Literature, 27 (Dec. 30, 1944), 10-11. [Harvey.]

Time, 95 (March 9, 1970), 54. [Harvey.]

Nation, 174 (March 15, 1952), 258. [Mrs. McThing.]

New York Times, March 2, 1952, sec. II, 1:1. [Mrs. McThing.]

New York Times, Nov. 4, 1945, sec. II, 1:1. [The Next Half Hour.]

New Yorker, 21 (Nov. 10, 1945), 44+. [The Next Half Hour.]

New York Times, March 6, 1937, 10:4. [Now You've Done It.]

CHILDRESS, ALICE (1920-)

Plays

The African Garden. Unpublished. Unproduced. One scene appears
in: Childress, Alice, ed. Black Scenes. New York: Doubleday,
1971.

Florence: A One Act Drama. In: Masses and Midstream, 31
(October 1950), 34-47. Produced off-Broadway, 1951.

The Freedom Drum. Unpublished. Produced by the Performing
Arts Repertory Theatre on tour, 1970.

Gold Thru the Trees. Unpublished. Produced off-Broadway, 1952.

Hero Ain't Nothin' but a Sandwich. New York: Coward, McCann &
Geoghegan, 1973. (Screenplay.)

Just a Little Simple. Unpublished. Produced off-Broadway, 1950.

Let's Hear It for the Queen. New York: Coward, McCann & Geoghegan, 1976. Never produced on the professional stage.

A Man Bearing a Pitcher. Unpublished. Never produced on the
professional stage.

Mojo. In: Mojo and String; Two Plays. New York: Dramatists
Play Service, 1971. Produced off-Broadway, 1970.

String. In: Mojo and String; Two Plays. New York: Dramatists
Play Service, 1971. Produced off-Broadway, 1969.

Trouble in Mind. In: Patterson, Lindsay, ed. Black Theatre: A
Twentieth Century Collection of the Work of its Best Playwrights.
New York: Dodd, Mead, 1971. Produced off-Broadway, 1955.

Wedding Band; A Love/Hate Story in Black and White. New York:
French, 1973. Produced off-Broadway, 1972.

When the Rattlesnake Sounds: A Play. New York: Coward, McCann
& Geoghegan, 1975. Never produced on the professional stage.

Wine in the Wilderness; A Comedy-Drama. New York: Dramatists
Play Service, 1969. Also in: Richards, Stanley, ed. Best Short
Plays, 1972. Philadelphia: Chilton, 1972. (Television play.)

The World on a Hill. In: Maloney, Henry B., ed. Plays to Re-
member. New York: Macmillan, 1967. Never produced on the
professional stage.

Biography

Contemporary Authors; A Bio-bibliographical Guide to Current Authors and Their Works. Clare D. Kinsman, ed. Vol. 45-48. Detroit: Gale, 1974.

Contemporary Dramatists. James Vinson, ed. 2nd. ed. New York: St. Martin, 1977.

Mitchell, Loften. "Three Writers and a Dream." Crisis, 72 (April 1965), 219-223.

Criticism

Evans, Donald. "Playwrights of the Fifties; Bring It All Back Home." Black World, 20 (February 1971), 41-5.

Mitchell, Loften. Black Drama. New York: Hawthorn, 1967, pp. 145-7, 168-9.

Reviews

New York Times, April 2, 1969, 37:1. [String.]

New Yorker, 45 (April 12, 1969), 131. [String.]

New York Times, Nov. 5, 1955, 23:2. [Trouble in Mind.]

Nation, 215 (Nov. 13, 1972), 475. [Wedding Band.]

New Republic, 167 (Nov. 25, 1972), 22+. [Wedding Band.]

New Yorker, 48 (Nov. 4, 1972), 105. [Wedding Band.]

COMDEN, BETTY (1919-   )

Plays

Applause. Book by Betty Comden and Adolph Green. Music by Charles Strouse. Lyrics by Lee Adams. New York: Random House, 1971. Also in: Guernsey, Otis L. , Jr. , ed. Best Plays of 1969-1970. New York: Dodd, Mead, 1971. (Condensation.) Produced Broadway, 1970.

Bells Are Ringing. Book and lyrics by Betty Comden and Adolph
Green. Music by Jule Styne. New York: Random House, 1957.
Produced Broadway, 1956.

Billion Dollar Baby. Book and lyrics by Betty Comden and Adolph
Green. Music by Morton Gould. Written 1945. Typescript at
the New York Public Library. Produced Broadway, 1945.

Bonanza Bound. Book and lyrics by Betty Comden and Adolph Green.
Music by Saul Chaplin. Unpublished. Produced Philadelphia,
1947.

Do Re Mi. Lyrics by Betty Comden and Adolph Green. Book by
Garson Kanin. Music by Jule Styne. New York: Chappell, 1961.
Produced Broadway, 1960.

Fade Out, Fade In. Book and lyrics by Betty Comden and Adolph
Green. Music by Jule Styne. New York: Random House, 1965.
Produced Broadway, 1964.

Hallelujah, Baby! Lyrics by Betty Comden and Adolph Green. Book
by Arthur Laurents. Music by Jule Styne. Vocal selections published by Stratford Music, 1967. Produced Broadway, 1967.

Leonard Bernstein's Theater Songs. Lyrics by Betty Comden and
others. Music by Leonard Bernstein. Unpublished. Produced
Broadway, 1965.

Lorelei. Lyrics by Betty Comden and Adolph Green. Book by
Kenny Solms and Gail Parent. Music by Jule Styne. Unpublished.
Produced Broadway, 1974.

On the Town. Book and lyrics by Betty Comden and Adolph Green.
Music by Leonard Bernstein. Written 1944. Typescript at the
New York Public Library. Produced Broadway, 1944.

On the Twentieth Century. Book and lyrics by Betty Comden and
Adolph Green. Music by Cy Coleman. New York: French, 1980.
Produced Broadway, 1978.

A Party with Betty Comden and Adolph Green. Music and lyrics by
Betty Comden and Adolph Green and others. Unpublished. Produced Broadway, 1958.

Peter Pan. Lyrics by Betty Comden, Adolph Green, and Carolyn
Leigh. Book by Richard Halliday. Music by Mark Charlap and
Jule Styne. Vocal score published by E. H. Morris, 1974. Pro-
duced Broadway, 1954.

Say, Darling. Lyrics by Betty Comden and Adolph Green. Book by
Richard Bissell, Abe Burrows, and Marian Bissell. Music by
Jule Styne. Unpublished. Produced Broadway, 1958.

Subways Are for Sleeping. Book and lyrics by Betty Comden and
Adolph Green. Music by Jule Styne. Unpublished. Produced
Broadway, 1951.

Two on the Aisle. Book and lyrics by Betty Comden, Adolph Green,
Nat Hiken, and William Friedberg. Music by Jule Styne. Unpublished. Produced Broadway, 1951.

Wonderful Town. Lyrics by Betty Comden and Adolph Green. Book
by Joseph Fields and Jerome Chodorov. Music by Leonard Bernstein. New York: Random House, 1953. Also in: Mantle, Robert B., ed. Best Plays of 1952-1953. New York: Dodd, Mead,
1953. (Condensation.) Produced Broadway, 1953.

Biography

Contemporary Authors; A Bio-bibliographical Guide to Current Authors and Their Works. Clare D. Kinsman, ed. Vol. 45-48.
Detroit: Gale, 1974.

Gelb, A., and B. Gelb. "On the Town with Comden and Green."
New York Times Magazine, Dec. 11, 1960, p. 39+.

Green, Stanley. World of Musical Comedy. 3rd. ed. South Bruns-
wick, N.J.: Barnes, 1974, pp. 311-27.

Lyon, P. "Two Minds That Beat as One." Holiday, 30 (December
1961), 149-52.

Reviews

New Republic, 162 (May 23, 1970), 20+. [Applause.]

New York Times, April 5, 1970, sec. II, 1:1. [Applause.]

New Yorker, 46 (April 11, 1970), 81. [Applause.]

Life, 42 (Feb. 11, 1957), 70+. [Bells Are Ringing.]

New York Times, Nov. 29, 1956, 43;4. [Bells Are Ringing.]

New Yorker, 32 (Dec. 1, 1956), 88+. [Bells Are Ringing.]

Life, 20 (Jan. 21, 1946), 67+. [Billion Dollar Baby.]

New York Times, Dec. 30, 1945, sec. II, 1:1. [Billion Dollar
Baby.]

New Yorker, 21, (Jan. 5, 1946), 40. [Billion Dollar Baby.]

Theatre Arts, 32 (February 1948), 19-23. [Bonanza Bound.]

Life, 50 (Feb. 10, 1961), 4+. [Do Re Mi.]

New York Times, Jan. 8, 1961, sec. II, 1:1. [Do Re Mi.]

New Yorker, 36 (Jan. 14, 1961), 68. [Do Re Mi.]

New York Times, May 27, 1964, 45:1. [Fade Out....]

Saturday Review, 47 (June 20, 1964), 28. [Fade Out....]

Commonweal, 86 (June 9, 1967), 342-5. [Hallelujah....]

New York Times, May 7, 1967, sec. II, 1:1. [Hallelujah....]

New Yorker, 43 (May 6, 1967), 150. [Hallelujah....]

Life, 59 (July 30, 1965), 12. [Leonard Bernstein's....]

New York Times, June 29, 1965, 27:2. [Leonard Bernstein's....]

New York Times, Jan. 28, 1974, 35:1. [Lorelei.]

New Yorker, 49 (Feb. 4, 1974), 46. [Lorelei.]

Life, 18 (Jan. 15, 1945), 49-51. [On the Town.]

New York Times, Jan. 7, 1945, sec. II, 1:1. [On the Town.]

Saturday Review, 28 (Feb. 17, 1945), 26-7. [On the Town.]

New York Times, Feb. 20, 1978, sec. III, 18:1. [On the Twentieth
    Century.]

New Yorker, 54 (March 6, 1978), 67+. [On the Twentieth Century.]

Saturday Review, 5 (April 15, 1978), 50+. [On the Twentieth Cen-
    tury.]

New York Times, Dec. 24, 1958, 2:7. [A Party with....]

New Yorker, 34 (Jan. 10, 1959), 70. [A Party with....]

Saturday Review, 42 (Jan. 10, 1959), 67. [A Party with....]

Life, 37 (Nov. 8, 1954), 109-10. [Peter Pan.]

New York Times, Oct. 21, 1954, 30:2. [Peter Pan.]

New Yorker, 30 (Oct. 30, 1954), 66+. [Peter Pan.]

New York Times, April 13, 1958, sec. II, 1:1. [Say, Darling.]

New Yorker, 34 (April 12, 1958), 67. [Say, Darling.]

Saturday Review, 41 (April 19, 1958), 28. [Say, Darling.]

New York Times, Dec. 28, 1961, 22:1. [Subways....]

New Yorker, 37 (Jan. 6, 1962), 56. [Subways....]

Theatre Arts, 46 (March 1962), 60. [Subways....]

Life, 31 (Sept. 10, 1951), 111-2. [Two on the Aisle.]

New York Times, July 20, 1951, 13:6. [Two on the Aisle.]

New Yorker, 27 (July 28, 1951), 48+. [Two on the Aisle.]

New York Times, March 8, 1953, sec. II, p. 1. [Wonderful Town.]

Time, 61 (March 30, 1953), 40-2. [Wonderful Town.]

CROTHERS, RACHEL (1878-1958)

Plays

As Husbands Go, A Comedy. New York: French, 1931. Also in:
Mantle, Robert B., ed. Best Plays of 1930-1931. New York:
Dodd, Mead, 1931. (Condensation.) Produced Broadway, 1931.

Bon Voyage. Unpublished. Produced New York City, 1929(?).

The Captain of the Gray Horse Troop; A Play in 5 Acts. Written
with L. M. Sill. ©1903. Typewritten copy at Harvard University
Library.

Caught Wet, A Comedy in Three Acts. New York: French, 1932.
Produced Broadway, 1931.

The Coming of Mrs. Patrick. ©1956. Microfilm of a typewritten
copy at the University of Chicago Library. Produced Broadway,
1907.

Criss Cross; A Play in One Act. New York: Dick & Fitzgerald,
1904. Produced Broadway, 1899.

Everyday, A Comedy Drama in Three Acts. New York: Co-National
Plays, 1930. Produced Broadway, 1921.

Expressing Willie. In: Crothers, Rachel. Expressing Willie, Nice

People, 39 East; Three Plays. New York: Brentano, 1924.
Also in: Cordell, R. A. , ed. Representative Modern Plays,
British and American. New York: Nelson, 1929. Produced
Broadway, 1924.

He and She. In: Quinn, Arthur H. , ed. Representative American
Plays. New York: Century, 1917. Produced Broadway, 1920.

The Heart of Paddy Whack; A Comedy in Three Acts. New York:
French, 1925. Produced Broadway, 1914.

Herfords. Variant title of He and She.

The Importance of Being a Woman. In: Crothers, Rachel. Six One
Act Plays. Boston: Baker, 1925. Never produced on the professional stage.

The Importance of Being Clothed. In: Crothers, Rachel. Six One
Act Plays. Boston: Baker, 1925. Never produced on the professional stage.

The Importance of Being Married. In: Crothers, Rachel. Six One
Act Plays. Boston: Baker, 1925. Never produced on the professional stage.

The Importance of Being Nice. In: Crothers, Rachel. Six One
Act Plays. Boston: Baker, 1925. Never produced on the professional stage.

Kiddies. Unpublished. Produced New York City, 1909(?).

A Lady's Virtue. Unpublished. Produced Broadway, 1925.

Let Us Be Gay, A Comedy. New York: French, 1929. Also in: Mantle,
Robert B. , ed. Best Plays of 1928-1929. New York: Dodd,
Mead, 1929. (Condensation.) Produced Broadway, 1929.

A Little Journey, A Comedy in Three Acts. New York: French,
1923. Produced Broadway, 1918.

A Man's World; A Play in Four Acts. Boston: Badger, 1915.
Produced Broadway, 1910.

Mary the Third. In: Crothers, Rachel. Mary the Third, Old Lady
31, A Little Journey; Three Plays. New York: Brentano, 1923.
Also in: Tucker, Samuel M. , ed. Twenty-five Modern Plays.
New York: Harper, 1931. Produced Broadway, 1923.

Mother Carey's Chickens; A Little Comedy of Home, in Three Acts.
Written with K. D. Wiggin. From the book of the same title by
K. D. Wiggin. New York: French, 1925. Produced Broadway,
1917.

Myself, Bettina. Unpublished. Produced Broadway, 1908.

Nice People. In: Everybody's Magazine, 45 (November 1921), 87-
94. Also in: Quinn, Arthur H. , ed. Contemporary American
Plays. New York: Scribner, 1923. Produced Broadway, 1921.

Nora. Unpublished. Produced New York City, 1903(?).

Old Lady 31; A Comedy. New York: French, 1923. Also in: Crothers,
Rachel. Mary the Third, Old Lady 31, A Little Journey; Three
Plays. New York: Brentano, 1923. Produced Broadway, 1916.

Once Upon a Time; A Comedy in Four Acts. New York: French,
1925. Produced Broadway, 1918.

Ourselves. Unpublished. Produced Broadway, 1913.

Peggy. In: Scribner's Magazine, 76 (August 1924), 175-83. Also
in: Crothers, Rachel. Six One Act Plays. Boston: Baker,
1925. Never produced on the professional stage.

Point of View. Unpublished. Produced Broadway, 1904.

The Rector, A Play in One Act. New York: French, 1905. Also
in: One Act Plays for Stage and Study. 1st series. New York:
French, 1925. Produced Broadway, 1902.

Susan and God. New York: Random House, 1938. Also in:
Mantle, Robert B. , ed. Best Plays of 1937-1938. New York: Dodd,
Mead, 1938. (Condensation.) Produced Broadway, 1937.

Talent. Unpublished. Produced New York City, 1934(?).

39 East; A Comedy in Three Acts. Boston: Baker, 1925. Also in:
Crothers, Rachel. Expressing Willie, Nice People, 39 East;
Three Plays. New York: Brentano, 1924. Produced Broadway,
1919.

The Three of Us; A Play in Four Acts. New York: Rosenfield,
1906. Produced Broadway, 1906.

The Valiant One; A Comedy. Minneapolis: Northwestern, 1937. Never
produced on the professional stage.

Venus. Unpublished. Produced Broadway, 1927.

What They Think. In: Crothers, Rachel. Six One Act Plays.
Boston: Baker, 1925. Also in: Ladies' Home Journal, 40 (February 1923), 12-3. Never produced on the professional stage.

When Ladies Meet, A Comedy. New York: French, 1932. Also
in: Mantle, Robert B. , ed. Best Plays of 1932-1933. New York:
Dodd, Mead, 1933. (Condensation.) Produced Broadway, 1933.

William Craddock. ©1956. Microfilm of typewritten copy at the
University of Chicago Library. Never produced on the professional
stage.

Young Wisdom. Unpublished. Produced Broadway, 1914.

Biography

Gottlieb, Lois C. Rachel Crothers. Boston: Twayne, 1979.

Kunitz, Stanley J. , and Howard Haycraft, eds. Twentieth Century
Authors; A Biographical Dictionary of Modern Literature. New
York: H. W. Wilson, 1942.

Criticism

Dickinson, Thomas H. Playwrights of the New American Theatre.
New York: Macmillan, 1925, pp. 182-7.

Flexner, Eleanor. American Playwrights 1918-1938: The Theatre
Retreats from Reality. New York: Simon & Schuster, 1938,
pp. 239-48.

Gottlieb, Lois C. Rachel Crothers. Boston: Twayne, 1979.

Quinn, Arthur H. A History of the American Drama from the Civil
War to the Present Day. Vol. 1: From William Vaughan Moody
to the Present Day. New York: Harper, 1927, pp. 50-61.

Reviews

Commonweal, 13 (March 18, 1931), 552-3. [As Husbands Go.]

New York Times, March 15, 1931, sec. IX, 1:1. [As Husbands Go.]

Catholic World, 134 (December 1931), 334-5. [Caught Wet.]

New York Times, Nov. 5, 1931, 29:1. [Caught Wet.]

Forum, 39 (January 1908), 372-4. [The Coming of Mrs. Patrick.]

Life, 50 (Nov. 21, 1907), 614-5. [The Coming of Mrs. Patrick.]

New York Times, Nov. 17, 1921, 15:1. [Everyday.]

New York Times, April 17, 1924, 22:1. [Expressing Willie.]

Theatre Arts, 9 (February 1925), 139-40. [Expressing Willie.]

New York Times, Feb. 13, 1920, 16:3. [He and She.]

New York Times, Nov. 24, 1914, 13:5. [The Heart of Paddy Whack.]

New York Times, Nov. 11, 1925, 28:2. [A Lady's Virtue.]

Commonweal, 9 (May 1, 1929), 750. [Let Us Be Gay.]

New York Times, Feb. 22, 1929, 19:1. [Let Us Be Gay.]

New York Times, Dec. 27, 1918, 9:2. [A Little Journey.]

Theatre Arts, 10 (June 1926), 423-4. [A Little Journey.]

Dial, 59 (Oct. 14, 1915), 325-6. [A Man's World.]

Life, 55 (Feb. 24, 1910), 324. [A Man's World.]

New York Times, Feb. 11, 1923, 1:1. [Mary the Third.]

Theatre Arts, 8 (June 1924), 425. [Mary the Third.]

New York Times, Sept. 26, 1917, 11:1. [Mother Carey's Chickens.]

New York Times, Oct. 6, 1908, 9:3. [Myself, Bettina.]

New York Times, March 3, 1921, 11:1. [Nice People.]

Review, 4 (April 13, 1921), 344-6. [Nice People.]

New York Times, Oct. 31, 1916, 11:1. [Old Lady 31.]

Theatre Arts, 8 (June 1924), 425. [Old Lady 31.]

Green Book, 20 (July 1981), 14-7. [Once Upon a Time.]

New York Times, April 16, 1918, 11:2. [Once Upon a Time.]

Drama, 5 (January 1914), 421-2. [Ourselves.]

New Republic, 92 (Oct. 27, 1937), 342-3. [Susan and God.]

New York Times, Oct. 17, 1937, sec. XI, 1:1. [Susan and God.]

New York Times, April 1, 1919, 9:1. [39 East.]

Theatre Arts, 9 (February 1925), 139-40. [39 East.]

Harper's Weekly, 50 (Nov. 3, 1906), 1578. [The Three of Us.]

New York Times, Oct. 18, 1906, 9:1. [The Three of Us.]

New York Times, Dec. 26, 1927, 26:5. [Venus.]

Commonweal, 16 (Oct. 26, 1932), 621. [When Ladies Meet.]

New York Times, Oct. 16, 1932, sec. IX, 1:1. [When Ladies Meet.]

Life, 63 (Jan. 22, 1914), 150-1. [Young Wisdom.]

New York Times, Jan. 6, 1914, 6:3. [Young Wisdom.]

CRYER, GRETCHEN (1936-   )

Plays

I'm Getting My Act Together and Taking It on the Road. Written with Nancy Ford. New York: French, 1980. Produced off-Broadway, 1978.

The Last Sweet Days of Isaac. Book and lyrics by Gretchen Cryer. Music by Nancy Ford. Unpublished. Produced off-Broadway, 1970.

Now Is the Time for All Good Men; A Musical. Revised and rewritten. New York: French, 1969, ©1967. Book and lyrics by Gretchen Cryer. Music by Nancy Ford. Produced off-Broadway, 1967.

Shelter. Book and lyrics by Gretchen Cryer. Music by Nancy Ford. New York: French, 1973. Produced off-Broadway, 1973.

Biography

Berg, Beatrice. "From School Days to Sweet Days." New York Times, Feb. 15, 1970, sec. II, 1:3.

Connely, Joan. "The Act Is Together and Thriving." Horizon, 22 (January/February 1979), 60-5.

Dworkin, Susan. "Cryer and Ford; Hang on to the Good Times." Ms., 6 (December 1977), 64-5.

Reviews

New York Times, June 15, 1978, sec. III, 17:1. [I'm Getting My Act Together....]

New Yorker, 54 (June 26, 1978), 51-2. [I'm Getting My Act Together....]

Nation, 210 (March 9, 1970), 284. [The Last Sweet Days. . . .]

New York Times, Feb. 8, 1970, sec. II, 1:1. [The Last Sweet
    Days. . . .]

New Yorker, 45 (Feb. 7, 1970), 73-4+. [The Last Sweet Days. . .]

America, 117 (Oct. 14, 1967), 421-2. [Now Is the Time. . . .]

New York Times, Sept. 27, 1967, 42:1. [Now Is the Time. . . .]

New Yorker, 43 (Oct. 7, 1967), 133-4. [Now Is the Time. . . .]

New York Times, Feb. 7, 1973, 31:1. [Shelter.]

New Yorker, 48 (Feb. 17, 1973), 79. [Shelter.]

CUSHING, CATHERINE CHISHOLM (1874-1952)

Plays

Between the Acts; A Play in One Act. ©1914. Typescript at the
    New York Public Library. Never produced on the professional
    stage.

Edgar Allan Poe. Unpublished. Produced Broadway, 1925.

Glorianna. Written with R. Friml. Unpublished. Produced Broad-
    way, 1918.

Jerry, A Comedy in Three Acts. New York: French, 1930. Pro-
    duced Broadway, 1914.

Kitty MacKay. Unpublished. Produced Broadway, 1914.

Lassie. Musical comedy by H. Felix founded on the comedy,
    Kitty MacKay. Unpublished. Produced Broadway, 1920.

Little Partners, A Three Act Play. Typescript at the New York
    Public Library.

Marge, A New Comedy. ©1923. Typescript at the New York Public
    Library. Produced Broadway, 1924.

Marjolaine. Written with H. Felix and B. Hooker. Founded on the
    play Pomander Walk, by L. N. Parker. Unpublished. Produced
    Broadway, 1922.

Master of the Inn. Unpublished. Produced Broadway, 1925.

Miss Ananias. Unpublished. Never produced on the professional
stage.

Nancy Stair; A Play. ©1923. Typescript at the New York Public
Library. Produced Broadway, 1905.

Pollyanna; A Comedy in Four Acts. Adapted from the story by
Eleanor H. Porter. New York: French, 1923. Produced Broadway, 1916.

The Poppy-Kiss; A Character Study. New York: Kaufman, 1923.
Produced Los Angeles, 1923.

The Princess Pretend; A Play in One Act. New York: Rosenfield,
1914. Never produced on the professional stage.

The Real Thing. Unpublished. Produced Broadway, 1911.

Sari. Operetta written with E. P. Heath and E. Kalman. Adapted
from the German, Der Zigeunerprimas, by J. Wilhelm and F.
Grunbaum. Unpublished. Produced Broadway, 1914.

Topsy and Eva. Unpublished. Produced Broadway, 1924.

Widow By Proxy, A Farce-Comedy in Three Acts. New York:
French, 1930. Produced Broadway, 1913.

Biography

Parsons, C. L. "Catherine Cushing." New York Dramatic Mirror,
67 (Jan. 17, 1912), 5+.

Patterson, Ada. "How Kitty MacKay and Jerry Were Born." Theatre, 19 (June 1914), 300+.

Reviews

New York Times, Oct. 6, 1925, 31:1. [Edgar Allan Poe.]

New York Times, Oct. 29, 1918, 9:3. [Glorianna.]

Theatre, 38 (December 1918), 339+. [Glorianna.]

Green Book, 11 (June 1914), 1017-8. [Jerry.]

New York Times, March 30, 1914, 9:1. [Jerry.]

Theatre, 19 (May 1914), 225-6. [Jerry.]

Bookman, 39 (March 1914), 65. [Kitty MacKay.]

Dramatist, 6 (October 1914), 504-5. [Kitty MacKay.]

New York Times, Jan. 8, 1914, 11:3. [Kitty MacKay.]

New York Times, April 7, 1920, 9:2. [Lassie.]

Theatre, 31 (May 1920), 401+. [Lassie.]

New York Times, Aug. 12, 1924, 12:2. [Marge.]

Life, 79 (Feb. 16, 1922), 18. [Marjolaine.]

New York Times, Jan. 25, 1922, 16:1. [Marjolaine.]

Theatre, 35 (April 1922), 229. [Marjolaine.]

New York Times, Dec. 23, 1925, 22:2. [Master of the Inn.]

Dramatist, 7 (July 1916), 708. [Pollyanna.]

Green Book, 16 (December 1916), 965-8. [Pollyanna.]

Theatre, 24 (November 1916), 277. [Pollyanna.]

Hampton, 27 (October 1911), 520. [The Real Thing.]

Theatre, 14 (September 1911), 78-9. [The Real Thing.]

Green Book, 11 (April 1914), 606-7. [Sari.]

International, 8 (February 1914), 68+. [Sari.]

New York Times, Jan. 29, 1930, 27:1. [Sari.]

New York Times, Dec. 24, 1924, 11:1. [Topsy and Eva.]

Theatre, 40 (March 1925), 16. [Topsy and Eva.]

Dramatist, 4 (April 1913), 346-7. [Widow by Proxy.]

Green Book, 9 (May 1913), 745-7. [Widow by Proxy.]

DAYTON, KATHARINE (1891-1945)

Plays

First Lady; A Play in Three Acts.   Written with George S. Kaufman.
New York: Random House, 1935.   Produced Broadway, 1935.

Save Me the Waltz.   1937.   Carbon copy of typescript at the Library
of Congress.   Produced Broadway, 1938.

Biography

Independent Woman, 15 (March 1936), 75.

New York Times, March 3, 1945, 21:3.   (Obituary.)

Reviews

Nation, 141 (Dec. 11, 1935), 694+.   [First Lady.]

Stage, 13 (January 1936), 22+.   [First Lady.]

New York Times, Dec. 8, 1935, sec. X, 3:1.   [First Lady.]

Theatre Arts, 20 (January 1936), 16+.   [First Lady.]

Nation, 146 (March 12, 1938), 310.   [Save Me the Waltz.]

New York Times, March 1, 1938, 19:2.   [Save Me the Waltz.]

Newsweek, 11 (March 14, 1938), 22.   [Save Me the Waltz.]

DONNELLY, DOROTHY (1880-1928)

Plays

Blossom Time.   Book and lyrics by Dorothy Donnelly.   Music adapted
from melodies of Schubert and Berete by Sigmund Romberg.   Play
adapted from Drei Madelhaus, by Willner and Reichert.   Lyrics
published by Leo Feist, 1921.   Produced Broadway, 1921.

The Call of Life. Adapted from a story by A. Schnitzler. Unpublished. Produced Broadway, 1925.

Fancy Free. Written with A. Barratt. Unpublished. Produced Broadway, 1918.

Forbidden. Unpublished. Produced Broadway, 1920.

Hello, Lola! Unpublished. Produced Broadway, 1926.

My Golden Girl. Variant title of My Princess.

My Maryland. Book and lyrics by Dorothy Donnelly. Music by Sigmund Romberg. New York: Harms, 1927. Produced Broadway, 1927.

My Princess; A Modern Operetta in Three Acts. Book and lyrics by Dorothy Donnelly. Music by Sigmund Romberg. Adapted from a play by Dorothy Donnelly and Edward Shelton. New York: Harms, 1927. Produced Broadway, 1927.

Poppy. Book and lyrics by Dorothy Donnelly. Music by Stephen Jones and Arthur Samuels. Unpublished. Produced Broadway, 1923.

The Proud Princess. Unpublished. Produced Baltimore, 1924.

The Riddle Woman. Unpublished. Produced Broadway, 1918.

The Student Prince. Book and lyrics by Dorothy Donnelly. Music by Sigmund Romberg. Piano-vocal score published by Harms, 1932. Produced Broadway, 1924.

Biography

"Dorothy Donnelly." Pearson (New York), 23 (April 1910), 557-8.

Kobbé, Gustav. Famous Actresses and Their Homes. Boston: Little, Brown, 1905, pp. 237-43.

Who Was Who in America. Vol. 1. Chicago: Marquis Who's Who, 1943.

Reviews

Life, 78 (Oct. 20, 1921), 18. [Blossom Time.]

New York Times, Sept. 30, 1921, 10:1. [Blossom Time.]

Theatre, 34 (December 1921), 388. [Blossom Time.]

Nation, 121 (Oct. 28, 1925), 494-5. [The Call of Life.]

New Republic, 44 (Oct. 28, 1925), 255-6. [The Call of Life.]

New York Times, Oct. 10, 1925, 10:1. [The Call of Life.]

Green Book, 20 (August 1918), 200+. [Fancy Free.]

Life, 71 (April 25, 1918), 682. [Fancy Free.]

New York Times, April 12, 1918, 11:1. [Fancy Free.]

Dramatist, 11 (January 1920), 904-5. [Forbidden.]

Life, 75 (Jan. 1, 1920), 27. [Forbidden.]

New York Times, Dec. 22, 1920, 19:1. [Forbidden.]

New York Times, Jan. 13, 1926, 30:1. [Hello, Lola.]

New York Times, Sept. 13, 1927, 37:2. [My Maryland.]

Vogue, 70 (Nov. 1, 1927), 126. [My Maryland.]

New York Times, Oct. 7, 1927, 24:2. [My Princess.]

Life, 82 (Sept. 20, 1923), 18. [Poppy.]

Nation, 119 (Sept. 19, 1923), 304. [Poppy.]

New York Times, Sept. 4, 1923, 14:2. [Poppy.]

New York Times, Feb. 17, 1924, sec. VII, 2:8. [The Proud Princess.]

Life, 72 (Nov. 7, 1918), 674. [The Riddle Woman.]

New York Times, Oct. 24, 1918, 11:3. [The Riddle Woman.]

Theatre, 28 (December 1918), 346. [The Riddle Woman.]

American Mercury, 4 (February 1925), 248-9. [The Student Prince.]

New York Times, Dec. 3, 1924, 25:3. [The Student Prince.]

Theatre, 41 (February 1925), 14-5. [The Student Prince.]

DREXLER, ROSALYN (1926-)

Plays

The Bed Was Full. In: Drexler, Rosalyn. The Line of Least Existence, and Other Plays. New York: Random House, 1967. Produced off-Broadway, 1972.

Home Movies. Music by Al Carmines. In: Drexler, Rosalyn. The Line of Least Existence, and Other Plays. New York: Random House, 1967. Also in: Poland, Albert, and Bruce Mailman, eds. The Off-Off Broadway Book. Indianapolis: Bobbs-Merrill, 1972. Produced off-Broadway, 1964.

Hot Buttered Roll. In: Drexler, Rosalyn. The Line of Least Existence, and Other Plays. New York: Random House, 1967. Also in: Benedikt, Michael, ed. Theatre Experiment. New York: Doubleday, 1967. Produced London, 1970.

The Investigation. In: Drexler, Rosalyn. The Line of Least Existence, and Other Plays. New York: Random House, 1967. Produced Boston, 1966; London, 1970.

The Line of Least Existence. New York: Random House, 1967. Produced off-Broadway, 1968.

She Who Was He. Unpublished. Produced off-Broadway, 1973.

Skywriting. In: Parone, Edward, ed. Collision Course. New York: Random House, 1968. Produced off-Broadway, 1968.

Softly, and Consider the Nearness. In: Drexler, Rosalyn. The Line of Least Existence, and Other Plays. New York: Random House, 1967. Produced off-Broadway, 1964.

Biography

Contemporary Dramatists. James Vinson, ed. 2nd ed. New York: St. Martin, 1977.

Goulianos, J. "Women and the Avant-Garde Theater: Interview." Massachusetts Review, 13 (Winter 1972), 257-67.

New York Times Biographical Edition, 2 (Nov. 7, 1971), 4055.

Criticism

Brown, Janet. Feminist Drama; Definition & Critical Analysis. Metuchen, N.J.: Scarecrow, 1979, pp. 22-36.

Olauson, Judith. The American Woman Playwright; A View of Criticism and Characterization. Troy, N.Y.: Whitston, 1981, pp. 114-8.

Reviews

New York Times, May 12, 1964, 32:1. [Home Movies.]

New Yorker, 40 (May 23, 1964), 134. [Home Movies.]

Plays and Players, 17 (April 1970), 43. [Hot Buttered Roll and Investigation.]

New York Times, March 25, 1968, 53:1. [The Line of Least Existence.]

Newsweek, 71 (April 1, 1968), 88. [The Line of Least Existence.]

New York Times, May 19, 1968, sec. II, 1:1. [Skywriting.]

New York Times, May 12, 1964, 32:1. [Softly, and Consider the Nearness.]

DUBOIS, SHIRLEY GRAHAM (1907-1977)

Plays

Coal Dust. Unpublished. Produced by the Gilpin Players, Cleveland, 1938.

Dust to Dust. Unpublished. Produced at Yale University, 1941(?).

Elijah's Ravens. Unpublished. Produced by the Gilpin Players, Cleveland, 1930.

I Gotta Home. Unpublished. Produced by the Gilpin Players, Cleveland, 1939.

It's Morning. Unpublished. Produced at Yale University, 1940.

Little Black Sambo. With Charlotte Chorpenning. Unpublished. Produced by the Federal Theater Project, Chicago, 1938.

The Swing Mikado. Unpublished. Produced by the Federal Theater Project, Chicago, 1938.

Tom-Tom. Unpublished. Produced as part of the Cleveland Opera Series, Summer 1932.

Track Thirteen. Boston: Expression, 1940. (Radio comedy.)

Biography

Chrisman, Robert. "The Black Scholar Hosts Shirley Graham Du-Bois." Black Scholar, 2 (December 1970), 50-2.

"Conversation: Ida Lewis and Shirley Graham DuBois." Essence, 1 (January 1971), 22-7.

Current Biography Yearbook 1946. New York: H. W. Wilson, 1947. (See under Graham, Shirley.)

Mason, Deborah. "DuBois Legend Carries on in Cairo." Sepia, 24 (January 1975), 45-53.

New York Times, April 5, 1977, p. 36. (Obituary.)

Reviews

Commonweal, 29 (March 17, 1939), 580. [The Swing Mikado.]

Nation, 148 (March 18, 1939), 328-9. [The Swing Mikado.]

Time, 33 (March 13, 1939), 57. [The Swing Mikado.]

ELLIS, EDITH (1876-1960)

Plays

The Amethyst Ring. Unpublished.

A Batch of Blunders. Unpublished.

Because I Love You. Unpublished.

Ben of Broken Bow; An Original American Comedy in Four Acts.
New York: French, 1925.

Betty's Last Bet; A Farce-Comedy in Three Acts. Chicago: Denison, 1921.

Bravo, Claudia. Unpublished.

Contrary Mary, A Comedy in Three Acts. New York: French, 1912.

Cupid's Ladder. Unpublished.

Dangerous Age. Variant title of White Villa. Produced London, 1937.

Devil's Garden. Based on the novel by W. B. Maxwell. Typescript at the New York Public Library. Produced Broadway, 1915.

Fields of Flax. Unpublished.

He Fell in Love with His Wife. Unpublished.

The Illustrious Tartarin; A Comedy in 3 Acts and 5 Scenes. Based on Alphonse Daudet's Tartarin in the Alps. New York: Rosenfield, ©1922.

The Judsons Entertain; A Comedy in Three Acts. New York: French, 1922.

Lady of LaPaz. Based on the novel These Generations, by Elinor Mordaunt. Unpublished. Produced London, 1936.

Last Chapter. Written with Edward Ellis. Unpublished. Produced London, 1930.

Love Wager. Unpublished.

Madame Is Amused. Unpublished.

Make-Believe. Unpublished.

Making Dick Over. Unpublished. Produced New York City, 1915.

The Man Higher Up. Unpublished. Produced Broadway, 1912.

The Man with Black Gloves. Unpublished.

Mary and John. Unpublished. Produced Broadway, 1905.

Mary Jane's Pa; A Play in Three Acts. New York: French, 1914. Produced Broadway, 1908.

Moon and Sixpence. Based on the novel by W. S. Maugham. Typewritten carbon copy at the Library of Congress. Produced London, 1925.

Mrs. B. O'Shaughnessy. Unpublished.

Mrs. Clancy's Car Ride. Written with Edward Ellis. Washington, D. C. : Commission on Training Camp Activities, Dept. of Dramatic Activities Among the Soldiers, 1918.

Mrs. Jimmie Thompson. Written with N. S. Rose. Unpublished. Produced Broadway, 1920.

My Man. Written with F. Halsey. Unpublished. Produced Broadway, 1910.

Partners. Unpublished.

Point of View. Unpublished. Produced Broadway, 1903.

Seven Sisters, A Farce Comedy in Three Acts. New York: Dramatists Play Service, 1933. Produced Broadway, 1911.

The Swallow. Typescript at the New York Public Library.

White Collars; A Comedy in Three Acts. Based on the novelette by Edgar Franklin. New York: French, 1926. Produced Broadway, 1925.

White Villa. Unpublished. Variant title of Dangerous Age. Produced Broadway, 1921.

Whose Little Bride Are You? A Farce Comedy in Three Acts. Chicago: Denison, 1919.

The Wrong Man. Unpublished.

Biography

American Women Writers; A Critical Reference Guide from Colonial Times to the Present. Lina Mainiero, ed. Vol. 1. New York: Ungar, 1979.

Mantle, Robert B. American Playwrights of Today. New York: Dodd, Mead, 1929, pp. 282-3.

New York Times, Dec. 28, 1960, 27:4. (Obituary.)

Criticism

American Women Writers; A Critical Reference Guide from Colonial Times to the Present. Lina Mainiero, ed. Vol. 1. New York: Ungar, 1979.

Reviews

New York Times, Oct. 6, 1937, 29:1. [Dangerous Age.]

Dramatist, 7 (January 1916), 645-6. [Devil's Garden.]

Green Book, 15 (March 1916), 439-40. [Devil's Garden.]

New York Times, Dec. 29, 1915, 11:1. [Devil's Garden.]

Theatre World, 26 (August 1936), 65-76. [Lady of LaPaz.]

The Times (London), July 3, 1936, p. 3, col. B. [Lady of LaPaz.]

London News, 176 (June 7, 1930), 1060. [Last Chapter.]

Saturday Review, 149 (June 7, 1930), 722. [Last Chapter.]

The Times (London), May 28, 1930, p. 14, col. B. [Last Chapter.]

New York Dramatic Mirror, 75 (Jan. 1, 1916), 9. [Making Dick Over.]

Collier's, 50 (Oct. 26, 1912), 15+. [The Man Higher Up.]

New York Times, Sept. 12, 1905, 9:1. [Mary and John.]

Theatre, 9 (January 1909), 4-5. [Mary Jane's Pa.]

Nation (London), 38 (Oct. 3, 1925), 16. [Moon and Sixpence.]

New York Times, Dec. 17, 1933, sec. IX, 4:3. [Moon and Sixpence.]

Saturday Review, 140 (Oct. 3, 1925), 269-70. [Moon and Sixpence.]

Dramatist, 11 (April 1920), 992-3. [Mrs. Jimmie....]

Life, 75 (April 15, 1920), 708-9. [Mrs. Jimmie....]

New York Times, March 30, 1920, 9:1. [Mrs. Jimmie....]

New York Dramatic Mirror, 64 (Oct. 5, 1910), 7+. [My Man.]

New York Times, Sept. 28, 1910, 11:3. [My Man.]

Theatre, 12 (November 1910), 5. [My Man.]

New York Times, April 16, 1903, 3:2. [Point of View.]

Collier's, 46 (March 11, 1911), 13+. [Seven Sisters.]

Theatre, 13 (April 1911), 136+. [Seven Sisters.]

New York Times, Feb. 24, 1925, 17:2. [White Collars.]

New York Times, Feb. 15, 1921, 7:1. [White Villa.]

Theatre, 33 (April 1921), 264+. [White Villa.]

Weekly Review, 4 (March 2, 1921), 209. [White Villa.]

EPHRON, PHOEBE (1916-1971)

Plays

Howie; A Comedy in Three Acts. New York: French, 1959. Produced Broadway, 1958.

My Daughter, Your Son; A Comedy in Two Acts. Written with Henry Ephron. New York: French, 1969. Produced Broadway, 1969.

Take Her, She's Mine; A Comedy. Written with Henry Ephron. New York: Random House, 1962. Also in: Theatre Arts, 47 (July 1963), 37-70. Produced Broadway, 1961.

Three's a Family; A Comedy in Three Acts. Written with Henry Ephron. New York: French, 1944. Produced London, 1944.

Biography

New York Times, Oct. 14, 1971, p. 48. (Obituary.)

Reviews

Theatre Arts, 42 (November 1958), 9. [Howie.]

New York Times, Sept. 18, 1958, 35:2. [Howie.]

New Yorker, 34 (Sept. 27, 1958), 74. [Howie.]

America, 121 (July 5, 1969), 18. [My Daughter....]

New York Times, May 14, 1969, 36:2. [My Daughter....]

New York Times, Dec. 22, 1961, 19:1. [Take Her....]

New Yorker, 37 (Jan. 6, 1962), 57. [Take Her....]

Newsweek, 59 (Jan. 1, 1962), 48. [Take Her....]

Life, 14 (June 28, 1943), 68+. [Three's a Family.]

New York Times, May 6, 1943, 24:2. [Three's a Family.]

FAY, MARY HELEN (1915?-)

Plays

Alice in Arms. Written with L. Bus-Fekete. Unpublished. Produced Broadway, 1945.

The Big Two. Written with L. Bus-Fekete. Unpublished. Produced Broadway, 1947.

Embezzled Heaven. Written with L. Bus-Fekete. Adapted from the novel by F. Werfel. Unpublished. Produced Broadway, 1944.

Faithfully Yours. Written with L. Bus-Fekete. Unpublished. Produced Broadway, 1951.

Girl Who Talked to God. Unpublished. Never produced on the professional stage.

Biography

Contemporary Authors; A Bio-bibliographical Guide to Current Authors and Their Works. Ann Evory, ed. Vol. 33-36, first revision. Detroit: Gale, 1978. (See under Fagyas, Maria.)

Reviews

New York Times, Feb. 1, 1945, 18:4. [Alice in Arms.]

Nation, 164 (Jan. 25, 1947), 110. [The Big Two.]

New York Times, Jan. 9, 1947, 21:2. [The Big Two.]

Theatre Arts, 31 (March 1947), 18. [The Big Two.]

Nation, 159 (Nov. 11, 1944), 598. [Embezzled Heaven.]

New York Times, Nov. 1, 1944, 20:2. [Embezzled Heaven.]

Theatre Arts, 29 (January 1945), 9-10. [Embezzled Heaven.]

New York Times, Oct. 19, 1951, 22:5. [Faithfully Yours.]

New Yorker, 27 (Oct. 27, 1951), 67. [Faithfully Yours.]

Theatre Arts, 35 (December 1951), 3. [Faithfully Yours.]

FERBER, EDNA (1887-1968)

Plays

Bravo! Written with George S. Kaufman. New York: Dramatists
Play Service, 1949. Produced Broadway, 1948.

Dinner at Eight, A Play in Three Acts. Written with George S.
Kaufman. New York: French, 1935. Also in: Mantle, Robert
B., ed. Best Plays of 1932-1933. New York: Dodd, Mead,
1933. (Condensation.) Produced Broadway, 1932.

The Eldest; A Drama of America Life. New York: Appleton, 1925.
Also in: Nicolson, Kenyon, ed. The Appleton Book of Short
Plays. 2nd series. New York: Appleton, 1927. Never pro-
duced on the professional stage.

The Land Is Bright. Written with George S. Kaufman. Garden
City, N.Y.: Doubleday, 1941. Produced Broadway, 1941.

Minick, A Comedy in Three Acts. Written with George S. Kaufman.
New York: French, 1925. Also in: Mantle, Robert B., ed. Best
Plays of 1924-1925. New York: Dodd, Mead, 1925. (Condensa-
tion.) Produced Broadway, 1924.

Our Mrs. McChesney. Written with George V. Hobart. N.p.,
191? Typescript copy at the New York Public Library. Produced
Broadway, 1915.

The Royal Family, A Comedy in Three Acts. Written with George
S. Kaufman. Garden City, N.Y.: Doubleday, 1928. Produced
Broadway, 1927.

Stage Door. Written with George S. Kaufman. Garden City, N.Y.:
Doubleday, 1936. Also in: Mantle, Robert B., ed. Best Plays of
1936-1937. New York: Dodd, Mead, 1937. (Condensation.)
Produced Broadway, 1936.

$1200 a Year; A Comedy in Three Acts. Written with Newman
Levy. Garden City, N.Y.: Doubleday, 1920. Never produced.
on the professional stage.

Biography

Contemporary Authors; A Bio-bibliographical Guide to Current Authors and Their Works. Clare D. Kinsman, ed. Vol. 5-8, first revision. Detroit: Gale, 1969.

Ferber, Edna. A Kind of Magic. Garden City, N. Y. : Doubleday, 1963. (Autobiography.)

Ferber, Edna. A Peculiar Treasure; Autobiography. Garden City, N. Y. : Doubleday, 1939.

Gilbert, Julie Goldsmith. Ferber; A Biography of Edna Ferber and Her Circle. Garden City, N. Y. : Doubleday, 1978.

Criticism

Bromfield, Louis. "Edna Ferber." Saturday Review of Literature, 12 (June 15, 1935), 10-12.

Overton, G. "Social Critic in Edna Ferber." Bookman, 64 (October 1926), 138-43.

Shaughnessy, Mary Rose. Women and Success in American Society in the Works of Edna Ferber. New York: Gordon, 1976.

Reviews

New York Times, Nov. 12, 1948, 31:2. [Bravo!]

Time, 52 (Nov. 22, 1948), 85. [Bravo!]

Nation, 135 (Nov. 9, 1932), 464-5. [Dinner at Eight.]

New Republic, 72 (Nov. 9, 1932), 355-7. [Dinner at Eight.]

New York Times, Oct. 24, 1932, 18:2. [Dinner at Eight.]

New York Times, Nov. 6, 1932, sec. IX, 1:1. [Dinner at Eight.]

Theatre Arts, 10 (April 1926), 280. [The Eldest.]

New York Times, Oct. 29, 1941, 26:2. [The Land is Bright.]

New York Times, Nov. 9, 1941, sec. IX, 1:1. [The Land Is Bright.]

Newsweek, 18 (Nov. 10, 1941), 70. [The Land Is Bright.]

American Mercury, 3 (November 1924), 376-7. [Minick.]

New York Times, Sept. 25, 1924, 20:1. [Minick.]

Theatre Arts, 9 (June 1925), 420. [Minick.]

Harper's Weekly, 61 (Nov. 6, 1915), 440. [Our Mrs. McChesney.]

Nation, 101 (Oct. 28, 1915), 527. [Our Mrs. McChesney.]

Life, 91 (Jan. 19, 1928), 21. [The Royal Family.]

New York Times, Dec. 29, 1927, 26:4. [The Royal Family.]

New York Times, Jan. 8, 1928, sec. VIII, 1:1. [The Royal Family.]

Saturday Review of Literature, 4 (Jan. 21, 1928), 531-2. [The Royal Family.]

New Republic, 89 (Nov. 11, 1936), 50. [Stage Door.]

New York Times, Sept. 29, 1936, 35:1. [Stage Door.]

New York Times, Oct. 4, 1936, sec. IX, 2:1. [Stage Door.]

Theatre Arts, 5 (January 1921), 86. [$1200 a Year.]

FIELDS, DOROTHY (1905-1974)

Plays

Annie Get Your Gun. Book by Dorothy and Herbert Fields. Music and lyrics by Irving Berlin. Chicago: Dramatic Publishing, 1952. Produced Broadway, 1946.

Arms and the Girl. Written with Herbert Fields and Rouben Mamoulian. N.Y. ?, 1950. Typewritten prompt book at the New York Public Library. Produced Broadway, 1950.

Blackbirds of 1928. Music by Jimmy McHugh. Lyrics by Dorothy Fields. New York: Jack Mills, 1928. Produced Broadway, 1928.

By the Beautiful Sea. Book by Dorothy and Herbert Fields. Music by Arthur Schwartz. Lyrics by Dorothy Fields. New York: Meyerson, 1954(?). Typescript at the New York Public Library. Produced Broadway, 1954.

Hello Daddy. Book by Herbert Fields. Music by Jimmy McHugh. Lyrics by Dorothy Fields. Unpublished. Produced Broadway, 1928.

International Revue. Book by Nat Dorfman and Lew Leslie. Music by Jimmy McHugh. Lyrics by Dorothy Fields. Unpublished. Produced Broadway, 1930.

Let's Face It! Music by Cole Porter. Book by Dorothy and Herbert Fields. Lyrics by Dorothy Fields. Unpublished. Produced Broadway, 1941.

Mexican Hayride. Written with Herbert Fields. Songs by Cole Porter. N.p., 1943. Typewritten copy at the New York Public Library. Produced Broadway, 1944.

Redhead. Book by Dorothy and Herbert Fields, Sidney Sheldon, David Shaw. Music by Albert Hague. Lyrics by Dorothy Fields. New York: Hart Stenographic Bureau, 1958(?). Typescript at the New York Public Library. Produced Broadway, 1959.

Seesaw: A Musical. Book by Michael Bennett. Music by Cy Coleman. Lyrics by Dorothy Fields. New York: French, 1975. Produced Broadway, 1973.

Singin' the Blues. Songs by Jimmy McHugh and Dorothy Fields. New York: Robbins Music, 1931. Produced Broadway, 1931.

Something for the Boys. Book by Dorothy and Herbert Fields. Music by Cole Porter. Unpublished. Produced Broadway, 1943.

Stars in Your Eyes; A Musical Comedy. Book by J. P. McEvoy. Music by Arthur Schwartz. Lyrics by Dorothy Fields. New York, 1939. Produced Broadway, 1939.

Sweet Charity. Book by Neil Simon. Music by Cy Coleman. Lyrics by Dorothy Fields. New York: Random House, 1966. Produced Broadway, 1966.

Swing to the Left. Variant title of Stars in Your Eyes.

A Tree Grows in Brooklyn. Book by Betty Smith and George Abbott. Music by Arthur Schwartz. Lyrics by Dorothy Fields. New York: Harper, 1951. Produced Broadway, 1951.

Up in Central Park. Book by Dorothy and Herbert Fields. Music by Sigmund Romberg. New York, 1945. Typescript at the New York Public Library. Produced Broadway, 1945.

Biography

Current Biography 1958. New York: H.W. Wilson, 1958.

New York Times, March 29, 1974, p. 38. (Obituary.)

Wilk, Max. They're Playing Our Song. New York: Atheneum, 1973, pp. 40-50.

Reviews

Life, 20 (June 3, 1946), 89-94. [Annie Get Your Gun.]

New York Times, May 26, 1946, sec. II, 1:1. [Annie Get Your Gun.]

Saturday Review, 29 (June 15, 1946), 30-2. [Annie Get Your Gun.]

New York Times, Feb. 3, 1950, 28:2. [Arms and the Girl.]

New Yorker, 25 (Feb. 11, 1950), 46-7. [Arms and the Girl.]

Life, 92 (July 12, 1928), 12. [Blackbirds.]

New York Times, May 10, 1928, 31:3. [Blackbirds.]

Life, 36 (May 17, 1954), 109-10. [By the Beautiful Sea.]

New York Times, April 18, 1954, sec. II, 1:1. [By the Beautiful Sea.]

New Yorker, 30 (April 17, 1954), 64-6. [By the Beautiful Sea.]

Life, 93 (Jan. 28, 1929), 12. [Hello Daddy.]

New York Times, Dec. 27, 1928, 26:5. [Hello Daddy.]

Life, 95 (March 28, 1930), 18. [International Revue.]

New York Times, Feb. 26, 1930, 22:2. [International Revue.]

Life, 11 (Oct. 10, 1941), 114-6+. [Let's Face It.]

New York Times, Oct. 10, 1941, 27:1. [Let's Face It.]

Life, 16 (Feb. 21, 1944), 83-4+. [Mexican Hayride.]

New York Times, Feb. 6, 1944, sec. II, 1:1. [Mexican Hayride.]

Theatre Arts, 28 (April 1944), 202+. [Mexican Hayride.]

Life, 46 (Feb. 23, 1959), 81-3. [Redhead.]

New York Times, Feb. 6, 1959, 21:1. [Redhead.]

Time, 73 (Feb. 16, 1959), 77. [Redhead.]

New York Times, March 25, 1973, sec. II, 1:1. [Seesaw.]

New Yorker, 49 (March 24, 1973), 74. [Seesaw.]

New York Times, April 12, 1931, sec. IX, 2:1. [Singin' the Blues.]

Life, 14 (Feb. 8, 1943), 79+. [Something for the Boys.]

New York Times, Jan. 17, 1943, sec. VIII, 1:1. [Something for the Boys.]

New Yorker, 18 (Jan. 16, 1943), 32. [Something for the Boys.]

New York Times, Feb. 10, 1939, 18:2. [Stars in Your Eyes.]

Time, 33 (Feb. 20, 1939), 54-5. [Stars in Your Eyes.]

Life, 60 (March 25, 1966), 99-100. [Sweet Charity.]

New York Times, Jan. 31, 1966, 22:1. [Sweet Charity.]

New Yorker, 41 (Feb. 5, 1966), 84. [Sweet Charity.]

New York Times, April 29, 1951, sec. II, 1:1. [A Tree....]

New Yorker, 27 (April 28, 1951), 56+. [A Tree....]

Life, 18 (Feb. 19, 1945), 41-2+. [Up in Central Park.]

New York Times, Jan. 29, 1945, 17:2. [Up in Central Park.]

New Yorker, 20 (Feb. 3, 1945), 40+. [Up in Central Park.]

FLINT, EVA K. (1902-)

Plays

Subway Express. Written with Martha Madison. Unpublished. Reproduction from a typewritten copy at the New York Public Library. Produced Broadway, 1929.

Under Glass; A Comedy in Three Acts. Written with George Bradshaw. New York: L. Salisbury, 193(?). Reproduction from a typewritten copy at the New York Public Library. Produced Broadway, 1933.

The Up and Up. Written with Martha Madison. Unpublished. Produced Broadway, 1930.

Reviews

New York Times, Sept. 25, 1929, 34:3. [Subway Express.]

Theatre, 50 (December 1929), 66. [Subway Express.]

New York Times, Oct. 31, 1933, 24:3. [Under Glass.]

New York Times, Sept. 9, 1930, 25:2. [The Up and Up.]

Theatre, 52 (November 1930), 25+. [The Up and Up.]

FORD, HARRIET (1868-1949)

Plays

Are Men Superior? A Farce Comedy in One Act. New York:
French, 1933. Also in: One Act Plays for Stage and Study. 7th
series. New York: French, 1932. Never produced on the professional stage.

The Argyle Case; A Play in Four Acts. Written with H. J. O'Higgins. New York: French, 1927. Produced Broadway, 1912.

Audrey. Written with E. F. Bodington. Unpublished. Produced
Broadway, 1902.

The Bride; A Comedy in One Act. New York: French, 1924. Produced Broadway, 1924.

Christopher Rand. Written with E. Robson in 1929. Unpublished.
Never produced on the professional stage.

The Dickey Bird. Written with H. J. O'Higgins. In: One Act
Plays for Stage and Study. 2nd series. New York: French,
1925. Produced Broadway, 1915.

The Divine Afflatus; A Comedy in One Act. New York: French,
1931. Never produced on the professional stage.

The Dummy; A Detective Comedy in Four Acts. Written with H. J.
O'Higgins and W. J. Burns. New York: French, 1925. Produced Broadway, 1914.

Fourth Estate. Written with J. M. Patterson. Unpublished. Produced Broadway, 1909.

A Gentleman of France. Adapted from the novel by Stanley Weyman. Typescript at the New York Public Library. Produced Broadway, 1901.

The Greatest Thing in the World; A Drama in Four Acts. Written with B. DeMille. Typescript at the New York Public Library. Produced Broadway, 1900.

The Happy Hoboes; A Comedy in One Act. Written with A. S. Tucker. New York: French, 1928. Never produced on the professional stage.

Heroic Treatment; A Comedy in One Act. New York: French, 1930. Never produced on the professional stage.

The Hold-Up; One Act Comedy. Written with A. G. O'Higgins. New York: French, 1930. Never produced on the professional stage.

In the Next Room; A Play in Three Acts. Written with E. Robson. New York: French, 1925. Produced Broadway, 1923.

In-Laws, A Comedy in One Act. In: One Act Plays for Stage and Study. 4th series. New York: French, 1928. Never produced on the professional stage.

Jacqueline. Written with C. Duer in 1909. Typescript at the New York Public Library.

The Land of the Free. Written with F. Hurst. Unpublished. Produced Asbury Park, N.J., 1917.

A Little Brother of the Rich. Written with J. M. Patterson. Unpublished. Produced Broadway, 1909.

Main Street. Written with H. J. O'Higgins. Adapted from the novel by Sinclair Lewis. Unpublished. Produced Broadway, 1921.

Mr. Lazarus; A Comedy in Four Acts. Written with H. J. O'Higgins. New York: French, 1916. Produced Broadway, 1916.

Mr. Susan Peters, A Comedy in One Act. New York: French, 1928. Never produced on the professional stage.

Mysterious Money, A Comedy in Three Acts. New York: French, 1929.

Old P. Q. : A Play in Three Acts. New York: French, 1928.

On the Hiring Line; A Comedy in Three Acts. Written with H. J.

O'Higgins. New York: French, 1923. Produced Broadway, 1918.
Produced London, 1921, under the title Wrong Number.

Orphan Aggie; A Romantic Comedy. Written with H. J. O'Higgins.
New York: French, 1927.

Polygamy. Written with H. J. O'Higgins. Unpublished. Produced
Broadway, 1914.

Sweet Seventeen. Unpublished. Produced Broadway, 1924.

Under Twenty; A Comedy in Three Acts. Written with L. Wester-
velt, J. Clements, and H. J. O'Higgins. New York: French,
1926.

Wanted--Money; A Comedy in One Act. Written with Althea Sprague
Tucker. New York: French, 1928. Produced Broadway, 1928.

What Are Parents For? New York: French, 1930. Never produced
on the professional stage.

What Imagination Will Do. New York: French, 1928. Never produced on the professional stage.

When a Feller Needs a Friend; A Play in Three Acts. Written with
H. J. O'Higgins. New York: French, 1920. Produced Broadway,
1918.

Where Julia Rules; A Comedy in Four Acts. Written with C. Duer.
New York: French, 1923.

The Woman He Married. Unpublished. Produced Denver, 1917.

The Wrong Number. Variant title of On the Hiring Line.

Youth Must Be Served; A Comedy in One Act. New York: French,
1934. Also in: One Act Plays for Stage and Study, 3rd series.
New York: French, 1927. Never produced on the professional
stage.

Biography

Dodge, W. P. "Sketch." Strand (New York), 49 (May 1915), 559-64.

"Greatest Gamble in the World." Strand (New York), 49 (May 1915),
553-9.

Mantle, Robert B. American Playwrights of Today. New York:
Dodd, Mead, 1929, pp. 248-50.

New York Times, Dec. 14, 1949, p. 31. (Obituary.)

Reviews

Green Book, 9 (March 1913), 389+. [The Argyle Case.]

New York Times, Dec. 25, 1912, 11:3. [The Argyle Case.]

New York Times, Feb. 20, 1915, 11:1. [The Dickey Bird.]

Green Book, 12 (July 1914), 102-4. [The Dummy.]

New York Times, April 14, 1914, 11:3. [The Dummy.]

Forum, 42 (November 1909), 438. [Fourth Estate.]

New York Times, Oct. 7, 1909, 9:3. [Fourth Estate.]

New York Times, Oct. 9, 1900, 5:1. [The Greatest Thing....]

New York Times, Oct. 3, 1923, 15:3. [In the Next Room.]

New York Times, Oct. 7, 1917, sec. II, 4:2. [The Land of the Free.]

Hampton, 24 (March 1910), 405-6. [A Little Brother....]

New York Times, Dec. 28, 1909, 9:3. [A Little Brother....]

Nation, 113 (Nov. 23, 1921), 603-4. [Main Street.]

New York Times, Oct. 2, 1921, sec. VII, 1:5. [Main Street.]

Nation, 103 (Sept. 14, 1916), 265. [Mr. Lazarus.]

New York Times, Sept. 6, 1916, 7:3. [Mr. Lazarus.]

Dramatist, 11 (January 1920), 986. [On the Hiring Line.]

Nation, 99 (Dec. 10, 1914), 698. [Polygamy.]

New York Times, Dec. 13, 1914, sec. VIII, 8:2. [Polygamy.]

New York Times, March 18, 1924, 24:2. [Sweet Seventeen.]

New York Times, July 17, 1921, sec. VI, 1:8. [Wrong Number.]

FORD, NANCY (1936-)

Plays

I'm Getting My Act Together and Taking It on the Road. Written
 with Gretchen Cryer. New York: French, 1980. Produced off-
 Broadway, 1978.

The Last Sweet Days of Isaac. Book and lyrics by Gretchen Cryer.
 Music by Nancy Ford. Unpublished. Produced off-Broadway,
 1970.

Now Is the Time for All Good Men; A Musical. Book and lyrics by
 Gretchen Cryer. Music by Nancy Ford. New York: French,
 1969, ©1967. Produced off-Broadway, 1967.

Shelter. Book and lyrics by Gretchen Cryer. Music by Nancy Ford.
 New York: French, 1973. Produced off-Broadway, 1973.

Biography

Berg, Beatrice. "From School Days to Sweet Days." New York
 Times, Feb. 15, 1970, sec. II, 1:3.

Connely, Joan. "The Act Is Together and Thriving." Horizon, 22
 (January/February 1979), 60-5.

Dworkin, Susan. "Cryer and Ford: Hang On to the Good Times."
 Ms., 6 (December 1977), 64-5.

Reviews

New York Times, June 15, 1978, sec. III, 17:1. [I'm Getting My
 Act Together....]

New Yorker, 54 (June 26, 1978), 51-2. [I'm Getting My Act Together....]

Nation, 210 (March 9, 1970), 284. [The Last Sweet Days....]

New York Times, Feb. 8, 1970, sec. II, 1:1. [The Last Sweet
 Days....]

New Yorker, 45 (Feb. 7, 1970), 73+. [The Last Sweet Days....]

America, 117 (Oct. 14, 1967), 421-2. [Now Is the Time....]

New York Times, Sept. 27, 1967, 42:1. [Now Is the Time....]

New Yorker, 43 (Oct. 7, 1967), 133-4. [Now Is the Time....]

New York Times, Feb. 7, 1973, 31:1. [Shelter.]

New Yorker, 48 (Feb. 17, 1973), 79. [Shelter.]

FORNES, MARIA IRENE (1930-)

Plays

The Annunciation. Unpublished. Produced off-Broadway, 1967.

Aurora. Music by John FitzGibbon. Unpublished. Produced off-Broadway, 1974.

Baboon!!! With others. Unpublished. Produced Cincinnati, 1972.

Cap-a-Pie. Music by Jose Raul Bernardo. Unpublished. Produced off-Broadway, 1975.

The Curse of the Langston House. Unpublished. Produced Playhouse in the Park, Cincinnati, 1972.

Dr. Kheal. New York, 1968. Typescript at the New York Public Library. Published in: Yale Theatre Review, September 1968. Also in: Fornes, Maria Irene. Promenade and Other Plays. New York: Winter House, 1971. Produced American Place Theatre, New York, 1974.

Molly's Dream. New York: Studio Duplicating Service, n.d. Mimeographed playscript at the library of the University of Indiana. In: Fornes, Maria Irene. Promenade and Other Plays. New York: Winter House, 1971. Never produced on the professional stage.

The Office. Unpublished. Produced off-Broadway, 1966.

Promenade. Music by Al Carmines. In: Fornes, Maria Irene. Promenade and Other Plays. New York: Winter House, 1971. Produced off-Broadway, 1965.

The Red Burning Light; or Mission XQ3. New York: Studio Duplicating Service, 1971, ©1968. Typescript at the New York Public

Library. In: Fornes, Maria Irene. Promenade and Other Plays. New York: Winter House, 1971. Produced off-Broadway, 1969.

The Successful Life of Three: A Skit for Vaudeville. In: Fornes, Maria Irene. Promenade and Other Plays. New York: Winter House, 1971. Produced off-Broadway, 1965.

Tango Palace. In: Fornes, Maria Irene. Promenade and Other Plays. New York: Winter House, 1971. Also in: Ballet, Arthur H. Playwrights for Tomorrow; A Collection of Plays. Vol. II. Minnesota: University of Minnesota Press, 1966. Produced as There! You Died in New York City, 1963.

There! You Died. Variant title of Tango Palace.

A Vietnamese Wedding. New York, 1971. Typescript at the New York Public Library. In: Fornes, Maria Irene. Promenade and Other Plays. New York: Winter House, 1971. Produced off-Broadway, 1967.

The Widow. Published as La Viuda in Cuatro Autores Cubanos. Havana: Casa de Las Americas, 1961. Produced off-Broadway, 1961.

Biography

Contemporary Authors; A Bio-bibliographical Guide to Current Authors and Their Works. Clare D. Kinsman, ed. Vol. 25-28, first revision. Detroit: Gale, 1977.

Harrington, Stephanie. "Irene Fornes, Playwright: Alice and the Red Queen." Village Voice, April 21, 1966, p. 1+.

Marranca, B. "Maria Irene Fornes: Interview." Performing Arts Journal, 2, 3 (1978), 106-11.

Reviews

New York Times, Sept. 30, 1974, 53:1. [Aurora.]

New York Times, March 21, 1974, 50:1. [Dr. Kheal.]

New York Times, June 5, 1969, 56:1. [Promenade.]

New Yorker, 45 (July 5, 1969), 63. [Promenade.]

Newsweek, 73 (June 16, 1969), 107. [Promenade.]

FRANKEN, ROSE (1895-)

Plays

Another Language; A Play in Three Acts. New York: French, 1932.
(Copyrighted 1929 under the title Hallam Wives.) Also in: Mantle,
Robert B., ed. Best Plays of 1931-1932. New York: Dodd,
Mead, 1932. (Condensation.) Produced Broadway, 1932.

Beyond the Farthest Star; A Comedy Drama in Three Acts. Variant
title of Outrageous Fortune.

Claudia; A Comedy Drama in Three Acts. New York: Farrar &
Rinehart, 1941. Also in: Mantle, Robert B., ed. Best Plays
of 1940-1941. New York: Dodd, Mead, 1941. (Condensation.)
Produced Broadway, 1941.

Doctors Disagree. Unpublished. Produced Broadway, 1943.

Hallam Wives. Variant title of Another Language.

The Hallams, A Play in Three Acts. New York: French, 1948.
Produced Broadway, 1948.

Mr. Dooley Jr.; A Comedy for Children. New York: French, 1932.
Never produced on the professional stage.

Outrageous Fortune, A Drama in Three Acts. New York: French,
1944. Also in: Mantle, Robert B., ed. Best Plays of 1943-
1944. New York: Dodd, Mead, 1944. (Condensation.) Produced
Broadway, 1943.

Soldier's Wife; A Comedy in Three Acts. New York: French, 1945.
In: Mantle, Robert B., ed. Best Plays of 1944-1945. New York:
Dodd, Mead, 1945. (Condensation.) Produced Broadway, 1944.

Biography

Current Biography 1947. New York: H. W. Wilson, 1948.

Franken, Rose D. When All Is Said and Done; An Autobiography.
New York: Doubleday, 1963.

Criticism

American Women Writers; A Critical Reference Guide from Colonial
Times to the Present. Lina Mainiero, ed. Vol. 2. New York:
Ungar, 1980.

Hughes, C. "Women Playmakers." New York Times Magazine, May 4, 1941, pp. 10-1+.

Olauson, Judith. The American Woman Playwright: A View of Criticism and Characterization. Troy, N.Y.: Whitston, 1981. pp. 24-6, 48-9, 55-7.

Reviews

Nation, 134 (May 18, 1932), 580+. [Another Language.]

New Republic, 70 (May 11, 1932), 351-2. [Another Language.]

New York Times, April 26, 1932, 25:3. [Another Language.]

Life, 10 (March 31, 1941), 120-3. [Claudia.]

New York Times, Feb. 13, 1941, 24:2. [Claudia.]

Time, 37 (Feb. 24, 1941), 58. [Claudia.]

New Yorker, 19 (Jan. 8, 1944), 38. [Doctors Disagree.]

Newsweek, 23 (Jan. 10, 1944), 89. [Doctors Disagree.]

Theatre Arts, 28 (March 1944), 141. [Doctors Disagree.]

New York Times, March 5, 1948, 18:2. [The Hallams.]

New Yorker, 24, (March 13, 1948), 48. [The Hallams.]

Time, 51 (March 15, 1948), 65. [The Hallams.]

New Republic, 109 (Nov. 15, 1943), 686. [Outrageous Fortune.]

Newsweek, 22 (Nov. 15, 1943), 96. [Outrageous Fortune.]

Theatre Arts, 28 (January 1944), 8-11. [Outrageous Fortune.]

Nation, 159 (Oct. 21, 1944), 482. [Soldier's Wife.]

New York Times, Oct. 5, 1944, 18:6. [Soldier's Wife.]

New Yorker, 20 (Oct. 14, 1944), 42. [Soldier's Wife.]

FRANKLIN, JENNIE ELIZABETH (1937-)

Plays

Black Girl; A Play in Two Acts. New York: Dramatists Play Service, 1971. Produced off-Broadway, 1971.

The Creation. Unpublished. Never produced on the professional stage.

Cut Out the Lights and Call the Law. Unpublished. Never produced on the professional stage.

The Enemy. Unpublished. Never produced on the professional stage.

A First Step to Freedom. Unpublished. Produced Sharon Waite Community Center, Harmony, Miss., 1964.

Four Women. Unpublished. Never produced on the professional stage.

The In-Crowd. Unpublished. Never produced on the professional stage.

Intercession. Unpublished. Never produced on the professional stage.

MacPilate. Unpublished. Never produced on the professional stage.

The Mau Mau Room. Unpublished. Produced by the Negro Ensemble Company, off-Broadway, 1969.

The Prodigal Sister. Book and lyrics by J. E. Franklin. Music and lyrics by Micki Grant. New York: French, 1974. Produced off-Broadway, 1974.

Things Our Way. Unpublished. Never produced on the professional stage.

Till the Well Run Dry. Unpublished. Never produced on the professional stage.

Biography

Beauford, Fred. "A Conversation with Black Girl's J. E. Franklin." Black Creation, 3 (Fall 1971), 38-40.

Contemporary Authors; A Bio-bibliographical Guide to Current Authors and Their Works. Cynthia R. Fadool, ed. Vol. 61-64. Detroit: Gale, 1976.

Hunter, Charlayne. "Two Black Women Combine Lives and Talent in Play." New York Times, July 13, 1971, 9:1.

Reviews

Nation, 213 (Nov. 1, 1971), 445. [Black Girl.]

New York Times, June 17, 1971, 49:1. [Black Girl.]

New Yorker, 47 (June 26, 1971), 76. [Black Girl.]

New York, 7 (Dec. 16, 1974), 96. [The Prodigal Sister.]

New York Times, Nov. 26, 1974, 30:1. [The Prodigal Sister.]

New Yorker, 50 (Dec. 9, 1974), 69-70. [The Prodigal Sister.]

FRINGS, KETTI (1915-1981)

Plays

Angel. Libretto by Ketti Frings and Peter Udell. Lyrics by Peter Udell. Music by Gary Geld. Based on the play Look Homeward, Angel by Ketti Frings. New York: French, 1979. Produced Broadway, 1978.

Long Dream. Dramatization of the novel by R. Wright. Unpublished. Produced Broadway, 1960.

Look Homeward, Angel; A Play Based on the Novel by Thomas Wolfe. New York: Scribner, 1948. Also in: Barnes, Clive, ed. 50 Best Plays of the American Theatre. Vol. 4. New York: Crown, 1969. Produced Broadway, 1957.

Mr. Sycamore; A New Play. From a story by Robert Ayre. New York: Rialto Service Bureau, 1942. Typescript at the New York Public Library, 1942. Produced Broadway, 1942.

Walking Happy. Book by Ketti Frings and Roger Hirson. Music by James Van Heusen. Lyrics by Sammy Cahn. Based on the play

Hobson's Choice, by Harold Brighouse.   New York: French, 1967.
Produced Broadway, 1966.

Biography

Current Biography Yearbook 1960.   New York: H. W. Wilson,
   ©1960, 1961.

New York Times, Feb. 13, 1981, 16:4.   (Obituary.)

Notable Names in the American Theatre.   Clifton, N.J.:   James T.
   White, 1976.

Reviews

New York Times, May 11, 1978, sec. III, 17:1.   [Angel.]

New Yorker, 54 (May 22, 1978), 91.   [Angel.]

New York Times, Feb. 18, 1960, 36:2.   [Long Dream.]

New Yorker, 36 (March 5, 1960), 120.   [Long Dream.]

Reporter, 22 (March 17, 1960), 38-9.   [Long Dream.]

Life, 43 (Dec. 16, 1957), 79-82.   [Look Homeward, Angel.]

New York Times, Nov. 29, 1957, 33:1.   [Look Homeward, Angel.]

New Yorker, 33 (Dec. 7, 1957), 93-5.   [Look Homeward, Angel.]

Saturday Review, 40 (Nov. 23, 1957), 27-8.   [Look Homeward,
   Angel.]

Commonweal, 37 (Nov. 27, 1942), 144.   [Mr. Sycamore.]

Nation, 155 (Nov. 28, 1942), 598.   [Mr. Sycamore.]

New York Times, Nov. 14, 1942, 13:2.   [Mr. Sycamore.]

New York Times, Nov. 28, 1966, 47:1.   [Walking Happy.]

Newsweek, 68 (Dec. 12, 1966), 100.   [Walking Happy.]

Time, 88 (Dec. 9, 1966), 60.   [Walking Happy.]

GALE, ZONA (1874-1938)

Plays

The Clouds. New York: French, 1936. Also in: New Plays for Women and Girls, Fifteen One-Act Plays. New York: French, 1932. Never produced on the professional stage.

Evening Clothes. Boston: Baker, 1932. Never produced on the professional stage.

Faint Perfume, A Play with a Prologue and Three Acts. New York: French, 1934. Never produced on the professional stage.

Miss Lulu Bett. New York, London: Appleton, 1921. Also in: Cordell, Kathryn (Coe), ed. Pulitzer Prize Plays, 1918-1934. New York: Random House, 1935. Produced Broadway, 1920.

Mister Pitt. New York: Appleton, 1925. Produced Broadway, 1924.

The Neighbors. New York: French, 1914. Also in: Dickinson, Thomas H., ed. Wisconsin Plays. New York: Huebsch, 1914. Also in: Kozelka, Paul, ed. Fifteen American One-Act Plays. New York: Washington Square, 1961. Produced Broadway, 1916.

Uncle Jimmy. Boston: Baker, 1922. Also in: Ladies' Home Journal, 38 (October 1921), 18-9. Also in: Hughes, Glenn. Short Plays for Modern Players. New York, London: Appleton, 1931. Never produced on the professional stage.

Biography

Derleth, August. Still Small Voice; The Biography of Zona Gale. New York, London: Appleton-Century, 1940.

Simonson, Harold P. Zona Gale. New York: Twayne, 1962.

Criticism

Forman, Henry James. "Zona Gale: A Touch of Greatness." Wisconsin Magazine of History, 46 (1962), 32-7.

Herron, Honaker. The Small Town in American Drama. Dallas: Southern Methodist University Press, 1969, pp. 202-5.

Smith, B. W. "Zona Gale." The Writer, 39 (March 1927), 95-6.

Reviews

Current Opinion, 70 (April 1921), 487-95. [Miss Lulu Bett.]

New York Times, Dec. 28, 1920, p. 9. [Miss Lulu Bett.]

American Mercury, 1 (March 1924), 374-5. [Mister Pitt.]

New York Times, Jan. 23, 1924, sec. VII, p. 15. [Mister Pitt.]

Dial, 50 (Aug. 15, 1915), 112-3. [The Neighbors.]

New York Times, Dec. 4, 1917, p. 11. [The Neighbors.]

GARSON, BARBARA (1941-)

Plays

The Co-op. Unpublished. Produced off-Broadway, 1972.

MacBird! New York: Grove, 1967. Also in: City Lights Journal, 3 (1966), 7-50. Produced off-Broadway, 1967.

Biography

Contemporary Authors; A Bio-bibliographical Guide to Current Authors and Their Works. Ann Evory, ed. Vol. 33-36. Detroit: Gale, 1978.

"Much Ado About Mac." Newsweek, 69 (Feb. 27, 1967), 99.

Reviews

Nation, 204 (March 13, 1967), 348-9. [MacBird!]

New York Times, March 12, 1967, sec. II, 1:1. [MacBird!]

New Republic, 156 (March 11, 1967), 30-2. [MacBird!]

Time, 89 (March 3, 1967), 52. [MacBird!]

GATES, ELEANOR (1875-1951)

Plays

Bird of Paradise. Written with Richard Walton Tully. Unpublished. Produced Broadway, 1912.

Darling of the World. Unpublished. Never produced on the professional stage.

Fire. Unpublished. Never produced on the professional stage.

Fish-Bait; A Farce in Three Acts. Typescript at the New York Public Library.

The Poor Little Rich Girl; A Play of Fact and Fancy in Three Acts. New York: Arrow, 1916. Produced Broadway, 1913.

Swat the Fly!; A One Act Fantasy. New York: Arrow, 1915. Never produced on the professional stage.

We Are Seven; A Three Act Whimsical Farce. New York: Arrow, 1915. Produced Broadway, 1913.

Biography

Brown, Edythe H. "Playing the Game of Writing." Editor, 64 (March 15, 1924), 82-3.

New York Times, March 8, 1951, 29:5. (Obituary.)

Smith, B. H. "Eleanor Gates Tully, Stock-breeder and Author." Sunset, 26 (March 1911), 317-20.

Criticism

Quinn, Arthur H. A History of the American Drama; From the Civil War to the Present Day. Vol. 1: From William Vaughan Moody to the Present Day. New York: Harper, 1927, pp. 144-5.

Reviews

American Playwright, 1 (April 1912), 119-21. [Bird of Paradise.]

Dramatist, 7 (July 1916), 715-6. [Bird of Paradise.]

New York Times, Jan 22, 1913, 11:1. [The Poor Little....]

Theatre Arts, 1 (February 1917), 92. [The Poor Little....]

American Playwright, 3 (January 1914), 7-8. [We Are Seven.]

New York Times, Dec. 25, 1913, 9:3. [We Are Seven.]

GERSTENBERG, ALICE (1885-1972)

Plays

Alice in Wonderland; A Dramatization of Lewis Carroll's "Alice's
Adventures in Wonderland" and "Through the Looking Glass."
Chicago: McClurg, 1915. Also in: Moses, Montrose J. A
Treasure of Plays for Children. Boston: Little, Brown, 1921.
Produced Broadway, 1915.

At the Club. In: Gerstenberg, Alice. Comedies All, Short Plays.
London, New York: Longmans, Green, 1930. Never produced
on the professional stage.

Attuned. In: Gerstenberg, Alice. Ten One-Act Plays. New York:
Brentano, 1921. Never produced on the professional stage.

Betty's Degree. In: Gerstenberg, Alice. A Little World; A Series
of College Plays for Girls. Chicago: Dramatic Publishing, 1908.
Never produced on the professional stage.

"Beyond." In: Mayorga, Margaret G. , ed. Representative One-
Act Plays by American Authors. Boston: Little, Brown, 1929.
Never produced on the professional stage.

The Buffer. In: Gerstenberg, Alice. Ten One-Act Plays. New
York: Brentano, 1921. Never produced on the professional stage.

Captain Joe; A Comedy in Four Acts. Chicago: Gerstenberg, ©1908.
Produced Academy of Dramatic Arts, New York, 1912.

The Class Play; A College Play for Twelve Girls. Chicago: Dramatic Publishing, 1908. Never produced on the professional stage.

The Class President, A College Play for Eleven Girls. Chicago: Dramatic Publishing, 1929. Never produced on the professional stage.

Ever Young. In: Drama, 12 (1922), 167-73. Never produced on
the professional stage.

Facing Facts. In: Gerstenberg, Alice. Comedies All, Short Plays.

London, New York: Longmans, Green, 1930. Never produced on the professional stage.

Fourteen, A One-Act Play. In: Drama, 10 (1920), 180-4. Never produced on the professional stage.

Glee Plays the Game, A Three Act Play with Women Characters Only. New York: French, 1934. Never produced on the professional stage.

He Said and She Said. In: Gerstenberg, Alice. Ten One-Act Plays. New York: Brentano, 1921. Never produced on the professional stage.

Hearts. In: Gerstenberg, Alice. Ten One-Act Plays. New York: Brentano, 1921. Never produced on the professional stage.

The Illuminati in Drama Libre. In: Gerstenberg, Alice. Ten One-Act Plays. New York: Brentano, 1921. Never produced on the professional stage.

Latch Keys. In: Gerstenberg, Alice. Comedies All, Short Plays. London, New York: Longmans, Green, 1930. Never produced on the professional stage.

London Town. Chicago, n.d. Typescript at the New York Public Library. Produced Chicago, 1937.

Mah-Jongg. In: Gerstenberg, Alice. Four Plays for Four Women. New York: Brentano, 1924. Never produced on the professional stage.

Mere Man. In: Gerstenberg, Alice. Comedies All, Short Plays. London, New York: Longmans, Green, 1930. Never produced on the professional stage.

The Opera Matinee; A Social Satire in One-Act for Fourteen Women. Summit, N.J.: Swartout, 1925. Also in: Gerstenberg, Alice. Comedies All, Short Plays. London, New York: Longmans, Green, 1930. Never produced on the professional stage.

Overtones, A One-Act Play. In: Washington Square Plays. Garden City, N.Y., 1917. Produced by the Washington Square Players, New York: Doubleday, Page, 1915.

A Patroness; A Monologue. Chicago, 191? Typescript at the New York Public Library. In: Shay, Frank, ed. A Treasury of Plays for Women. Boston: Little, Brown, 1922. Never produced on the professional stage.

The Pot Boiler; A Satire. In: Shay, Frank, ed. Fifty Contemporary One-Act Plays. Cincinnati: Stewart & Kidd, 1921. Produced Brooklyn, N.Y., 1923.

The Puppeteer. In: Gerstenberg, Alice. Comedies All, Short Plays. London, New York: Longmans, Green, 1930. Never produced on the professional stage.

The Queen's Christmas, A Play in One-Act. Chicago: Dramatic Publishing, 1939. Never produced on the professional stage.

Rhythm. In: Gerstenberg, Alice. Comedies All, Short Plays. London, New York: Longmans, Green, 1930. Never produced on the professional stage.

Sentience, A One-Act Comedy. New York: French, 1933. (Variant title: Tuning In.) Never produced on the professional stage.

Setback. In: Gerstenberg, Alice. Comedies All, Short Plays. London, New York: Longmans, Green, 1930. Never produced on the professional stage.

... Something in the Air. Written with Maude Fealy. Chicago: Dramatic Publishing, 1942. Never produced on the professional stage.

Sound-Effects Man. In: Mayorga, Margaret G. , ed. The World's a Stage; Short Plays for Juniors. New York: French, 1943. Never produced on the professional stage.

Star Dust; A Royalty Play. New York: French, 1931. Never produced on the professional stage.

Their Husband. In: Gerstenberg, Alice. Four Plays for Four Women. New York: Brentano, 1924. Never produced on the professional stage.

... Time for Romance. Chicago: Dramatic Publishing, 1941. Never produced on the professional stage.

The Trap. In: Twelve One-Act Plays. New York: Longmans, Green, 1926. Never produced on the professional stage.

Tuning In. Variant title of Sentience.

The Unseen. In: Goldstone, George A. , ed. One-Act Plays. Boston: Allyn & Bacon, 1926. Never produced on the professional stage.

Upstage. In: Gerstenberg, Alice. Comedies All, Short Plays. London, New York: Longmans, Green, 1930. Never produced on the professional stage.

Victory Belles; A Farce Comedy. Written with Henry Adrian. N. p. , n. d. Typescript at the New York Public Library. Produced Broadway, 1943.

The Water Babies, A Dramatization of Charles Kingsley's Classic
Story. New York: Longmans, Green, 1930. Never produced on
the professional stage.

When Chicago Was Young. Unpublished. Produced Chicago, 1932.

Where Are Those Men? A Sketch for Girls. Chicago: Dramatic
Publishing, 1912. Never produced on the professional stage.

Within the Hour, A Story Play in Seven Scenes. Chicago: Dramatic
Publishing, 1934. Never produced on the professional stage.

Biography

"About Alice's Stage Mother." New York Times, April 4, 1915,
sec. VIII, 5:1.

The Biographical Cyclopaedia of American Women. Volume 1. Re-
print of annual periodical published 1924. Detroit: Gale, 1974.

Reviews

Book News, 33 (May 1915), 454-5. [Alice in Wonderland.]

New York Times, March 24, 1915, 11:1. [Alice in Wonderland.]

New Republic, 5 (Nov. 20, 1915), 74. [Overtones.]

New York Times, Nov. 10, 1915, 13:5. [Overtones.]

New York Times, May 11, 1923, 20:3. [The Pot Boiler.]

New York Times, Oct. 27, 1943, 26:3. [Victory Belles.]

New York Times, Nov. 13, 1932, sec. IX, 3:8. [When Chicago Was
Young.]

GLASPELL, SUSAN (1882-1948)

Plays

Alison's House; A Play in Three Acts. New York: French, 1930.
Also in: Cordell, K. H. C., and W. H. Cordell, eds. The Pul-
itzer Prizes. New York: Random House, 1935. Produced Civic
Repertory Theatre, New York, 1930.

Bernice, A Play in Three Acts. London: Benn, 1924. Also in: Theatre Arts Magazine, 3 (October 1919), 264-300. Also in: Glaspell, Susan. Plays. Boston: Small, Maynard, 1920. Never produced on the professional stage.

Chains of Dew; A Comedy in Three Acts. 1920(?). Carbon copy of typescript at the Library of Congress. Produced Provincetown Playhouse, New York, 1922.

Close the Book. In: Glaspell, Susan. Plays. Boston: Small, Maynard, 1920. Produced Broadway, 1918.

The Comic Artist, A Play in Three Acts. Written with Norman Matson. London: Benn, 1927. Produced Broadway, 1933.

Inheritors; A Play in Three Acts. Boston: Small, Maynard, 1921. Produced Provincetown Playhouse, New York, 1921.

The Outside. In: Clements, C. C., ed. Sea Plays. Boston: Small, Maynard, 1925. Produced in Provincetown, Mass., 1916(?).

The People; A Play in One Act. New York(?), 1916(?). Typescript at the New York Public Library. In: Glaspell, Susan. The People and Close the Book. Two One Act Plays. New York: Shay, 1918. Produced Neighborhood Playhouse, New York, 1916-17.

Suppressed Desires; A Comedy in Two Episodes. In collaboration with George Cram Cook. Boston: Baker, 1924. In: Weiss, M. Jerry, ed. Ten Short Plays. New York: Dell, 1967. Produced Provincetown, Mass., 1914.

Tickless Time, A Comedy in One Act. In: Glaspell, Susan. Plays. Boston: Small, Maynard, 1920. Produced Provincetown, Mass., 1916(?).

Trifles, A Play in One Act. New York: Shay/Washington Square Players, 1916. Also in: Kriegel, Harriet. Women in Drama; An Anthology. New York: American Library, 1975. Produced Provincetown Playhouse, New York, 1920.

The Verge; A Play in Three Acts. Boston: Small, Maynard, 1922. Produced Provincetown Playhouse, New York, 1921.

Woman's Honor. In: Glaspell, Susan. Plays. Boston: Small, Maynard, 1920. Produced by the Greenwich Village Players, 1918.

Biography

Lewisohn, L. "Susan Glaspell." Nation, 111 (Nov. 3, 1920), 509-10.

94 : American Women Dramatists

Waterman, Arthur E. Susan Glaspell. New York: Twayne, 1966.

Waterman, Arthur E. "Susan Glaspell and The Provincetown."
Modern Drama, 7 (1964), 174-84.

Criticism

Gould, J. R. "Susan Glaspell and the Provincetown Players," in
Modern American Playwrights. New York: Dodd, Mead, 1966,
pp. 26-49.

Noe, Marcia. "Susan Glaspell's Analysis of the Midwestern Character." Books at Iowa, 27 (1977), 3-14.

Waterman, Arthur E. Susan Glaspell. New York: Twayne, 1966.

Reviews

Nation, 132 (May 27, 1931), 590-1. [Alison's House.]

New York Times, May 10, 1931, sec. VII, 1:1. [Alison's House.]

Theatre Arts, 15 (February 1931), 101-2. [Alison's House.]

Theatre Arts, 4 (October 1920) 349. [Bernice.]

New York Times, April 28, 1922, 20:2. [Chains of Dew.]

Theatre, 27 (June 1918), 358. [Close the Book.]

Nation, 136 (May 10, 1933), 539-40. [The Comic Artist.]

New Republic, 74 (May 10, 1933), 365-6. [The Comic Artist.]

New York Times, April 20, 1933, 20:3. [The Comic Artist.]

Nation, 112 (April 6, 1921), 515. [Inheritors.]

New York Times, March 27, 1921, sec. VII, 1:2. [Inheritors.]

Forum, 64 (September/October 1920), 237. [Suppressed Desires.]

Theatre Arts, 1 (February 1917), 93. [Suppressed Desires.]

Forum, 64 (September/October 1920), 237. [Trifles.]

New York Times, Feb. 13, 1927, sec. VII, 4:6. [Trifles.]

New York Times, Jan. 30, 1932, 13:6. [Trifles.]

Nation, 113 (Dec. 14, 1921), 708-9. [The Verge.]

New York Times, Nov. 20, 1921, sec. VI, 1:1. [The Verge.]

GOETZ, RUTH GOODMAN (1912-)

Plays

Heiress, A Play. Suggested by the Henry James novel Washington
  Square. Written with Augustus Goetz. New York: Dramatists
  Play Service, 1948. In: Chapman, John, ed. Best Plays of
  1947-1948. New York: Dodd, Mead, 1948. (Condensation.)
  Produced Broadway, 1947.

The Hidden River; A Play from the Novel by Storm Jameson. Written with Augustus Goetz. New York: Dramatists Play Service,
  1957. Produced Broadway, 1957.

Immoralist; A Drama in Three Acts. Based on the novel by André
  Gide. Written with Augustus Goetz. New York: Dramatists Play
  Service, 1954. Also in: Kronenberger, Louis, ed. Best Plays
  of 1953-1954. New York: Dodd, Mead, 1954. (Condensation.)
  Produced Broadway, 1954.

One-Man-Show. New York, 1945(?). Written with Augustus Goetz.
  Typescript at the New York Public Library. Produced Broadway,
  1945.

Play on Love. Written with Bart Howard. Unpublished. Produced
  London, 1970.

Biography

Who's Who in the Theatre. Ian Herbert, ed. 16th ed. Detroit:
  Gale, 1977.

Criticism

Bentley, Eric R. "Homosexuality." Dramatic Event. New York:
  Horizon, 1954, pp. 205-8.

McCarthy, Mary T. "Four Well-Made Plays." Sights and Specta-
  cles, 1937-1956. New York: Farrar, Straus and Cudahy, 1956,
  pp. 121-30.

Reviews

Life, 23 (Nov. 3, 1947), 149-50. [Heiress.]

New York Times, Oct. 5, 1947, sec. II, 1:1. [Heiress.]

Theatre Arts, 31 (December 1947), 12-3. [Heiress.]

New York Times, Jan. 24, 1957, 32:1. [The Hidden River.]

Saturday Review, 40 (Feb. 9, 1957), 25. [The Hidden River.]

Theatre Arts, 41 (April 1957), 14. [The Hidden River.]

Nation, 178 (Feb. 20, 1954), 156. [Immoralist.]

New York Times, Feb. 14, 1954, sec. II, 1:1. [Immoralist.]

New Yorker, 29 (Feb. 13, 1954), 61. [Immoralist.]

New York Times, Feb. 18, 1945, sec. II, 1:1. [One Man Show.]

New York Times, Jan. 16, 1970, 31:1. [Play on Love.]

GOODRICH, FRANCES (1890-   )

Plays

Bridal Wise. Written with Albert Hackett. Unpublished. Produced
    Broadway, 1932.

The Diary of Anne Frank. Written with Albert Hackett. Based on
    the book Anne Frank: Diary of a Young Girl. New York: Ran-
    dom House, 1956. In: Chapman, John, ed. Theatre, 1953-1956.
    New York: Random House, 1956. Also in: Gassner, John, ed.
    Best American Plays; Supplementary Volume, 1918-1958. New
    York: Crown, 1961. Produced Broadway, 1955.

Father's Day. Variant title of Western Union, Please.

The Great Big Doorstep. Written with Albert Hackett. Chicago:
    Dramatic Publishing, 1943. Produced Broadway, 1942.

Up Pops the Devil, A Comedy in Three Acts. Written with Albert
    Hackett. New York: French, 1933. Produced Broadway, 1930.

Western Union, Please, A Comedy in Three Acts.   Written with Albert Hackett.   New York: French, 1942.   Produced Cape Cod,
Mass. , 1937.

Biography

Current Biography 1956.   New York: H. W. Wilson, 1956.

Reviews

Commonweal, 16 (June 15, 1932), 188.   [Bridal Wise.]

New York Times, May 31, 1932, 15:5.   [Bridal Wise.]

Commonweal, 63 (Oct. 28, 1955), 91-2.   [The Diary of Anne Frank.]

New Republic, 134 (Jan. 2, 1956), 20.   [The Diary of Anne Frank.]

New York Times, Oct. 16, 1955, sec. II, 1:1.   [The Diary of Anne
Frank.]

New Yorker, 31 (Oct. 15, 1955), 75-6.   [The Diary of Anne Frank.]

New York Times, Nov. 27, 1942, 26:2.   [The Great Big Doorstep.]

Theatre Arts, 27 (January 1943), 17.   [The Great Big Doorstep.]

Time, 40 (Dec. 7, 1942), 54.   [The Great Big Doorstep.]

Life, 96 (Sept. 19, 1930), 16.   [Up Pops the Devil.]

New York Times, Sept. 14, 1930, sec. VIII, 1:1.   [Up Pops the
Devil.]

Theatre, 52 (November 1930), 25-6.   [Up Pops the Devil.]

New York Times, July 13, 1937, p. 22.   [Western Union, Please.]

GORDON, RUTH (1896-)

Plays

Leading Lady; A Play in Three Acts.   New York: Dramatists Play

Service, 1949. Also in: Theatre Arts, 34 (February 1950), 57-88. Produced Broadway, 1948.

Over Twenty-one, A Comedy. New York: Random House, 1944. In: Mantle, Robert B., ed. Best Plays of 1943-1944. New York: Dodd, Mead, 1944. (Condensation.) Produced Broadway, 1944.

A Very Rich Woman. New York: French, 1964. Produced Broadway, 1965.

Years Ago, A Play. New York: Viking, 1947. Also in: Mantle, Robert B., ed. Best Plays of 1946-1947. New York: Dodd, Mead, 1947. (Condensation.) Produced Broadway, 1946.

Biography

Current Biography Yearbook 1972. New York: H. W. Wilson, 1972.

Gordon, Ruth. My Side; The Autobiography of Ruth Gordon. New York: Harper & Row, 1976.

Reviews

New Republic, 119 (Nov. 8, 1948), 25-6. [Leading Lady.]

New York Times, Oct. 19, 1948, 38:1. [Leading Lady.]

New Yorker, 24 (Oct. 30, 1948), 42+. [Leading Lady.]

New York Times, Jan 4, 1944, 20:2. [Over Twenty-one.]

New Yorker, 19 (Jan. 15, 1944), 36. [Over Twenty-one.]

New York Times, Oct. 5, 1965, 5:8. [A Very Rich Woman.]

Saturday Review, 48 (Oct. 16, 1965), 75. [A Very Rich Woman.]

Time, 86 (Oct. 8, 1965), 68. [A Very Rich Woman.]

Life, 22 (Jan. 6, 1947), 58-60. [Years Ago.]

New York Times, Dec. 4, 1946, 44:2. [Years Ago.]

New York Times, Dec. 15, 1946, sec. II, 3:1. [Years Ago.]

New Yorker, 22 (Dec. 16, 1946), 94. [Years Ago.]

GRANT, MICKI (193?-)

Plays

Croesus and the Witch. Written with Vinnette Carroll. Unpublished.
Produced off-Broadway, 1971.

Don't Bother Me, I Can't Cope. Written with Vinnette Carroll. New
York: French, 1972. Produced off-Broadway, 1970; Broadway,
1971.

I'm Laughin' but I Ain't Tickled. Unpublished. Produced off-
Broadway, 1976.

It's So Nice to Be Civilized. Unpublished. Produced Broadway,
1980.

Moon on a Rainbow Shawl. Written with Errol John. Music by
Micki Grant. Unpublished. Produced off-Broadway, 1962; 1970.

Old Judge Mose Is Dead. Written with Vinnette Carroll. Unpublished.
Produced off-Broadway, 1969.

The Prodigal Sister. Book and lyrics by J. E. Franklin. Music
and lyrics by Micki Grant. New York: French, 1974. Produced
off-Broadway, 1974.

Step Lively, Boy. Written with Vinnette Carroll. Unpublished.
Produced off-Broadway, 1973.

The Ups and Downs of Theophilus Maitland. Written with Vinnette
Carroll. Unpublished. Produced off-Broadway, 1975.

Your Arms Too Short to Box with God. Written with Vinnette Carroll and Alex Bradford. Unpublished. Produced Italy, 1975;
Broadway, 1976.

Biography

New York Times Biographical Edition, 3 (1972), 960.

Peterson, M. "Micki Grant." Essence, 3 (November 1972), 32.

"She Can Cope." Ebony, 4 (February 1973), 100-9.

Reviews

New York Times, Aug. 27, 1971, 18. [Croesus and the Witch.]

New Yorker, 47 (Sept. 4, 1971) 54. [Croesus and the Witch.]

Ebony, 28 (February 1973), 100-2+. [Don't Bother Me....]

Nation, 214 (May 8, 1972), 604. [Don't Bother Me....]

New York Times, April 20, 1972, 51:1. [Don't Bother Me....]

New Yorker, 48 (April 29, 1972), 104. [Don't Bother Me....]

New York, 13 (June 16, 1980), 88. [It's So Nice....]

New Yorker, 56, (June 16, 1980), 96. [It's So Nice....]

New York Times, Dec. 18, 1970, 52:1. [Moon on a Rainbow....]

New Yorker, 37 (Jan. 27, 1962), 73. [Moon on a Rainbow....]

Saturday Review, 45 (March 10, 1962), 32. [Moon on a Rainbow....]

New York Times, April 29, 1969, 25:1. [Old Judge Mose Is Dead.]

New York, 7 (Dec. 16, 1974), 96. [The Prodigal Sister.]

New York Times, Nov. 26, 1974, 30:1. [The Prodigal Sister.]

New York, 10 (Jan. 10, 1977), 63. [Your Arms....]

New York Times, Dec. 23, 1976, 20:1. [Your Arms....]

Newsweek, 89 (Jan. 10, 1977), 66. [Your Arms....]

Time, 109 (Jan. 10, 1977), 55. [Your Arms....]

HAMILTON, NANCY (1908-   )

Plays

Count Me In. Book and lyrics by Nancy Hamilton, Walter Kerr, and Leo Brady. Music by Ann Ronell and Will Irwin. Unpublished. Produced Broadway, 1942.

New Faces. Sketches and lyrics by Nancy Hamilton, Viola Brothers Shore, and June Sillman. Music by Warburton Gilbert and others. Unpublished. Produced Broadway, 1934.

One for the Money; An Intimate Revue. Written with Morgan Lewis. Typescript at the New York Public Library. Produced Broadway, 1939.

Three to Make Ready; An Intimate Revue. Written with Morgan Lewis. Typescript at the New York Public Library. Produced Broadway, 1946.

Two for the Show; An Intimate Revue. Written with Morgan Lewis. Typescript at the New York Public Library. Produced Broadway, 1940.

Biography

Pringle, F. "The Story of Nancy Hamilton." Collier's, 105 (April 13, 1940), 11.

Reviews

New York Times, Oct. 9, 1942, p. 24. [Count Me In.]

Theatre Arts, 26 (December 1942), 742. [Count Me In.]

Commonweal, 19 (March 30, 1934), 609. [New Faces.]

New York Times, March 16, 1934, p. 24. [New Faces.]

Newsweek, 3 (March 24, 1934), 39. [New Faces.]

New York Times, Feb. 6, 1939, 9:2. [One for the Money.]

Life, 20 (March 25, 1946), 67-70. [Three to Make Ready.]

New York Times, March 17, 1946, sec. II, 1:1. [Three to Make Ready.]

Theatre Arts, 30 (May 1946), 261-2. [Three to Make Ready.]

New York Times, Feb. 18, 1940, sec. IX, 1:1. [Two for the Show.]

Theatre Arts, 24 (April 1940), 232. [Two for the Show.]

HANSBERRY, LORRAINE (1930-1965)

Plays

Les Blancs. In: Hansberry, Lorraine. Les Blancs; The Collected Last Plays of Lorraine Hansberry. Robert Nemiroff, ed. New York: Random House, 1972. Produced Broadway, 1970.

The Drinking Gourd. A television drama. In: Hansberry, Lorraine. Les Blancs.... New York: Random House, 1972. Produced on TV, 1969.

A Raisin in the Sun; A Drama in Three Acts. New York: Random House, 1959. Also in: Patterson, Lindsay, ed. Black Theater. New York: New American Library, 1971. Also in: Cerf, Bennett, ed. Four Contemporary American Plays. New York: Random House, 1961. Produced Broadway, 1959.

The Sign in Sidney Brustein's Window, A Drama in Three Acts. New York: Random House, 1965. Also in: Gassner, John, ed. Best American Plays; 6th Series, 1963-1967. New York: Crown, 1971. Produced Broadway, 1964.

To Be Young, Gifted and Black. Robert Nemiroff, ed. Englewood Cliffs, N.J.: Prentice-Hall, 1969. Produced off-Broadway, 1969.

What Use Are Flowers. In: Hansberry, Lorraine. Les Blancs.... New York: Random House, 1972. Also in: Richards, Stanley, ed. The Best Short Plays of 1973. Radnor, Pa.: Chilton, 1973. Never produced on the professional stage.

Biography

Baldwin, James. "Sweet Lorraine." Esquire, 72 (November 1969), 139-40.

Contemporary Authors; A Bio-bibliographical Guide to Current Authors and Their Works. Christine Nasso, ed. Vol. 25-28, first revision. Detroit: Gale, 1977.

Current Biography Yearbook 1959. New York: H. W. Wilson, 1960.

New York Times, Jan. 13, 1965, 25:1. (Obituary.)

"Playwright." New Yorker 35 (May 9, 1959), 33-5.

Criticism

American Women Writers; A Critical Reference Guide from Colonial
Times to the Present. Lina Mainiero, ed. Vol. 2. New York:
Ungar, 1980.

Brown, Lloyd W. "Lorraine Hansberry as Ironist; A Reappraisal of
A Raisin." Journal of Black Studies, 4 (1974), 237-47.

Olauson, Judith. The American Woman Playwright; A View of Criticism and Characterization. Troy, N.Y.: Whitston, 1981, pp.
89-92, 102-8.

Phillips, Elizabeth C. The Works of Lorraine Hansberry. New
York: Simon & Schuster, 1973.

Reviews

Nation, 211 (Nov. 30, 1970), 573. [Les Blancs.]

New York Times, Nov. 16, 1970, 48:4. [Les Blancs.]

New Yorker, 46 (Nov. 21, 1970), 124. [Les Blancs.]

Commentary, 27 (June 1959), 527-30. [A Raisin....]

Nation, 188 (April 4, 1959), 301-2. [A Raisin....]

New York Times, March 29, 1959, sec. II, 1:1. [A Raisin....]

Theatre Arts, 43 (May 1959), 22-3. [A Raisin....]

New York Times, Nov. 1, 1964, sec. II, 1:1. [The Sign in Sidney
Brustein's Window.]

New Yorker, 40 (Oct. 24, 1964), 93. [The Sign in Sidney Brustein's
Window.]

Saturday Review, 47 (Oct. 31, 1964), 31. [The Sign in Sidney Brustein's Window.]

New York Times, Jan. 3, 1969, 15:1. [To Be Young....]

New Yorker, 44 (Jan. 11, 1969), 58. [To Be Young....]

Time, 39 (Jan. 10, 1969), 43. [To Be Young....]

HATTON, FANNY LOCKE (1869-1930)

Plays

The Blue Devil; A Comedy in Three Acts. Written with Frederick
Hatton. Typescript at the New York Public Library. Never produced on the professional stage.

Brimstone and Hell-Fire; A Little Satire in One Act. Written with
Frederick Hatton. Typescript at the New York Public Library.
Produced in Boston, 1915.

The Checkerboard. Written with Frederick Hatton. Unpublished.
Produced Broadway, 1920.

The Dancing Partner. Written by A. Engel and A. Grunwald.
Adapted by Fanny and Frederick Hatton. Unpublished. Produced
Broadway, 1930.

The Fatal Woman. Written with Frederick Hatton. Unpublished.
Produced Broadway, 1930.

The Great Lover. Written with L. Dietrichstein and Frederick Hatton. Unpublished. Produced Broadway, 1915.

The Indestructible Wife. Written with Frederick Hatton. Unpublished.
Produced Broadway, 1918.

Lombardi, Ltd; A Comedy in Three Acts. Written with Frederick
Hatton. New York: French, 1928. Produced Broadway, 1927.

Long Island Love. Written with Frederick Hatton. Unpublished.
Produced Broadway, 1936.

Love, Honor and Betray. Written with Frederick Hatton. Unpublished. Produced Broadway, 1930.

Madame Milo. Written with Frederick Hatton. Unpublished. Produced Atlantic City, 1921.

Mastery of Kats; A Society Comedy in Three Acts. Written with
Frederick Hatton. Typescript at the New York Public Library.
Never produced on the professional stage.

Playthings; A Play. Written with Frederick Hatton. Typescript at
the New York Public Library. Produced Los Angeles, 1925.

The Songbird; A Play in Four Acts. Written with Frederick Hatton.
Ottawa, Canada: Popham, 1915. Never produced on the professional
stage.

The Squab Farm, A Play in Four Acts. Written with Frederick Hatton. Typescript at the Library of Congress. Never produced on the
professional stage.

Synthetic Sin; A Comedy in Four Episodes. Written with Frederick
Hatton. Unpublished. Produced Broadway, 1927.

Tonight or Never. Written with Frederick Hatton. Unpublished.
Produced Broadway, 1930.

"Treat 'em Rough," A New Comedy. Written with Frederick Hatton.
New York: Co-National Plays, 1930. Produced Broadway, 1926.

Upstairs and Down; A Comedy in Three Acts. Written with Frederick Hatton. Prompt book at the New York Public Library.
Produced Broadway, 1916.

The Walk-Off's. Written with Frederick Hatton. Only copy at the
New York Public Library. Produced Broadway, 1918.

We Girls, A Comedy. Written with Frederick Hatton. New York:
Dramatists Play Service, 1937. Produced Broadway, 1921.

Years of Discretion; A Comedy in Three Acts. Written with Frederick Hatton. Dublin: Maunsel, 1913. Produced Broadway, 1913.

Biography

Mantle, Robert B. Contemporary American Playwrights. New York:
Dodd, Mead, 1938, pp. 235-6.

New York Times, Nov. 28, 1939, 25:5. (Obituary.)

Sumner, K. "Happy Hattons and Their Creed." American Mercury,
86 (October 1918), 36-7.

Criticism

Collins, C. W. "Fanny Hatton as Dramatist." Green Book Magazine, 9 (February 1913), 222-34.

Reviews

Dramatic Mirror, Aug. 28, 1920, p. 371+. [The Checkerboard.]

New York Times, Aug. 20, 1920, 7:2. [The Checkerboard.]

Drama, 21 (November 1930), 9+. [The Dancing Partner.]

New York Times, July 27, 1930, sec. VIII, 2:3. [The Dancing
Partner.]

New York Times, March 2, 1930, sec. IX, 4:7. [The Fatal Woman.]

Nation, 101 (Nov. 18, 1915), 605. [The Great Lover.]

New York Times, Oct. 12, 1932, 27:3. [The Great Lover.]

Green Book, 19 (April 1918), 592-5. [The Indestructible Wife.]

New York Times, Jan. 31, 1918, 7:1. [The Indestructible Wife.]

New York Times, June 7, 1927, 27:3. [Lombardi, Ltd.]

New York Times, Aug. 1, 1926, sec. VII, 4:1. [Long Island....]

New York Times, March 13, 1930, 22:2. [Love, Honor....]

Theatre, 51 (May 1930), 42-3. [Love, Honor....]

Green Book, 19 (June 1918), 971+. [The Squab Farm.]

New York Times, March 14, 1918, 11:1. [The Squab Farm.]

New York Times, Oct. 11, 1927, 26:2. [Synthetic Sin.]

Theatre, 46 (December 1927), 44. [Synthetic Sin.]

New York Times, Nov. 19, 1930, 19:3. [Tonight or Never.]

Theatre, 53 (January 1931), 26. [Tonight or Never.]

New York Times, May 23, 1926, sec. VIII, 1:1. [Treat 'em....]

Green Book, 16 (December 1916), 972-4. [Upstairs....]

Nation, 103 (Oct. 5, 1916), 330. [Upstairs....]

Life, 72 (Oct. 3, 1918), 488-9. [The Walk-Off's.]

New York Times, Sept. 18, 1918, 11:1. [The Walk-Off's.]

New York Times, Nov. 10, 1921, 26:3. [We Girls.]

Redbook, 20 (March 1913), 881-5. [Years of Discretion.]

Theatre, 17 (April 1913), 119-20. [Years of Discretion.]

HELBURN, THERESA (1887-1959)

Plays

Allison Makes Hay; A Comedy in Three Acts. Boston: Baker, 1919.
Produced on Broadway in 1918 under the title Crops and Croppers.

Denbigh. Written 1927. Typescript at the New York Public Library.
Produced Broadway, 1927.

Enter the Hero. In: Knickerbocker, E. van Berghen, ed. Twelve
Plays. New York: H. Holt, 1924. Produced by the Washington
Square Players, New York City, 1917.

A Hero Is Born. Complete working script at the New York Public
Library. Produced Broadway, 1937.

Little Dark Horse. Unpublished. Produced Broadway, 1941.

Other Lives. Written with E. Goodman. Produced Washington,
D. C., 1921.

Biography

Current Biography 1944. New York: H. W. Wilson, 1944.

Helburn, Theresa. Wayward Quest; Autobiography. New York:
Little, Brown, 1960.

New York Times, Aug. 19, 1959, p. 29. (Obituary.)

Reviews

New York Times, Sept. 13, 1918, 9:1. [Crops and Croppers.]

New York Times, Oct. 2, 1937, 18:6. [A Hero Is Born.]

Time, 30 (Oct. 11, 1937), 54. [A Hero Is Born.]

New York Times, Nov. 17, 1941, 14:4. [Little Dark Horse.]

Dramatist, 12 (October 1921), 1883. [Other Lives.]

New York Times, Sept. 11, 1921, sec. VI, 1:6. [Other Lives.]

HELLMAN, LILLIAN (1906-)

Plays

Another Part of the Forest. New York: Viking, 1947. Also in:
Hellman, Lillian. Collected Plays. Boston: Little, Brown,
1972. Produced Broadway, 1946.

Autumn Garden. Boston: Little, Brown, 1951. Also in: Hellman,
Lillian. Collected Plays. Boston: Little, Brown, 1972. Produced Broadway, 1951.

Broadway Revue. Contributed sketches. Unpublished. Produced
Broadway, 1968.

Candide: A Comic Operetta Based on Voltaire's Satire. Book by
Lillian Hellman. Music by Leonard Bernstein. New York: Ran-
dom House, 1957. Also in: Hellman, Lillian. Collected Plays.
Boston: Little, Brown, 1972. Produced Broadway, 1956.

The Children's Hour. New York: Knopf, 1934. Also in: Hellman,
Lillian. Collected Plays. Boston: Little, Brown, 1972. Produced Broadway, 1934.

Days to Come. New York: Knopf, 1936. Also in: Hellman, Lillian.
Collected Plays. Boston: Little, Brown, 1972. Produced Broadway, 1936.

Dear Queen. Written with L. Kronenberger. Unpublished. Never
produced on the professional stage.

The Lark. Based on a play by Jean Anouilh. New York: Random
House, 1956. Also in: Hellman, Lillian. Collected Plays.
Boston: Little, Brown, 1972. Produced Broadway, 1955.

The Little Foxes. New York: Random House, 1939. Also in:
Hellman, Lillian. Collected Plays. Boston: Little, Brown,
1972. Produced Broadway, 1939.

Montserrat, A Play in Two Acts. Based on a novel by Emmanuel
Robles. New York: Dramatists Play Service, 1950. Also in:
Hellman, Lillian. Collected Plays. Boston: Little, Brown,
1972. Produced Broadway, 1949.

My Mother, My Father, and Me. Based on the novel How Much?,
by Burt Blechman. New York: Random House, 1963. Also in:
Hellman, Lillian. Collected Plays. Boston: Little, Brown,
1972. Produced Broadway, 1963.

The Searching Wind, A Play in Two Acts. New York: Viking, 1944.
Also in: Hellman, Lillian. Collected Plays. Boston: Little,
Brown, 1972. Produced Broadway, 1944.

Toys in the Attic, A New Play. New York: Viking, 1960. Also
in: Hellman, Lillian. Collected Plays. Boston: Little, Brown,
1972. Produced Broadway, 1960.

Watch on the Rhine, A Play in Three Acts. New York: Random
House, 1941. Also in: Hellman, Lillian. Collected Plays. Boston: Little, Brown, 1972. Produced Broadway, 1941.

Biography

Contemporary Authors; A Bio-bibliographical Guide to Current Authors and Their Works. Clare D. Kinsman, ed. Vol. 13-16,
first revision. Detroit: Gale, 1975.

Falk, Doris V. Lillian Hellman. New York: Ungar, 1978.

Hellman, Lillian. Pentimento: A Book of Portraits. Boston:
Little, Brown, 1974. (Autobiography.)

Hellman, Lillian. Scoundrel Time. Boston: Little, Brown, 1976.
(Autobiography.)

Hellman, Lillian. An Unfinished Woman. Boston: Little, Brown,
1969. (Autobiography.)

Criticism

Clark, Barrett H. "Lillian Hellman." College English, 6 (1940),
127-33.

Falk, Doris V. Lillian Hellman. New York: Ungar, 1978.

Gould, Jean. "Lillian Hellman." Modern American Playwrights.
New York: Dodd, Mead, 1966, pp. 168-85.

Lederer, Katherine. Lillian Hellman. Boston: Twayne, 1979.

Riordan, Mary M. Lillian Hellman, a Bibliography: 1926-1978.
Metuchen, N.J.: Scarecrow, 1980.

Reviews

Life, 21 (Dec. 9, 1946), 71-2. [Another Part of the Forest.]

New York Times, Dec. 12, 1946, sec. II, 1:1. [Another Part....]

Saturday Review, 29 (Dec. 14, 1946), 20-3. [Another Part....]

New Republic, 124 (March 26, 1951), 21-2. [Autumn Garden.]

New York Times, March 18, 1951, sec. II, 1:1. [Autumn Garden.]

New Yorker, 27 (March 17, 1951), 52. [Autumn Garden.]

Commonweal, 65 (Dec. 28, 1956), 333-4. [Candide.]

New Republic, 135 (Dec. 17, 1956), 30-1. [Candide.]

New York Times, Dec. 3, 1956, 40:2. [Candide.]

Nation, 139 (Dec. 5, 1934), 656-7. [The Children's Hour.]

New Republic, 81 (Dec. 19, 1934), 169. [The Children's Hour.]

New York Times, Dec. 2, 1934, sec. X, 1:1. [The Children's Hour.]

Nation, 143 (Dec. 26, 1936), 769-70. [Days to Come.]

New Republic, 89 (Dec. 30, 1936), 274. [Days to Come.]

New York Times, Dec. 16, 1936, 35:1. [Days to Come.]

Life, 39 (Dec. 12, 1955), 113+. [The Lark.]

New York Times, Nov. 27, 1955, sec. II, 1:1. [The Lark.]

New Yorker, 31 (Dec. 3, 1955), 112+. [The Lark.]

New Republic, 98 (April 12, 1939), 279. [The Little Foxes.]

New York Times, Feb. 26, 1939, sec. IX, 1:1. [The Little Foxes.]

Theatre Arts, 23 (April 1939), 244+. [The Little Foxes.]

Commonweal, 51 (Nov. 18, 1949), 179-80. [Montserrat.]

New York Times, Oct. 31, 1949, 21:4. [Montserrat.]

Saturday Review, 32 (Nov. 19, 1949), 53-4. [Montserrat.]

New York Times, March 25, 1963, 5:5. [My Mother....]

New Yorker, 39 (April 20, 1963), 334. [My Mother....]

Theatre Arts, 47 (May 1963), 69-70. [My Mother....]

Life, 16 (May 1, 1944), 43-4+. [The Searching Wind.]

New York Times, April 23, 1944, sec. II, 1:1. [The Searching Wind.]

New Yorker, 20 (April 22, 1944), 42+. [The Searching Wind.]

Life, 48 (April 4, 1960), 53-4+. [Toys in the Attic.]

New York Times, March 6, 1960, sec. II, 1:1. [Toys in the Attic.]

New Yorker, 36 (March 5, 1960), 124-5. [Toys in the Attic.]

Commonweal, 34 (April 25, 1941), 15-6. [Watch on the Rhine.]

Life, 10 (April 14, 1941), 81-2+. [Watch on the Rhine.]

New Republic, 104 (April 14, 1941), 498-9. [Watch on the Rhine.]

HENLEY, BETH (1952-   )

Plays

Am I Blue. Unpublished. Produced off-Broadway, 1982.

Crimes of the Heart. Unpublished. Produced Louisville, Ky.,
1979; off-Broadway, 1979; Broadway, 1981.

The Miss Firecracker Concert, A Play in Two Acts. New York:
Theatre Communications Group, 1979. Produced Buffalo, N.Y.,
1981.

Wake of Jamie Foster. Unpublished. Never produced on the professional stage.

Biography

Berkvist, Robert. "Act I: the Pulitzer, Act II: Broadway." New
York Times, Oct. 25, 1981, sec. II, p. 4+.

Haller, S. "Her First Play, Her First Pulitzer Prize." Saturday
Review, 8 (November 1981), 40+.

Reviews

New York Times, Jan. 11, 1982, sec. C, p. 14. [Am I Blue.]

New York, 14 (Jan. 12, 1981), 42+. [Crimes of the Heart.]

New York Times, Dec. 22, 1980, sec. III, 16:1. [Crimes of the
Heart.]

New Yorker, 56 (Jan. 12, 1981), 81+. [Crimes of the Heart.]

Newsweek, 93 (March 19, 1979), 92-3. [Crimes of the Heart.]

Time, 113 (March 5, 1979), 73. [Crimes of the Heart.]

HEYWARD, DOROTHY HARTZELL (1890-1961)

Plays

Babar the Elephant; A Children's Opera in One Act, Five Scenes. Libretto by Dorothy Heyward. Lyrics by J. Randal. Music by N. Berezowski. New York: Fisher, 1953. Never produced on the professional stage.

Cinderelative. Unpublished. Produced Broadway, 1930.

Jonica. Unpublished. Produced Broadway, 1930.

The Lighted House; A Play in Prologue and Three Sets. Written 1925. Typescript at the New York Public Library. Never produced on the professional stage.

Little Girl Blue; A Romantic Comedy in a Prologue and Three Sets. Written with D. DeJagers. New York: French, 1931. Never produced on the professional stage.

Love in a Cupboard; A Comedy in One Act. New York: French, 1926. Never produced on the professional stage.

Mamba's Daughters; A Play. Written with DuBose Heyward. New York: Farrar & Rinehart, 1939. Produced Broadway, 1939.

Nancy Ann; A Comedy in Three Acts. New York: French, 1927. Produced Broadway, 1924.

Porgy; A Play in Four Acts. Written with DuBose Heyward. Garden City, N.Y.: Published for the Theatre Guild by Doubleday, Page, 1927. Also in: Mantle, Robert B., ed. Best Plays of 1927/28. New York: Dodd, Mead, 1928. (Condensation.) Also in: Gassner, John, and Olive Barnes, comps. 50 Best Plays of the American Theatre. New York: Crown, 1969. Produced Broadway, 1927.

Set My People Free; A Play. New York: Rialto Service Brueau, 1948(?). Typescript at the New York Public Library. Produced Broadway, 1948.

South Pacific. Written with H. Rigsby. Typescript at the New
York Public Library. Produced Broadway, 1943.

Biography

Mantle, Robert B. Contemporary American Playwrights. New York:
Dodd, Mead, 1938, pp. 231-2.

New York Times, Nov. 20, 1961, p. 31. (Obituary.)

Who Was Who in America. Vol. 4. Chicago: Marquis Who's Who,
1968.

Reviews

New York Times, Sept. 19, 1930, 18:4. [Cinderelative.]

New York Times, March 30, 1930, sec. VIII, 2:7. [Jonica.]

New York Times, Jan. 15, 1939, sec. IX, 1:1. [Mamba's Daughters.]

Newsweek, 13 (Jan. 16, 1939), 26. [Mamba's Daughters.]

Time, 33 (Jan. 16, 1939), 41. [Mamba's Daughters.]

Life, 83 (April 17, 1924), 20. [Nancy Ann.]

New York Times, April 1, 1924, 18:1. [Nancy Ann.]

Nation, 125 (Oct. 26, 1927), 457-8. [Porgy.]

New Republic, 52 (Oct. 26, 1927), 261-2. [Porgy.]

New York Times, Oct. 16, 1927, sec. IX, 1:1. [Porgy.]

New Republic, 119 (Nov. 22, 1948), 28. [Set My People Free.]

New York Times, Nov. 14, 1948, sec. II, 1:1. [Set My People
Free.]

New York Times, Dec. 30, 1943, 11:2. [South Pacific.]

Time, 43 (Jan. 10, 1944), 72. [South Pacific.]

HINTON, JANE

Plays

Good Fairy. Adapted from the work by Ferenc Molnár. Unpublished.
Produced Broadway, 1931.

Meet a Body, A Mystery Play. New York: Longmans, Green, 1947.
Produced Broadway, 1944.

Obsession. Adapted from the play Jealousy, by L. Verneuil. Unpublished. Produced Broadway, 1946.

Sex Fable. Translated from the French comedy by E. Bourdet. Unpublished. Produced Broadway, 1931.

Reviews

New York Times, Nov. 25, 1931, 17:1. [Good Fairy.]

Nation, 159 (Nov. 4, 1944), 568. [Meet a Body.]

New York Times, Oct. 17, 1944, 19:5. [Meet a Body.]

New York Times, Oct. 2, 1946, 39:2. [Obsession.]

Theatre World, 42 (November 1946), 23+. [Obsession.]

Time, 48 (Oct. 14, 1946), 100. [Obsession.]

New York Times, Oct. 21, 1931, 26:1. [Sex Fable.]

Vanity Fair, 36 (April 1931), 90+. [Sex Fable.]

Vogue, 78 (Dec. 15, 1931), 57+. [Sex Fable.]

HOWE, TINA (193?-)

Plays

The Art of Dining: A Comedy. New York: French, 1980. Produced off-Broadway, 1979.

Birth and After Birth. In: Moore, Honor, ed. The New Women's Theatre: Ten Plays by Contemporary Women. New York: Random House, 1977. Produced off-Broadway, 1974.

Museum, A Drama. New York: French, 1978. Produced off-Broadway, 1978.

The Nest. Unpublished. Produced off-Broadway, 1970.

Biography

Brown, Janet. Feminist Drama; Definition & Critical Analysis. Metuchen, N.J.: Scarecrow, 1979, pp. 72-3.

Criticism

Brown, Janet. Feminist Drama; Definition & Critical Analysis. Metuchen, N.J.: Scarecrow, 1979, pp. 69-85.

Reviews

Nation, 230 (Jan. 5, 1980), 30. [The Art of Dining.]

New York Times, Dec. 7, 1979, sec. C, 6:1. [The Art of Dining.]

New Yorker, 44 (Dec. 17, 1979), 100-1. [The Art of Dining.]

America, 138 (April 8, 1978), 286. [Museum.]

New York Times, Feb. 28, 1978, 28:4. [Museum.]

New Yorker, 54 (March 6, 1978), 67-8. [Museum.]

New York Times, April 10, 1970, 46:1. [The Nest.]

HURLBUT, GLADYS (1898?-)

Plays

By Your Leave. Unpublished. Produced Broadway, 1934.

Higher and Higher. Book by Gladys Hurlbut and Josh Logan. Lyrics by Lorenz Hart. Music by Richard Rodgers. Typewritten copy at the New York Public Library. Produced Broadway, 1940.

Mad Morning. Unpublished. Produced Broadway, 1935.

Ring Two; A Comedy. Written 1939. Typewritten prompt book at the New York Public Library. Produced Broadway, 1939.

Yankee Point. Unpublished. Produced Broadway, 1942.

Biography

Hurlbut, Gladys. Next Week East Lynne! New York: Dutton, 1950. (Autobiography.)

Reviews

New York Times, Jan. 25, 1934, 15:3. [By Your Leave.]

Time, 23 (Feb. 5, 1934), 34-5. [By Your Leave.]

Life, 8 (April 15, 1940), 42+. [Higher and Higher.]

New York Times, April 5, 1940, 24:3. [Higher and Higher.]

New York Times, June 25, 1935, 14:1. [Mad Morning.]

New York Times, Nov. 14, 1939, 20:3. [Ring Two.]

New York Times, Nov. 23, 1939, 38:2. [Ring Two.]

New York Times, Nov. 24, 1942, 28:2. [Yankee Point.]

Theatre Arts, 27 (January 1943), 17+. [Yankee Point.]

HURST, FANNIE (1889-1968)

Plays

Back Pay. Based on her short story of the same name. Story in: Cosmopolitan, 67 (November 1919), 35-40+. Produced Broadway, 1921.

Humoresque. Based on the motion-picture scenario and story of the same name. Story in: Cosmopolitan, 66 (March 1919), 32-9. Produced Broadway, 1923.

It Is to Laugh. Unpublished. Produced Broadway, 1927.

Land of the Free. Written with Harriet Ford. Unpublished. Produced Asbury Park, N. J. , 1917.

Biography

Dodd, Loring H. Celebrities at Our Hearthside. Boston: Dresser, Chapman, & Grimes, 1959, pp. 248-52.

Hurst, Fannie. Anatomy of Me; A Wanderer in Search of Herself. Garden City, N. Y. : Doubleday, 1958.

New York Times, Feb. 24, 1968, p. 1. (Obituary.)

Criticism

Cranmer, Catherine. "Little Visits with Literary Missourians: Fannie Hurst." Missouri Historical Review, 19 (April 1925), 389-96.

Salpeter, Harry. "Fannie Hurst: Sob Sister of American Fiction." Bookman, 78 (August 1931), 612-5.

Reviews

New York Times, Aug. 21, 1921, sec. VI, 1:8. [Back Pay.]

Review, 5 (Sept. 10, 1921), 234-5. [Back Pay.]

New York Times, March 4, 1923, sec. VII, 1:1. [Humoresque.]

New York Times, Dec. 27, 1927, 24:2. [It Is to Laugh.]

Theatre, 47 (March 1928), 40+. [It Is to Laugh.]

JACKER, CORINNE L. (1933-)

Plays

Bits and Pieces. In: Jacker, Corinne L. Two Plays. New York:

Dramatists Play Service, 1975. Also in: Moore, Honor, ed. The New Women's Theatre: Ten Plays by Contemporary American Women. New York: Random House, 1977. Produced off-Broadway, 1974.

Breakfast, Lunch, Dinner. In: Jacker, Corinne L. Two Plays. New York: Dramatists Play Service, 1975. Never produced on the professional stage.

A Happy Ending. Unpublished. Produced off-Broadway, 1959.

Harry Outside. New York: Dramatists Play Service, 1975. Produced off-Broadway, 1975.

The Island. Unpublished. Produced off-Broadway, 1978.

Jennifer, Jemima and the Machine. Unpublished. Produced off-Broadway, 1970.

Later. New York: Dramatists Play Service, 1979. Produced off-Broadway, 1979.

My Life. New York: Dramatists Play Service, 1977. Produced off-Broadway, 1977.

Night Thoughts. In: Jacker, Corinne L. Night Thoughts and Terminal. New York: Dramatists Play Service, 1977. Produced off-Broadway, 1973.

Other People's Tables. Unpublished. Produced off-Broadway, 1976.

Pale Horse, Pale Rider. Unpublished. Produced off-Broadway, 1958.

A Picture of Love. Unpublished. Produced on CBS, 1959.

Project Omega: Lillian. Unpublished. Produced off-Broadway, 1971.

The Scientific Method. Unpublished. Produced Shakespeare Festival, Stratford, Conn. , 1970.

Seditious Acts. Unpublished. Produced off-Broadway, 1969.

Taking Care of Harry. Variant title of Harry Outside.

Terminal. In: Jacker, Corinne L. Night Thoughts and Terminal. New York: Dramatists Play Service, 1977. Produced off-Broadway, 1973.

Travelers. Unpublished. Produced off-Broadway, 1974.

Biography

Contemporary Authors; A Bio-bibliographical Guide to Current Authors and Their Works. Clare D. Kinsman, ed. Vol. 17-20, first revision. Detroit: Gale, 1976.

Moore, Honor, ed. The New Women's Theatre: Ten Plays by Contemporary American Women. New York: Random House, 1977.

Who's Who of American Women. 11th ed., 1979-80. Chicago: Marquis Who's Who, 1979.

Reviews

New York Times, Nov. 19, 1974, 52:1. [Bits and Pieces.]

Nation, 220 (May 31, 1975), 669. [Harry Outside.]

New York Times, May 13, 1975, 31:1. [Harry Outside.]

New Yorker, 51 (May 26, 1975), 77-8. [Harry Outside.]

New York Times, Jan. 16, 1979, sec. III, 8:5. [Later.]

Nation, 224 (Feb. 12, 1977), 190-1. [My Life.]

New York, 10 (Feb. 14, 1977), 88-9. [My Life.]

New York Times, Jan. 24, 1977, 19:1. [My Life.]

New York Times, Oct. 29, 1976, sec. III, 5:1. [Other People's Tables.]

New York Times, Oct. 30, 1957, 26:1. [Pale Horse....]

New York Times, May 24, 1970, sec. II, 3:1. [Terminal.]

JANIS, ELSIE (1889-1956)

Plays

Elsie Janis and Her Gang. Unpublished. Produced Broadway, 1919.

It's All Wrong. Unpublished. Produced London, 1920.

Puzzles of 1925. Unpublished. Produced Broadway, 1925.

A Star for a Night; A Story of Stage Life. New York: Rickey, 1911. Produced off-Broadway for the Actors' Fund, 1911.

Biography

Janis, Elsie. So Far, So Good! New York: Dutton, 1932. (Autobiography.)

New York Times, Feb. 28, 1956, p. 1+. (Obituary.)

Who Was Who in the Theatre: 1912-1976. Detroit: Gale, 1978.

Reviews

New York Times, Dec. 2, 1919, 11:1. [Elsie Janis....]

New York Times, Feb. 3, 1925, 25:3. [Puzzles of 1925.]

New York Dramatic Mirror, April 5, 1911, p. 10. [A Star for a Night.]

JONES, ELINOR

Plays

Colette. Adapted from Earthly Paradise, by Colette, Robert Phelps, ed. New York: Studio Duplicating Service, 1970. Typescript at the New York Public Library. Produced off-Broadway, 1970.

A Voice of My Own. New York: Dramatists Play Service, 1979. Produced off-Broadway, 1979.

Reviews

New York Times, May 7, 1970, 60:1. [Colette.]

New York Times, May 17, 1970, sec. II, 1:1. [Colette.]

New York Times, May 9, 1979, sec. III. 17:4. [A Voice....]

KANIN, FAY (1915-)

Plays

Gay Life. Book by Fay and Michael Kanin. Music by Arthur
  Schwartz. Lyrics by Howard Dietz. Unpublished. Produced
  Broadway, 1961.

Goodbye, My Fancy; A Comedy. New York: French, 1949. Produced Broadway, 1948.

His and Hers; A Comedy in Three Acts. Written with Michael Kanin.
  New York: French, 1954. Produced Broadway, 1954.

M'Lord and Lady. Written with Michael Kanin. Unpublished. Produced Los Angeles, 1974.

Most Likely to Succeed. Variant title of Goodbye, My Fancy.

Rashomon, A Drama in Two Acts. Written with Michael Kanin.
  Based on stories by Ryunosuke Akutagawa. New York: French,
  1959. Produced Broadway, 1959.

Biography

The Biographical Encyclopedia and Who's Who of the American Theatre. Walter Rigdon, ed. New York: Heineman, 1966.

Froug, William. Screenwriter Looks at the Screenwriter. New
  York: Macmillan, 1972, pp. 327-52.

Reviews

New York Times, Nov. 20, 1961, 38:1. [Gay Life.]

New Yorker, 37 (Dec. 2, 1961), 118. [Gay Life.]

Theatre Arts, 46 (February 1962), 11-2. [Gay Life.]

New York Times, Nov. 18, 1948, 35:2. [Goodbye, My Fancy.]

New Yorker, 24 (Nov. 27, 1948), 56+. [Goodbye, My Fancy.]

Saturday Review, 32 (Jan. 8, 1949), 30-2. [Goodbye, My Fancy.]

New York Times, Jan. 8, 1954, 18:2. [His and Hers.]

New Yorker, 29 (Jan. 16, 1954), 54-6. [His and Hers.]

Saturday Review, 37 (Jan. 30, 1954), 27. [His and Hers.]

New York Times, Feb. 8, 1959, sec. II, 1:1. [Rashomon.]

New Yorker, 34 (Feb. 7, 1959), 81-2. [Rashomon.]

Theatre Arts, 43 (February 1959), 12-3. [Rashomon.]

KAUFMAN, BEATRICE (1895-1945)

Plays

Divided by Three. Written with M. Leech. Original manuscript at the New York Public Library. Produced Broadway, 1934.

The White Haired Boy. Written with C. Martin. Unpublished. Produced Broadway, 1940.

Biography

Publishers' Weekly, 148 (Oct. 20, 1945), 1858. (Obituary.)

Reviews

New York Times, Sept. 28, 1934, 26:3. [Divided by Three.]

Stage, 12 (November 1934), 10+. [Divided by Three.]

Theatre Arts, 18 (November 1934), 821. [Divided by Three.]

New York Times, Oct. 29, 1940, 32:6. [The White Haired Boy.]

KAZAN, MOLLY (1906-1963)

Plays

The Alligators. In: Kazan, Molly. Rosemary. The Alligators.
Two One-Hour Plays. New York: French, 1960. Produced off-
Broadway, 1960.

Egghead; A Play in Three Acts. New York: Dramatists Play Service, 1958. Produced Broadway, 1957.

Rosemary. In: Kazan, Molly. Rosemary. The Alligators. Two
One-Hour Plays. New York: French, 1960. Produced off-
Broadway, 1960.

Biography

Biographical Encyclopedia and Who's Who of the American Theatre.
Walter Rigdon, ed. New York: Heineman, 1966.

New York Times, Dec. 18, 1963, p. 37. (Obituary.)

Reviews

New York Times, Nov. 15, 1960, 47:1. [The Alligators and Rosemary.]

New Yorker, 36 (Nov. 26, 1960), 107-8. [The Alligators and Rosemary.]

New York Theatre Critics Reviews, 1957, p. 231. [Egghead.]

New York Times, Oct. 10, 1957, 39:1. [Egghead.]

New Yorker, 33 (Oct. 19, 1957), 81-3. [Egghead.]

KENNEDY, ADRIENNE (1931-)

Plays

A Beast Story. In: Kennedy, Adrienne. Cities in Bezique; Two

One-Act Plays: The Owl Answers and A Beast Story. New York: French, 1969. Produced off-Broadway, 1969.

Boats. Unpublished. Produced Los Angeles, 1969.

Cities in Bezique. Title of two plays: A Beast Story and The Owl Answers.

An Evening with Dead Essex. Unpublished. Produced off-Broadway, 1973.

Funnyhouse of a Negro, A Play in One Act. New York: French, 1969. Also in: Oliver, Clinton S., and Stephanie Sills, eds. Contemporary Black Drama. New York: Scribner, 1970. Produced off-Broadway, 1964.

The Lennon Play: In His Own Write. Adapted from John Lennon's In His Own Write and A Spaniard in the Works. London: Cape, 1968. In: Richards, Stanley, ed. Best Short Plays of the World Theatre, 1968-1973. New York: Crown, 1973. Produced London, 1968.

A Lesson in a Dead Language. In: Parone, Edward, comp. Collison Course. New York: Random House, 1968. Never produced on the professional stage.

The Owl Answers. In: Kennedy, Adrienne. Cities in Bezique; Two One-Act Plays: The Owl Answers and A Beast Story. New York: French, 1969. Also in: Hoffman, William M., ed. New American Plays. Vol. 2. New York: Hill & Wang, 1968. Produced off-Broadway, 1969.

The Pale Blue Flower. Unpublished. Never produced on the professional stage.

A Rat's Mass. In: Couch, William, Jr., ed. New Black Playwrights. Baton Rouge: Louisiana State University Press, 1968. Produced at LaMama, N.Y., 1969.

Sun. In: Scripts; A Monthly of Plays and Theater Pieces, 1, 1 (November 1971), 51-4. Never produced on the professional stage.

Biography

Contemporary Dramatists. James Vinson, ed. 2nd ed. New York: St. Martin, 1977.

Shockley, Ann A. Living Black American Authors: A Biographical Directory. New York: Bowker, 1973.

Criticism

Benston, K. W. "Cities in Bezique: Adrienne Kennedy's Expression-
istic Vision." CLA Journal, 20 (December 1976), 235-44.

Brown, Lorraine A. "For the Characters Are Myself: Adrienne
Kennedy's Funnyhouse of a Negro." Negro American Literature
Forum, 9 (1975), 86-8.

Tener, R. L. "Theatre of Identity: Adrienne Kennedy's Portrait
of the Black Woman." Studies in Black Literature, 6 (Summer
1975), 1-5.

Reviews

New York Times, Jan. 13, 1969, 26:1. [Cities in Bezique.]

New Yorker, 44 (Jan. 25, 1969), 77. [Cities in Bezique.]

New Yorker, 39 (Jan. 25, 1964), 76+. [Funnyhouse of a Negro.]

New York Times, Nov. 1, 1969, 39:1. [A Rat's Mass.]

Plays and Players, 17 (November 1969), 14-5. [A Rat's Mass.]

KERR, JEAN (1924-)

Plays

The Big Help, A Comedy in Three Acts. Chicago: Dramatic Publishing, 1947. Never produced on the professional stage.

Finishing Touches. New York: Dramatists Play Service, 1973.
Also in: Guernsey, Otis L., Jr., ed. Best Plays of 1972-1973.
New York: Dodd, Mead, 1973. (Condensation.) Produced Broad-
way, 1972.

Franz Werfel's The Song of Bernadette; A Play in Three Acts.
Dramatized from his novel. Written with W. Kerr. Chicago:
Dramatic Publishing, 1944. Produced Broadway, 1944.

Goldilocks. Written with W. Kerr. Music by Leroy Anderson.
Garden City, N.Y.: Doubleday, 1958. Produced Broadway, 1958.

Jenny Kissed Me; A Comedy in Three Acts. New York: Dramatists
Play Service, 1949. Produced Broadway, 1948.

John Murray Anderson's Almanac. Contributed sketches. Unpublished. Produced Broadway, 1953.

King of Hearts. Written with E. Brooke. Garden City, N.Y. : Doubleday, 1954. Also in: Theatre Arts, 39, 7 (July 1955), 35-62. Produced Broadway, 1954.

Lunch Hour. New York: French, 1981. Produced Broadway, 1980.

Mary, Mary. Garden City, N.Y. : Doubleday, 1963. Also in: Kerr, Jean. Mary, Mary, and Other Plays. Greenwich, Conn. : Fawcett, 1964. Produced Broadway, 1961.

Our Hearts Were Young and Gay. Dramatized from the book by Cornelia Otis Skinner and Emily Kimbrough. Chicago: Dramatic Publishing, 1946. Motion picture, 1944.

Poor Richard. Garden City, N.Y. : Doubleday, 1965. Produced Broadway, 1964.

Thank You, Just Looking. Variant title of Touch and Go.

Touch and Go. Unpublished. Produced Broadway, 1949.

Biography

Contemporary Authors; A Bio-bibliographical Guide to Current Authors and Their Works. Barbara Harte, ed. Vol. 5-8, first revision. Detroit: Gale, 1969.

Current Biography 1958. New York: H. W. Wilson, 1958.

New York Times, Feb. 18, 1973, 1:1.

Reviews

National Review, 25 (March 16, 1973), 316-7. [Finishing Touches.]

New Yorker, 48 (Feb. 17, 1973), 79. [Finishing Touches.]

Saturday Review of the Arts, 1 (March 1973), 55. [Finishing Touches.]

New York Times, Oct. 13, 1958, 33:1. [Goldilocks.]

New Yorker, 34 (Oct. 18, 1958), 55. [Goldilocks.]

Reporter, 19 (Nov. 13, 1958), 37-8. [Goldilocks.]

New York Times, Dec. 24, 1948, 12:2. [Jenny Kissed Me.]

New Yorker, 24 (Jan. 1, 1949), 36. [Jenny Kissed Me.]

Time, 53 (Jan. 3, 1949), 49. [Jenny Kissed Me.]

New York Times, Dec. 11, 1953, 42:2. [John Murray....]

New Yorker, 29 (Dec. 19, 1953), 75. [John Murray....]

Theatre Arts, 38 (January 1954), 76-8. [John Murray....]

Life, 36 (April 26, 1954), 97-8+. [King of Hearts.]

New York Times, April 11, 1954, sec. II, 1:1. [King of Hearts.]

New Yorker, 30 (April 10, 1954), 60+. [King of Hearts.]

New York Times, Nov. 13, 1980, sec. III, 19:1. [Lunch Hour.]

New Yorker, 56 (Nov. 24, 1980), 134. [Lunch Hour.]

Commonweal, 74 (April 14, 1961), 79-80. [Mary, Mary.]

New York Times, March 9, 1961, 24:2. [Mary, Mary.]

Theatre Arts, 45 (May 1961), 58. [Mary, Mary.]

New York Times, Dec. 3, 1964, 59:1. [Poor Richard.]

New Yorker, 40 (Dec. 12, 1964), 152+. [Poor Richard.]

Saturday Review, 47 (Dec. 19, 1964), 25. [Poor Richard.]

America, 99 (May 3, 1958), 179. [... Song of Bernadette.]

New York Times, July 27, 1944, 15:3. [... Song of Bernadette.]

New Yorker, 25 (Oct. 22, 1949), 60+. [Touch and Go.]

Saturday Review, 33 (Jan. 14, 1950), 4-5. [Touch and Go.]

KUMMER, CLARE (1888-1958)

Plays

Amourette. Unpublished. Produced Broadway, 1933.

Annie Dear. Unpublished. Produced Broadway, 1924.

Banco. Adapted from the French of A. Savoir. Unpublished. Produced Broadway, 1922.

Be Calm, Camilla! New York: French, 1922. Produced Broadway, 1918.

Bridges. New York: French, 1922. Produced Broadway, 1921.

Chinese Love; A Play in One Act. New York: French, 1922. Produced Broadway, 1921.

The Choir Rehearsal; A Play in One Act. New York: French, 1922. Produced Broadway, 1921.

Good Gracious, Annabelle, A Romantic Farce in Three Acts. New York: French, 1922. Also in: Mantle, Robert B., ed. Best Plays of 1909-1919. New York: Dodd, Mead, 1919. (Condensation.) Produced Broadway, 1916.

Her Master's Voice; A Comedy in Two Acts. New York: French, 1934. Also in: Mantle, Robert B., ed. Best Plays of 1933-1934. New York: Dodd, Mead, 1934. (Condensation.) Produced Broadway, 1933.

The Lights of Duxbury. Unpublished. Produced Brooklyn, N.Y., 1918.

Madame Pompadour. Musical play by R. Schanzer and E. Welisch, adapted by Clare Kummer. Unpublished. Produced Broadway, 1924.

Many Happy Returns. Unpublished. Produced Broadway, 1945.

The Mountain Man. Unpublished. Produced Broadway, 1921.

One Kiss. Unpublished. Produced Broadway, 1923.

Open Storage; A Comedy in One Act. New York: French, 1938. In: One Act Plays for Stage and Study. 9th series. New York: French, 1938. Never produced on the professional stage.

Opera Ball. Adapted from the German of Victor Leon and H. von Waldberg by Clare Kummer and Sydney Rosenfeld. Music by Richard Heubergen. Unpublished. Produced Broadway, 1912.

Papers; A Comedy in One Act. New York: French, 1934. Also in: One Act Plays for Stage and Study. 3rd series. New York: French, 1927. Never produced on the professional stage.

Pomeroy's Past; A Comedy in Three Acts. New York: French, 1926. Produced Broadway, 1926.

The Rescuing Angel; A Comedy in Three Acts. New York: French, 1923. Produced Broadway, 1917.

The Robbery, A Comedy in One Act. New York: French, 1921. Also in: Mayorga, M.G., ed. Representative One-Act Plays by American Authors. Boston: Little, Brown, 1937. Produced Broadway, 1921.

Rollo's Wild Oat; A Comedy in Three Acts. New York: French, 1922. Also in: Collier's, 66 (Dec. 25, 1920), 11+. Produced Broadway, 1920.

Roxy. Unpublished. Produced Chicago, 1919.

So's Your Old Antique; A Comedy in One Act. New York: French, 1920. Also in: One Act Plays for Stage and Study. 4th series. New York: French, 1928. Never produced on the professional stage.

Spring Thaw; A Comedy in Three Acts. New York: French, 1937. Produced Broadway, 1938.

A Successful Calamity; A Comedy in Two Acts. New York: French, 1922. Produced Broadway, 1917.

Three Waltzes. Musical play by Clare Kummer and Rowland Leigh. Based on the play by P. Knepler and A. Robinson. Music by J. Strauss, Sr., J. Strauss, Jr., and O. Straus. Unpublished. Produced Broadway, 1937.

Biography

"Clare Kummer." New Republic, 26 (April 20, 1921), 233-5.

"Kummer." Forum, 61 (March 1919), 307-16.

Criticism

Beckhard, A. J. "Clare Kummer." Bookman, 53 (May 1921), 276-7.

Mantle, Robert B. Contemporary American Playwrights. New York: Dodd, Mead, 1938, pp. 292-3.

Reviews

Commonweal, 18 (Oct. 13, 1933), 564. [Amourette.]

New York Times, Sept. 28, 1933, 25:2. [Amourette.]

New York Times, Nov. 5, 1924, 25:3. [Annie Dear.]

Life, 80 (Oct. 12, 1922), 10. [Banco.]

New York Times, Sept. 21, 1922, 18:1. [Banco.]

Life, 72 (Nov. 14, 1918), 72. [Be Calm....]

New York Times, Nov. 1, 1918, p. 13. [Be Calm....]

Dramatic Mirror, 83 (March 5, 1921), 408. [Bridges.]

New York Times, March 1, 1921, 18:1. [Chinese Love.]

New York Times, March 1, 1921, 18:1. [Choir Rehearsal.]

Green Book, 17 (January 1917), 10+. [Good Gracious....]

New Republic, 9 (Jan. 20, 1917), 331. [Good Gracious....]

Nation, 137 (Nov. 8, 1933), 550. [Her Master's Voice.]

New York Times, Oct. 24, 1933, 24:3. [Her Master's Voice.]

New York Times, Nov. 12, 1924, 20:6. [Madame Pompadour.]

Theatre, 41 (January 1925), 19. [Madame Pompadour.]

New York Times, Jan. 6, 1945, 15:5. [Many Happy Returns.]

New Yorker, 20 (Jan. 13, 1945), 40. [Many Happy Returns.]

New Republic, 29 (Feb. 8, 1922), 309-10. [The Mountain Man.]

New York Times, Dec. 13, 1921, 24:2. [The Mountain Man.]

New York Times, Nov. 28, 1923, 14:2. [One Kiss.]

Green Book, 7 (March 1912), 459-61. [Opera Ball.]

New York Times, April 20, 1926, 24:4. [Pomeroy's Past.]

Vogue, 67 (June 15, 1926), 79+. [Pomeroy's Past.]

Life, 70 (Oct. 25, 1917), 672. [The Rescuing Angel.]

New York Times, Oct. 9, 1917, p. 9. [The Rescuing Angel.]

New York Times, March 1, 1921, 18:1. [The Robbery.]

New York Times, Nov. 24, 1920, 14:1. [Rollo's Wild Oat.]

Theatre, 33 (February 1921), 83+. [Rollo's Wild Oat.]

New York Times, May 8, 1930, 32:5. [So's Your Old Antique.]

New York Times, March 22, 1938, 18:1. [Spring Thaw.]

Newsweek, 11 (April 4, 1938), 25. [Spring Thaw.]

Nation, 104 (Feb. 15, 1917), 198. [A Successful Calamity.]

New York Times, March 19, 1921, 11:2. [A Successful Calamity.]

New York Times, Nov. 15, 1937, 15:6. [Three Waltzes.]

Time, 31 (Jan. 3, 1938), 24. [Three Waltzes.]

LAMB, MYRNA (193?-)

Plays

Apple Pie. Book by Myrna Lamb. Music by Nicholas Meyers.
  Unpublished. Produced by the New York Shakespeare Festival
  Public Theatre, 1975.

Because I Said So. Unpublished. Produced off-Broadway, 1974.

But What Have You Done for Me Lately. In: Ravitz, Abe C. , ed.
  The Disinherited: Plays. Belmont, Calif. : Dickenson, 1974.
  Produced by the New Feminist Theatre, New York, 1969.

Crab Quadrille. Unpublished. Produced off-Broadway, 1976.

I Lost a Pair of Gloves. ©1972. In: Moore, Honor, ed. The New
  Women's Theatre: Ten Plays by Contemporary American Women.
  New York: Random House, 1977. Never produced on the profes-
  sional stage.

Mod Donna. In: Lamb, Myrna. Mod Donna and Scyklon Z. New
  York: Pathfinder, 1971. Produced by the New York Shakespeare
  Festival Public Theatre, 1970.

Olympic Park. Unpublished. Produced off-Broadway, 1978.

Scyklon Z. This is the collective name for several "playlets" in-
  cluding: In the Shadow of the Crematoria, Monologia, Pas de
  Deux, and The Butcher Shop. In: Ravitz, Abe C. , ed. The
  Disinherited: Plays. Belmont, Calif. : Dickenson, 1974.

The Serving Girl and the Lady. In: Ravitz, Abe C. , ed. The Disinherited: Plays. Belmont, Calif. : Dickenson, 1974. Produced
  off-Broadway, 1970(?).

Biography

National Playwrights Directory. Phyllis J. Kaye, ed. New York:
  Drama Book Specialists, 1977.

Criticism

Olauson, Judith. The American Woman Playwright; A View of Criticism and Characterization. Troy, N. Y. : Whitston, 1981, pp.
126-31.

Reviews

New York Times, Aug. 25, 1974, 49:2. [Apple Pie.]

New York Times, Feb. 22, 1976, sec. II, 7:4. [Apple Pie.]

Village Voice, 19 (Jan. 24, 1974), 75:1. [Because I Said So.]

New York Times, May 18, 1969, sec. II, 1:4. [But What Have You
Done for Me Lately.]

New York Times, Dec. 6, 1976, 46:4. [Crab Quadrille.]

New York Times, May 4, 1970, 48:1. [Mod Donna.]

Village Voice, 15, 19 (May 7, 1970), 53. [Mod Donna.]

Village Voice, 15, 22 (May 28, 1970), 47. [Mod Donna.]

New York Times, Dec. 21, 1978, sec. III, 16:1. [Olympic Park.]

LENNART, ISOBEL (1915-1971)

Plays

Funny Girl; A New Musical. Book by Isobel Lennart. Music by
Jule Styne. Lyrics by Bob Merrill. New York: Random House,
1964. Produced Broadway, 1964.

Biography

New York Times, Jan. 26, 1971, p. 36. (Obituary.)

Reviews

New York Times, March 27, 1964, 15:1. [Funny Girl.]

Newsweek, 63 (April 6, 1964), 76-7. [Funny Girl.]

Saturday Review, 47 (April 11, 1964), 34. [Funny Girl.]

LOOS, ANITA (1894-1981)

Plays

The Amazing Adele. Unpublished. Produced Philadelphia, 1955.

Cheri; Dramatization of Two Novels by Colette. Typescript at the
New York Public Library. Produced Broadway, 1959.

The Fall of Eve. Written with John Emerson. New York: Dodd,
Mead, 1926. Produced Broadway, 1925.

Gentlemen Prefer Blondes, A Play in Three Acts. Written with J.
Emerson. Typescript at the New York Public Library. Produced
Broadway, 1926; musical version, 1949.

Gigi. New York: Random House, 1952. Also in: Chapman, John,
ed. Best Plays of 1951-1952. (Condensation.) New York: Dodd,
Mead, 1952. Produced Broadway, 1951.

Gogo Loves You. Unpublished. Produced off-Broadway, 1964.

Happy Birthday. New York: French, 1947. Produced Broadway,
1946.

King's Mare: A Play in Three Acts. Written by J. Canolle. Translated and adapted by Anita Loos. London: Evans, 1967. Produced London, 1966, under the title Something About Anne.

Nine Fifteen Revue. Unpublished. Produced Broadway, 1930.

Social Register. Unpublished. Produced Broadway, 1931.

Something About Anne. Variant title of King's Mare.

The Whole Town's Talking; A Farce in Three Acts. Written with
J. Emerson. New York: Longmans, Green, 1925. Produced
Broadway, 1925.

Biography

Contemporary Authors; A Bio-bibliographical Guide to Current

Authors and Their Works. Christine Nasso, ed. Vol. 21-24, first revision. Detroit: Gale, 1977.

Loos, Anita. A Girl Like I. New York: Viking, 1966. (Autobiography.)

Loos, Anita. Kiss Hollywood Goodbye. New York: Viking, 1974. (Autobiography.)

New York Times Biographical Edition, 4 (1973), 639-40.

Reviews

New York Times, Oct. 13, 1959, 44:1. [Cheri.]

New Yorker, 35 (Oct. 24, 1959), 91-2. [Cheri.]

New Republic, 44 (Sept. 16, 1925), 95-6. [The Fall of Eve.]

New York Times, Sept. 1, 1925, 18:1. [The Fall of Eve.]

Harper's Bazaar, 60 (October 1926), 117+. [Gentlemen Prefer Blondes.]

New York Times, April 25, 1926, sec. VIII, 1:8. [Gentlemen Prefer Blondes.]

Life, 27 (Dec. 26, 1949), 68-71. [Gentlemen Prefer Blondes (musical).]

New York Times, Dec. 9, 1949, p. 35. [Gentlemen Prefer Blondes (musical).]

New York Times, Nov. 26, 1951, 20:4. [Gigi.]

Saturday Review, 34 (Dec. 15, 1951), 32-3. [Gigi.]

New York Times, Oct. 10, 1964, 19:2. [Gogo Loves You.]

Life, 21 (Nov. 18, 1946), 79-82. [Happy Birthday.]

New York Times, Nov. 1, 1946, 31:2. [Happy Birthday.]

New York Times, July 21, 1966, 23:1. [King's Mare.]

New York Times, Feb. 12, 1930, p. 26. [Nine Fifteen Revue.]

New York Times, Oct. 4, 1931, sec. VIII, 2:3. [Social Register.]

Metropolitan, 58 (December 1923), 38-9. [The Whole Town's Talking.]

New York Times, Aug. 30, 1923, 8:2. [The Whole Town's Talking.]

LUCE, CLARE BOOTHE (1903-)

Plays

Abide with Me. Typescript at the New York Public Library. Produced Broadway, 1935.

Child of the Morning. Typescript at the New York Public Library.
Produced Boston, 1951.

A Doll's House. Variant title of Slam the Door Softly.

Kiss the Boys Goodbye. New York: Random House, 1939. Also
in: Mantle, Robert B. , ed. Best Plays of 1938-1939. New
York: Dodd, Mead, 1939. (Condensation.) Produced Broadway,
1938.

Margin for Error. New York: Random House, 1940. Produced
Broadway, 1939.

Slam the Door Softly. New York: Dramatists Play Service, 1970.
Also in: Life, 69 (Oct. 16, 1970), 54-6+ (under the title A
Doll's House). Never produced on the professional stage.

The Women. New York: Random House, 1937. Also in: Sullivan,
Victoria, ed. Plays By and About Women; An Anthology. New
York: Random House, 1974. Produced Broadway, 1936.

Biography

Contemporary Authors; A Bio-bibliographical Guide to Current Authors and Their Works. Clare D. Kinsman, ed. Vol. 45-48.
Detroit: Gale, 1974.

Roosevelt, Felicia W. Doers and Dowagers. Garden City, N. Y. :
Doubleday, 1975, pp. 157-75.

Shadegg, Stephen C. Clare Boothe Luce; A Biography. New York:
Simon & Schuster, 1970.

Sheed, Wilfrid. Clare Boothe Luce. New York: Dutton, 1982.

Reviews

New York Times, Nov. 22, 1935, 19:2. [Abide with Me.]

Time, 26 (Dec. 2, 1935), 68. [Abide with Me.]

Commonweal, 68 (May 9, 1958), 153-4. [Child of the Morning.]

New York Times, Nov. 17, 1951, 9:7. [Child of the Morning.]

New York Times, Sept. 29, 1938, 30:2. [Kiss the Boys Goodbye.]

Theatre Arts, 22 (November 1938), 778+. [Kiss the Boys Goodbye.]

New York Times, Oct. 15, 1939, 48:7. [Margin for Error.]

Theatre Arts, 24 (January 1940), 18-9. [Margin for Error.]

New York Times, Dec. 8, 1936, 30:6. [The Women.]

New York Times, Dec. 28, 1936, 13:1. [The Women.]

Newsweek, 9 (Jan. 2, 1937), 22-3. [The Women.]

McCULLERS, CARSON (1917-1967)

Plays

The Ballad of the Sad Café. Based on her novel of the same name. Dramatization by Edward Albee. Narration written by Carson McCullers. Published: Albee, Edward. The Play, The Ballad of the Sad Café. Boston: Houghton Mifflin, 1963. Produced Broadway, 1963.

The Member of the Wedding; A Play. Boston: Houghton Mifflin, 1951. Also in: Gassner, John, ed. Best American Plays. 3rd series, 1941-1951. New York: Crown, 1952. Also in: Gassner John, and Clive Barnes, comps. Fifty Best Plays of the American Theater. New York: Crown, 1969. Produced Broadway, 1950.

The Square Root of Wonderful; A Play. Boston: Houghton Mifflin, 1958. Produced Broadway, 1957.

Biography

Carr, Virginia S. The Lonely Hunter: A Biography of Carson McCullers. Garden City, N.Y.: Doubleday, 1975.

Contemporary Authors; A Bio-bibliographical Guide to Current Authors and Their Works. Barbara Harte, ed. Vol. 5-8, first revision. Detroit: Gale, 1969.

Evans, Oliver. The Ballad of Carson McCullers. New York: Co-ward-McCann, 1966.

McDowell, Margaret. Carson McCullers. Boston: Twayne, 1980.

Criticism

Dedmond, F. B. "Doing Her Own Thing: Carson McCullers' Dram-atization of The Member of the Wedding." South Atlantic Bulletin, 40, 2 (1975), 47-52.

Dusenbury, Winifred L. The Theme of Loneliness in Modern Amer-ican Drama. Gainesville: University of Florida Press, 1960, pp. 57-85.

McDowell, Margaret. Carson McCullers. Boston: Twayne, 1980.

Phillips, Robert S. "The Gothic Architecture of The Member of the Wedding." Renascence, 16 (1964), 59-72.

Rubin, L. D. "Carson McCullers: The Aesthetic of Pain." Vir-ginia Quarterly Review, 53 (Spring 1977), 265-83.

Weales, Gerald. American Drama Since World War II. New York: Harcourt, Brace, and World, 1962, pp. 154-81.

Reviews

Nation, 197 (Nov. 23, 1963), 333-4. [The Ballad....]

New Republic, 149 (Nov. 16, 1963), 28-9. [The Ballad....]

New York Times, Oct. 31, 1963, 27:1. [The Ballad....]

New Yorker, 39 (Nov. 9, 1963), 95. [The Ballad....]

New York Times, Jan. 6, 1950, 26:6. [The Member of the Wedding.]

New Yorker, 25 (Jan. 14, 1950), 46. [The Member of the Wedding.]

Saturday Review, 33 (Jan. 28, 1950), 27-9. [The Member of the Wedding.]

New York Times, Oct. 31, 1957, 40:1. [The Square Root....]

New Yorker, 33 (Nov. 9, 1957), 103-5. [The Square Root....]

Time, 70 (Nov. 11, 1957), 93-4. [The Square Root....]

McFADDEN, ELIZABETH APTHORP (1875-1961)

Plays

Beggarman, Thief. Unpublished. Never produced on the professional
stage.

The Boy Who Discovered Easter; A Play in Three Scenes. New
York: French, 1926. Never produced on the professional stage.

Double Door, A Play in Three Acts. New York: French, 1934.
Produced London and Broadway, 1933.

If Liberty Dies Here, A Play in One Act. New York: French,
1944. Never produced on the professional stage.

Knights of the Silver Shield; A Play in One Act. New York: French,
1929. Never produced on the professional stage.

Man Without a Country; A Play in a Prologue, Three Acts and an
Epilogue. Written with A. Crimmins. Adapted from the story
of the same name by Edward Everett Hale. New York: French,
1918. Never produced on the professional stage.

The Palace of Knossos, A Play of Theseus and the Minotaur. New
York: French, 1931. Never produced on the professional stage.

The Product of the Mill; A Play in Four Acts. New York: French,
1927. Never produced on the professional stage.

A Salute to the Fourth. New York: Dramatists Play Service, 1939.
Never produced on the professional stage.

Signature. Unpublished. Produced Broadway, 1945.

Tidings of Joy, A Christmas Play in One Act. New York: French,
1933. Never produced on the professional stage.

Why the Chimes Rang: A Play in One Act. New York: French,
1915. Never produced on the professional stage.

Biography

New York Times, July 18, 1961, 29:4. (Obituary.)

Reviews

New York Times, Sept. 22, 1933, 15:5. [Double Door.]

Newsweek, 2 (Sept. 30, 1933), 45-6. [Double Door.]

New York Times, Feb. 15, 1945, 25:2. [Signature.]

Newsweek, 25 (Feb. 26, 1945), 81. [Signature.]

Theatre Arts, 29 (April 1945), 206. [Signature.]

McLAURIN, KATE L. (1885-1933)

Plays

The Alien Breed. Unpublished. Typescript at the New York Public
  Library.

Caught. Unpublished. Produced Broadway, 1925.

A Discussion with Interruptions. In: Smart Set, 26 (December
  1908), 125-7. Never produced on the professional stage.

It All Depends. Unpublished. Produced Broadway, 1925.

The Six-fifty. Unpublished. Produced Broadway, 1921.

When We Were Young. Unpublished. Produced Broadway, 1920.

Whispering Wires: A Play in Three Acts. From the novel of the
  same name by Henry Leverage. Boston: Baker, 1934. Produced Broadway, 1922.

Biography

Mantle, Robert B. American Playwrights of Today. New York:
  Dodd, Mead, 1929, pp. 300-1.

New York Times, March 2, 1933, 17:1. (Obituary.)

Who's Who on the Stage 1908. New York: Dodge, 1908.

Reviews

New York Times, Oct. 6, 1925, 31:2. [Caught.]

New York Times, Aug. 11, 1925, 16:4. [It All Depends.]

New York Times, Oct. 2, 1921, sec. VII, 1:8. [The Six-fifty.]

New York Times, Nov. 23, 1920, 11:1. [When We Were Young.]

Life, 80 (Aug. 24, 1922), 18. [Whispering Wires.]

New York Times, Aug. 8, 1922, 26:2. [Whispering Wires.]

MADISON, MARTHA

Plays

The Night Remembers. Unpublished. Produced Broadway, 1934.

Subway Express. Written with Eva K. Flint. Unpublished. Reproduction from a typewritten copy at the New York Public Library.
Produced Broadway, 1929.

The Up and Up. Written with Eva K. Flint. Unpublished. Produced Broadway, 1930.

Reviews

New York Times, Nov. 28, 1934, 24:3. [The Night Remembers.]

New York Times, Sept. 25, 1929, 34:3. [Subway Express.]

Theatre, 50 (December 1929), 66. [Subway Express.]

New York Times, Sept. 9, 1930, 25:2. [The Up and Up.]

Theatre, 52 (November 1930), 25+. [The Up and Up.]

MANNES, MARYA (1904-   )

Plays

Cafe. Unpublished. Produced Broadway, 1930.

Dance Me a Song, A Revue in Two Acts and Two Dozen Scenes.
Contributed sketches. Unpublished. Produced Broadway, 1950.

She Stoops to Conquer. Written by Oliver Goldsmith. New epilogue
by Marya Mannes. This version unpublished. Produced Washington, D. C. , 1968.

Biography

Current Biography 1959. New York: H. W. Wilson, 1959.

Mannes, Marya. Out of My Time. Garden City, N. Y. : Doubleday,
1971. (Autobiography.)

Wakeman, John, ed. World Authors: 1950-1970. New York:
H. W. Wilson, 1975.

Reviews

New York Times, Aug. 29, 1930, 11:1. [Cafe.]

New York Times, Jan. 21, 1950, 10:5. [Dance Me a Song.]

New Yorker, 25 (Jan. 28, 1950), 48. [Dance Me a Song.]

Time, 55 (Jan. 30, 1950), 40. [Dance Me a Song.]

New York Times, April 1, 1968, 58:3. [She Stoops to Conquer.]

MARSHALL, ARMINA (1900-)

Plays

Dr. Knock: A Comedy in Three Acts. Adapted by Armina Marshall
and Laurence Langner from the French play by Jules Romains.
New York: French, 1925. Produced Broadway, 1936.

On to Fortune. Written with Laurence Langner. Unpublished.
Typescript at the New York Public Library. Produced Broadway,
1935.

Pursuit of Happiness, An American Comedy. Written with Laurence
Langner. New York: French, 1934. Produced Broadway, 1933.

Suzanne and the Elder; An American Comedy. Written with Laurence
   Langner. New York: Random House, 1940. Produced Broadway,
   1940.

Biography

Notable Names in the American Theatre. Clifton, N. J. : James T.
   White, 1976.

Who's Who in the Theatre. Ian Herbert, ed. 16th ed. Detroit:
   Gale, 1977.

Reviews

Literary Digest, 122 (July 25, 1936), 19. [Dr. Knock.]

New York Times, July 14, 1936, 22:1. [Dr. Knock.]

New York Times, Jan. 15, 1935, 23:2. [On to Fortune.]

Nation, 137 (Oct. 25, 1933), 493-4. [Pursuit of Happiness.]

New Republic, 76 (Oct. 25, 1933), 307-8. [Pursuit....]

New York Times, June 24, 1934, sec. IX, 1:4. [Pursuit....]

New York Times, Oct. 13, 1940, 47:7. [Suzanne.]

Theatre Arts, 25 (January 1941), 13-4. [Suzanne.]

MATTHEWS, ADELAIDE (1886-?)

Plays

An Errand for Polly, A Character Comedy in Three Acts. Written
   with William C. Duncan. New York: French, 1926. Never produced on the professional stage.

The First Mrs. Chiverick; A Comedy in Three Acts. Written with
   Martha Stanley. New York: French, 1930.

Heart's Desire. Written with Ann Nichols. Unpublished. Never
   produced on the professional stage.

Innocent Anne; A Light Comedy in Four Acts. Written with Martha
Stanley. New York: French, 1930.

It Never Happens Twice; A Comedy in Three Acts. Minneapolis:
Northwestern, 1938. Never produced on the professional stage.

Just Married; A Comedy in Three Acts. Written with Anne Nichols.
New York: French, 1929. Produced Broadway, 1921.

Marrying Anne, A Comedy in Three Acts. Boston: Baker, 1930.
Never produced on the professional stage.

Nearly Married. Written with Anne Nichols. Unpublished. Produced Broadway, 1929.

Nightie Night; A Farce in a Prologue and Three Acts. Written with
Martha Stanley. New York: French, 1929. Produced Broadway,
1919.

Puppy Love; A Farcical Comedy in Three Acts. Written with Martha
Stanley. New York: French, 1927. Produced Broadway, 1925.

Scrambled Wives. Written with Martha Stanley. Unpublished. Produced Broadway, 1920.

Sunset Glow, A Comedy in Three Acts. Boston: Baker, 1929.
Never produced on the professional stage.

The Teaser. Written with Martha Stanley. Unpublished. Produced
Broadway, 1921.

The Wasp's Nest; A Mystery Comedy in Three Acts. Written with
Martha Stanley. New York: French, 1929. Produced Broadway,
1927.

Where Innocence Is Bliss, A Light Comedy in Four Acts. Written
with Martha Stanley. New York: French, 1929.

Biography

Mantle, Robert B. American Playwrights of Today. New York:
Dodd, Mead, 1929, p. 297.

Mantle, Robert B. Contemporary American Playwrights. New York:
Dodd, Mead, 1938, p. 318.

Reviews

New York Times, April 27, 1921, 21:1. [Just Married.]

Theatre, 34 (July 1921), 9+. [Just Married.]

New York Times, Sept. 22, 1929, sec. IX, 4:1. [Nearly Married.]

Forum, 62 (October/November 1919), 500. [Nightie Night.]

Life, 74 (Sept. 25, 1919), 548. [Nightie Night.]

New York Times, Sept. 10, 1919, 16:1. [Nightie Night.]

New York Times, Oct. 4, 1925, sec. IX, 2:1. [Puppy Love.]

Vogue, 67 (April 1, 1926), 95+. [Puppy Love.]

New York Times, Aug. 6, 1920, 16:1. [Scrambled Wives.]

Theatre, 32 (October 1920), 165+. [Scrambled Wives.]

Nation, 113 (Sept. 3, 1921), 215. [The Teaser.]

New York Times, July 28, 1921, 8:3. [The Teaser.]

New York Times, Oct. 26, 1927, 26:3. [The Wasp's Nest.]

MAY, ELAINE (1932-   )

Plays

Adaptation. New York: Dramatists Play Service, 1971. Also in:
Guernsey, Otis L. Best Plays of 1968-1969. New York: Dodd,
Mead, 1969. (Condensation.) Produced Broadway, 1969.

An Evening with Mike Nichols and Elaine May. Written with Mike
Nichols. Unpublished. Produced Broadway, 1960.

Biography

"Behind the Lens." Time, 99 (March 20, 1972), 92-3.

Current Biography 1961. New York: H. W. Wilson, 1961.

Thompson, T. "Whatever Happened to Elaine May?" Life, 63
(July 28, 1967), 54+.

Vinson, James, ed. Contemporary Dramatists. New York: St.
Martin, 1973, pp. 519-20.

Reviews

New York Times, Feb. 11, 1969, 27:1. [Adaptation.]

New Yorker, 45 (Feb. 22, 1969), 90+. [Adaptation.]

Time, 93 (Feb. 21, 1969), 42. [Adaptation.]

New York Times, Oct. 10, 1960, 37:1. [An Evening....]

Theatre Arts, 44 (December 1960), 12. [An Evening....]

Time, 76 (Oct. 24, 1960), 73. [An Evening....]

MAYO, MARGARET (1882-1951)

Plays

The Austrian Dancer. Unpublished. Never produced on the professional stage.

Baby Mine; A Farce in Three Acts. New York: French, 1924. Produced Broadway, 1910.

Be Careful, Baby. Written with Salisbury Field. Unpublished. Produced London, 1918.

Behind the Scenes. Unpublished. Never produced on the professional stage.

Being Fitted. Unpublished. Never produced on the professional stage.

Commencement Days. Unpublished. Produced Broadway, 1908.

Cyprienne; A Comedy in Three Acts. Adapted from the French of Victorien Sardou. New York: French, 1941. Never produced on the professional stage.

The Debtors. Written by F. von Schoenthau. Translated by Margaret Mayo. Produced Broadway, 1909.

The Flirt. Unpublished. Never produced on the professional stage.

Heads Up. Written with Zellah Covington. Unpublished. Produced 1929(?).

His Bridal Night. Written with Laurence Rising. Unpublished. Produced Broadway, 1916.

The Jungle. Unpublished. Never produced on the professional stage.

Loving Ladies. Written with Aubrey Kennedy. Unpublished. Produced 1926(?).

The Marriage of William Ashe. Adapted from the novel by H. Ward. Unpublished. Produced Broadway, 1906.

Nip and Tuck. Unpublished. Produced (?).

Pettie Darling. Unpublished. Produced (?).

Polly of the Circus, A Comedy-Drama in Three Acts. New York: Longmans, Green, 1933. Produced Broadway, 1907.

Prisoner of the World. Unpublished. Never produced on the professional stage.

Rock-a-Bye Baby, A Musical Comedy. Written by Margaret Mayo, E. A. Woolf, J. Kern, and H. Reynolds. Based on Baby Mine. Unpublished. Produced Broadway, 1918.

Seeing Things. Written with Aubrey Kennedy. Unpublished. Produced Broadway, 1920.

Twin Beds. Written with Salisbury Field. New York: French, 1931. Produced Broadway, 1914.

Under Two Flags. Adapted from the novel by Ouida. Unpublished. Produced London, 1913.

The Wall Street Girl. Book written with E. Selwyn. Lyrics by Otto Harbach. Music by K. Hoschna. Unpublished. Typescript of libretto at the New York Public Library. Produced Broadway, 1912.

The White Way. Unpublished. Produced(?).

Biography

New York Times, Feb. 26, 1951, 23:1. (Obituary.)

"Successful Woman Dramatist." McClure, 39 (September 1912), 597-9.

Who Was Who in the Theatre, 1912-1976. Detroit: Gale, 1978.

Wolf, R. "Biographical Sketch." Green Book, 10 (October 1913), 616-26.

Reviews

Good Housekeeping, 51 (December 1910), 702-3. [Baby Mine.]

New York Times, April 3, 1927, sec. VIII, 2:1. [Baby Mine.]

Life, 54 (Oct. 28, 1909), 584. [Debtors.]

Nation, 103 (Aug. 24, 1916), 183. [His Bridal Night.]

Theatre, 6 (January 1906), 3-4. [The Marriage of William Ashe.]

Green Book, 20 (August 1918), 202+. [Rock-a-Bye Baby.]

New York Times, May 23, 1918, p. 11. [Rock-a-Bye Baby.]

Theatre, 28 (July 1918), 23. [Rock-a-Bye Baby.]

Dramatist, 11 (July 1920), 1008-9. [Seeing Things.]

Theatre, 32 (July/August 1920), 31+. [Seeing Things.]

Dramatist, 6 (Janaury 1915), 533-4. [Twin Beds.]

Green Book, 12 (October 1914), 697-9. [Twin Beds.]

Red Book, 19 (August 1912), 766-8. [The Wall Street Girl.]

Theatre, 15 (May 1912), 16. [The Wall Street Girl.]

MERCHANT, ABBY (1882-)

Plays

The Bride's Rival, A One Act Play. New York: French, 1934.
Never produced on the professional stage.

The Ever Green Lady. Unpublished. Produced Broadway, 1922.

The New Englander. Unpublished. Produced Broadway, 1919.

A New Frock for Pierrette, A Revue. New York: French, 1933.
Never produced on the professional stage.

Your Loving Son. Unpublished. Produced Broadway, 1941.

Biography

Who's Who of American Women. Vol. 1, 1958-1959. Chicago:
Marquis Who's Who, 1959.

Reviews

New York Times, Oct. 12, 1922, 25:2. [The Ever Green Lady.]

American Mercury, 1 (April 1924), 502. [The New Englander.]

New Republic, 37 (Feb. 20, 1924), 336. [The New Englander.]

New York Times, Feb. 8, 1924, 22:2. [The New Englander.]

New York Times, April 5, 1941, 13:2. [Your Loving Son.]

MERRIAM, EVE (1916-   )

Plays

And I Ain't Finished Yet. Unpublished. Produced off-Broadway,
1981.

The Club. Book by Eve Merriam. Musical arrangements by A.
Ivanoff. New York: French, 1977. Produced off-Broadway,
1976.

Dialogue for Lovers. Unpublished. Produced off-Broadway, 1980.

Inner City. Unpublished. Produced Broadway, 1971.

Out of Our Father's House. Written with P. Wagner and J. Hofsiss.
In: Moore, Honor, ed. The New Women's Theatre. New York:
Vintage, 1977. Produced off-Broadway, 1977.

Viva Reviva. Book and lyrics by Eve Merriam. Music by Amy
Rubin. Unpublished. Produced off-Broadway, 1977.

Biography

Contemporary Authors; A Bio-bibliographical Guide to Current Authors and Their Works. Barbara Harte and Carolyn Riley, eds.
Vol. 5-8, first revision. Detroit: Gale, 1969.

Reviews

Ms. , 5 (March 1977), 34+. [The Club.]

New Republic, 176 (Feb. 5, 1977), 38. [The Club.]

New York Times, Oct. 15, 1976, sec. III, 10:3. [The Club.]

New York Times, April 29, 1980, sec. III, 10:4. [Dialogue for Lovers.]

New Yorker, 56 (May 5, 1980), 113. [Dialogue for Lovers.]

New York Theatre Critics' Reviews, 32, 24 (1971), 147-9. [Inner City.]

New York Times, Dec. 20, 1971, 48:1. [Inner City.]

New York Times, Nov. 4, 1977, sec. III, 2:3. [Out of Our Father's House.]

New York Times, Oct. 19, 1977, sec. III, 22:1. [Viva Reviva.]

MEYER, ANNIE NATHAN (1867-1951)

Plays

Advertising of Kate. Unpublished. Produced Broadway, 1922.

Black Souls: A Play in Six Scenes. New Bedford, Mass. : Reynolds, 1932. Produced at the Provincetown Playhouse, New York, 1932.

Dinner of Herbs, A Comedy. Unpublished. Produced off-Broadway, 1909.

The District Attorney. Unpublished. Produced Buffalo, N. Y. , 1921.

The Dominant Sex. New York: Brandu, 1911. Never produced on the professional stage.

The Dreamer. New York: Broadway Publishing, 1912. Never produced on the professional stage.

The New Way; A Comedy in Three Acts. New York: French, 1925. Produced Broadway, 1923.

P's and Q's, A Farce in One Act. New York: French, 1921.
Never produced on the professional stage.

The Scientific Mother. In: Bookman, 5 (July 1897), 381-2. Never
produced on the professional stage.

The Spur. Unpublished. Produced Broadway, 1914.

Biography

Meyer, Annie Florance (Nathan). It's Been Fun; An Autobiography.
New York: Schuman, 1951.

New York Times, Sept. 24, 1951, 27:1. (Obituary.)

Notable American Women: The Modern Period. A Biographical
Dictionary. Cambridge, Mass.: Belknap Press of Harvard University Press, 1980.

Taylor, R. L. "Doctor, the Lady, and Columbia University." New
Yorker, 19 (Oct. 23, 1943), 27-32. Continued in next issue:
Oct. 31, 1943, 28-32+.

Reviews

New York Times, May 9, 1922, 22:2. [Advertising of Kate.]

New York Times, March 31, 1932, 25:1. [Black Souls.]

Theatre, 9 (April 1909), 117. [Dinner of Herbs.]

New York Times, Dec. 5, 1923, 23:6. [The New Way.]

New York Dramatic Mirror, 72 (Nov. 4, 1914), 9. [The Spur.]

New York Times, Oct. 27, 1914, 11:7. [The Spur.]

MIELE, ELIZABETH (1900-)

Plays

An Angel Comes East! Typescript at the New York Public Library.

Anybody's Game; A Comedy in Three Acts. Boston: Baker, 1933.
Produced Broadway, 1932.

The Big Shot. Variant title of Ever So Happy.

Brains of the Family; A Comedy. Typescript at the New York Public
    Library. Produced off-Broadway, 1932.

City Haul. Typescript at the New York Public Library. Produced
    Broadway, 1929.

Did I Say--No? Boston: Baker, 1934. Produced Broadway, 1931.

Ever So Happy. Unpublished. Produced off-Broadway, 1932.

High Hat 'em. Typescript at the New York Public Library.

Hit the Trail. Lyrics by Elizabeth Miele. Book by Frank O'Neill.
    Music by F. Valerio. Unpublished. Produced Broadway, 1954.

The Red-Checker; A Play. Typescript at the New York Public Li-
    brary.

Biography

Mantle, Robert B. Contemporary American Playwrights. New York:
    Dodd, Mead, 1938, p. 319.

Reviews

New York Times, Dec. 22, 1932, 21:4. [Anybody's Game.]

New York Times, Dec. 31, 1929, 14:4. [City Haul.]

New York Times, Sept. 23, 1931, 19:4. [Did I Say--No?]

New York Times, Dec. 3, 1954, 31:2. [Hit the Trail.]

New Yorker, 30 (Dec. 11, 1954), 98. [Hit the Trail.]

Theatre Arts, 39 (February 1955), 16+. [Hit the Trail.]

MILLAY, EDNA ST. VINCENT (1892-1950)

Plays

Aria da Capo; A Play in One Act. New York: Harper, 1920.

Also in: Kozeeka, Paul, ed. Fifteen American One Act Plays. New York: Pocket, 1975. Also in: Gassner, John, ed. Twenty-five Best Plays of the Modern American Theatre. New York: Crown, 1949. Produced at the Provincetown Playhouse, New York, 1919.

Conversation at Midnight. New York: Harper, 1937. Produced Los Angeles, 1961; New York, 1964.

The King's Henchman; A Play in Three Acts. New York: Harper, 1927. Also in: Tucker, Samuel M., ed. Modern American and British Plays. New York: Harper, 1931. Produced at the Metropolitan Opera House, New York, 1927.

The Lamp and the Bell; A Drama in Five Acts. New York: Harper, 1921. Also in: Shay, Frank, ed. A Treasury of Plays for Women. Boston: Little, Brown, 1922. Produced Broadway, 1921.

Launzi. Unpublished. Produced Broadway, 1923.

Lovely Light (selected letters and poems by Millay). Unpublished. Produced Broadway, 1960.

The Princess Marries the Page. New York: Harper, 1932.

Two Slatterns and a King; A Moral Interlude. Cincinnati: Kidd, 1921. Also in: Millay, Edna St. Vincent. Three Plays. New York: Harper, 1926.

Biography

American Writers: A Collection of Literary Biographies. Leonard Unger, ed. Vol. III. New York: Scribner, 1974.

Brittin, Norman A. Edna St. Vincent Millay. New York: Twayne, 1967.

Gray, James. Edna St. Vincent Millay. Minneapolis: University of Minnesota Press, 1967.

Criticism

Brittin, Norman A. Edna St. Vincent Millay. New York: Twayne, 1967.

Nierman, Judith. Edna St. Vincent Millay: A Reference Guide. Boston: Hall, 1977.

Orel, Harold. "Tarnished Arrows: The Last Phase of Edna St. Vincent Millay." Kansas Magazine, 1 (1960), 73-8.

Patton, John Joseph. "Edna St. Vincent Millay As a Verse Dramatist." Ph.D. dissertation, University of Colorado, 1962.

Reviews

New York Times, Dec. 14, 1919, sec. 8, p. 2. [Aria da Capo.]

New York Times, May 13, 1923, 16:2. [Aria da Capo.]

Los Angeles Herald & Express, Dec. 1, 1961, sec. B, p. 6. [Conversation at Midnight.]

New York Times, Nov. 13, 1964, 27:1. [Conversation at Midnight.]

Nation, 124 (March 9, 1927), 267-8. [The King's Henchman.]

New Republic, 50 (March 16, 1927), 101-2. [The King's Henchman.]

Yale Review, 17 (October 1927), 174-5. [The King's Henchman.]

The Measure, 7 (September 1921), 18. [The Lamp and the Bell.]

New York Evening Post Literary Review, July 16, 1921, p. 3. [The Lamp and the Bell.]

New York Times, Oct. 11, 1923, 16:3. [Launzi.]

New York Times, Feb. 9, 1960, 27:4. [Lovely Light.]

New Yorker, 36 (Feb. 20, 1960), 102. [Lovely Light.]

Time, 75 (Feb. 22, 1960), 100. [Lovely Light.]

Christian Science Monitor, Dec. 31, 1932, p. 13. [The Princess Marries the Page.]

New York Times Book Review, Dec. 18, 1932, p. 8. [The Princess Marries the Page.]

Booklist, 18 (June 1922), 324. [Two Slatterns and a King.]

Boston Evening Transcript, Aug. 26, 1922, sec. 4, p. 7. [Two Slatterns and a King.]

MILLER, ALICE DUER (1874-1942)

Plays

Charm School; A Comedy in Three Acts. Written with Robert Miller. New York: French, 1922. Produced Broadway, 1920.

Come Out of the Kitchen; A Comedy in Three Acts. Written with A. E. Thomas. Based on a story of the same name by Alice Miller. New York: French, 1921. Produced Broadway, 1916.

June Days. Musical based on a play by Alice Miller and Robert Miller. Book by Cyrus Wood. Music by J. Fred Coots. Lyrics by Clifford Grey. Unpublished. Produced Broadway, 1925.

Little Scandal; A Comedy. Written with Florence Ryerson. New York: French, 1951.

Magnolia Lady. Musical comedy based on Come Out of the Kitchen. Book and lyrics by Anne Caldwell. Music by Harold Levey. Unpublished. Produced Broadway, 1924.

The Rehearsal. Original draft at the New York Public Library. Produced New York, 1915/16(?).

Roberta. Musical comedy based on the novel Gowns by Roberta, by Alice Miller. Musical by J. Kern and O. Harbach. Piano-vocal score published in 1950 by Harms (New York). Produced Broadway, 1933.

Sky High, A Comedy. Written with Florence Ryerson. New York: French, 1950. Produced New York, 1925(?).

The Springboard; A Comedy in Three Acts. New York: French, 1928. Produced Broadway, 1927.

Biography

Current Biography 1941. New York: H. W. Wilson, 1941.

New Yorker, 2 (Feb. 19, 1927), 25-7.

Overton, Grant. The Women Who Make Our Novels. New York: Dodd, Mead, 1928, pp. 206-13.

Reviews

London News, 158 (Jan. 22, 1921), 118. [Charm School.]

New York Times, Aug. 3, 1920, 12:1. [Charm School.]

Dramatist, 8 (January 1917), 761-2. [Come Out of the Kitchen.]

Green Book, 17 (January 1917), 8. [Come Out of the Kitchen.]

New York Times, Oct. 24, 1916, 14:1. [Come Out of the Kitchen.]

New York Times, Aug. 23, 1925, sec. VII, 1:1. [June Days.]

New York Times, Nov. 26, 1924, 17:2. [Magnolia Lady.]

Catholic World, 138 (March 1934), 733. [Roberta.]

New York Times, Nov. 20, 1933, 18:4. [Roberta.]

Stage, 11 (December 1933), 8. [Roberta.]

New York Times, Oct. 2, 1927, sec. VIII, 4:6. [The Springboard.]

Theatre, 46 (December 1927), 44. [The Springboard.]

MITCHELL, FANNY TODD

Plays

Angela. Unpublished. Produced Broadway, 1928.

Boom-Boom. Musical comedy. Book by Fanny Mitchell. Music by W. Janssen. Lyrics by M. Holiner and J. Keirn Brennan. Unpublished. Produced Broadway, 1929.

Music in May. Musical comedy. Book by Fanny Mitchell. Music by E. Berte and K. Rubens. Lyrics by J. Keirn Brennan. Unpublished. Produced Broadway, 1929.

Wonderful Night. Adapted from Die Fledermaus by J. Strauss. Unpublished. Produced Broadway, 1929.

Reviews

New York Times, Dec. 4, 1928, 28:2. [Angela.]

New York Times, Jan. 29, 1929, 26:4. [Boom-Boom.]

Theatre, 49 (May 1929), 47. [Boom-Boom.]

New York Times, April 2, 1929, 29:1. [Music in May.]

New York Times, Jan. 7, 1929, sec. IX, p. 1. [Music in May.]

New York Times, Nov. 1, 1929, 23:3. [Wonderful Night.]

MITCHELL, NORMA (189?-1967)

Plays

Autumn Hill. Written with John Harris. Unpublished. Produced
    Broadway, 1942.

Buy, Buy, Baby. Written with R. Medcraft. Unpublished. Produced
    Broadway, 1926.

Cradle Snatchers; A Farce-Comedy in Three Acts. Written with R.
    Medcraft. New York: French, 1931. Produced Broadway, 1925.

I Can't Bear It. Written with R. Medcraft. Based on a play by F.
    Bellamy and L. MacKall. Typescript at the New York Public Li-
    brary.

Post Road; A Play in Two Acts. Written with Wilbur D. Steele.
    New York: French, 1936. Produced Broadway, 1934.

When Hell Froze. Written with Wilbur D. Steele. Unpublished.
    Produced Boston, 1930.

Biography

Mantle, Robert B. Contemporary American Playwrights. New York:
    Dodd, Mead, 1938, pp. 236-7.

New York Times, May 30, 1967, 19:5. (Obituary.)

Reviews

New York Times, April 14, 1942, 17:4. [Autumn Hill.]

New Yorker, 18 (April 25, 1942), 30. [Autumn Hill.]

Life, 88 (Oct. 28, 1926), 19. [Buy, Buy, Baby.]

New York Times, Oct. 8, 1926, 26:2. [Buy, Buy, Baby.]

Dramatist, 17 (July 1926), 1303-4. [Cradle Snatchers.]

Life, 86 (Nov. 5, 1925), 22. [Cradle Snatchers.]

New York Times, Sept. 8, 1925, 28:2. [Cradle Snatchers.]

New York Times, Dec. 5, 1934, 28:3. [Post Road.]

New York Times, July 23, 1935, 24:3. [Post Road.]

New York Times, Oct. 5, 1930, sec. IX, 4:6. [When Hell Froze.]

MOORE, HONOR (1945-)

Plays

Mourning Pictures. In: Moore, Honor, ed. The New Women's Theatre: Ten Plays by Contemporary American Women. New York: Random House, 1977. Produced off-Broadway, 1974.

Years. Unpublished. Received a staged reading at the American Place Theatre, New York City, 1978.

Biography

Contemporary Authors; A Bio-bibliographical Guide to Current Authors and Their Works. Frances C. Locher, ed. Vol. 85-88. Detroit: Gale, 1980.

Reviews

Ms., 3 (November 1974), 100+. [Mourning Pictures.]

New York Times, Nov. 11, 1974, 41:1. [Mourning Pictures.]

New Yorker, 50 (Nov. 18, 1974), 113. [Mourning Pictures.]

MORRISON, ANNE (189?-)

Plays

Jonesy; A Comedy in Three Acts. Written with P. Toohey. New York: French, 1929. Produced Broadway, 1929.

Pigs; A Comedy in Three Acts. Written with P. McNutt. New York: French, 1924. Produced Broadway, 1924.

Their First Anniversary; A One Act Play. In: One Act Plays for Stage and Study. 8th series. New York: French, 1934. Never produced on the professional stage.

The Wild Westcotts; A Comedy in Three Acts. New York: French, 1926. Produced Broadway, 1923.

Biography

Mantle, Robert B. American Playwrights of Today. New York: Dodd, Mead, 1929, p. 301.

Reviews

Life, 93 (May 3, 1929), 24. [Jonesy.]

New York Times, April 10, 1929, 32:2. [Jonesy.]

Theatre, 49 (June 1929), 45. [Jonesy.]

Dramatist, 16 (April 1925), 1259-60. [Pigs.]

New York Times, June 8, 1924, sec. VII, 1:8. [Pigs.]

New York Times, Sept. 2, 1924, 22:5. [Pigs.]

New York Times, Dec. 25, 1923, 26:2. [The Wild Westcotts.]

NANUS, SUSAN (1950?-)

Plays

Playing Dolls. Unpublished. Produced off-Broadway, 1978.

The Survivor. Unpublished. Produced Broadway, 1981.

Where Memories Are Magic and Dreams Are Invented. Unpublished.
Produced off-Broadway, 1978.

Reviews

New York, 14 (March 16, 1981), 44. [The Survivor.]

New York Times, Dec. 19, 1980, sec. 3, 16:1. [The Survivor.]

Variety, 302 (March 11, 1981), 228. [The Survivor.]

NICHOLS, ANNE (1891-1966)

Plays

Abie's Irish Rose; A Comedy in Three Acts. New York: French,
1937. Also in: Cerf, Bennett A., and Van H. Cartmell, comps.
S.R.O.; The Most Successful Plays in the History of the American
Stage. Garden City, N.Y.: Doubleday, Doran, 1944. Produced
Broadway, 1922.

Down Limerick Way. Unpublished. Produced Broadway, 1919.

The Gilded Cage. Typescript at the New York Public Library.
Produced Los Angeles, 1920.

The Happy Cavalier. Unpublished. Produced N.Y., 1920(?).

Heart's Desire. Written with Adelaide Matthews. Unpublished.
Never produced on the professional stage.

Her Weekend. Unpublished. Produced Broadway, 1936.

Just Married; A Comedy in Three Acts. Written with Adelaide Matthews. New York: French, 1929. Produced Broadway, 1921.

The Land of Romance. Written 1922. Unpublished. Never produced on the professional stage.

Linger Longer Letty. Musical comedy. Written with A. Goodman and B. Grosman. Music by Alfred Goodman. Unpublished. Produced Broadway, 1919.

Love Dreams. Musical comedy. Book by Anne Nichols. Music by W. Janssen. Lyrics by O. Morosco. Unpublished. Produced Broadway, 1921.

Nearly Married. Written with Adelaide Matthews. Unpublished. Produced Broadway, 1929.

Pre-Honeymoon. Written with A. van Ronkel. Unpublished. Produced Broadway, 1936.

Seven Miles to Arden. Written in 1919. Unpublished. Never produced on the professional stage.

Biography

Drewry, J. E. "Interview with Author." National Magazine, 55 (September 1926), 12+.

Lincoln, N. "Ladies Behind the Scenes." Everybody's Magazine, 54 (April 1926), 88-93.

Mullett, Mary B. "Interview with Anne Nichols." American Mercury, 98 (August 1924), 18-9.

Reviews

Life, 89 (Feb. 3, 1927), 19. [Abie's Irish Rose.]

New Republic, 42 (March 18, 1925), 98-9. [Abie's Irish Rose.]

New York Times, May 24, 1922, 22:4. [Abie's Irish Rose.]

New York Times, March 29, 1927, 23:3. [Abie's Irish Rose.]

New York Clipper, 67 (Feb. 4, 1920), 25. [Down Limerick Way.]

New York Times, March 20, 1936, 28:5. [Her Weekend.]

New York Times, April 27, 1921, 21:1. [Just Married.]

Theatre, 34 (July 1921), 9+. [Just Married.]

New York Times, Nov. 21, 1919, 14:1. [Linger Longer Letty.]

Theatre, 31 (January 1920), 20+. [Linger Longer Letty.]

New York Times, Oct. 11, 1921, 22:2. [Love Dreams.]

Theatre, 34 (December 1921), 416+. [Love Dreams.]

New York Times, Sept. 22, 1929, sec. IX, 4:1. [Nearly Married.]

New York Times, May 1, 1936, 19:4. [Pre-Honeymoon.]

Time, 27 (May 11, 1936), 28. [Pre-Honeymoon.]

NORDSTROM, FRANCES (188?-)

Plays

All Wrong. Written 1919. Unpublished.

Her Market Price. Written 1924. Unpublished.

It Pays to Flirt. Written with Joseph McManus in 1918. Unpublished.

Lady Bug; A Comedy in Three Acts. New York: French, 1935.
    Produced Broadway, 1922.

Little Doctor Love; A One-Act Play. New York: French, 1935.
    Never produced on the professional stage.

Music Box Revue. Written by Irving Berlin, Frances Nordstrom,
    and others. Unpublished. Produced Broadway, 1921.

On the Ragged Edge. Written 1919. Unpublished.

Room 44. Unpublished. Produced Atlantic City, N.J., 1912.

The Ruined Lady. Typescript at the University of Chicago. Pro-
    duced Broadway, 1920.

Snapshots of 1921. Written with Glen MacDonough and others. Un-
    published. Produced Broadway, 1921.

Some Lawyer. Written 1919. Unpublished.

Biography

Who Was Who in the Theatre: 1912-1976. Detroit: Gale, 1978.

Reviews

Life, 79 (May 4, 1922), 18. [Lady Bug.]

New York Times, April 18, 1922, 15:3. [Lady Bug.]

Independent, 107 (Dec. 31, 1931), 856. [Music Box Revue.]

New York Times, Sept. 23, 1921, 18:2. [Music Box Revue.]

Life, 75 (Feb. 12, 1920), 276. [The Ruined Lady.]

Nation, 110 (Feb. 14, 1920), 210. [The Ruined Lady.]

New York Times, Jan. 21, 1920, 10:2. [The Ruined Lady.]

New York Times, June 3, 1921, 19:2. [Snapshots of 1921.]

Theatre, 34 (August 1921), 97-9. [Snapshots of 1921.]

NORMAN, MARSHA (1948-)

Plays

Getting Out: A Play in Two Acts. Garden City, N.Y.: Doubleday,
1979. In: Guernsey, Otis L., Jr., ed. Best Plays of 1978-
1979. New York: Dodd, Mead, 1979. (Condensation.) Produced
Louisville, Ky., 1977; off-Broadway, 1978.

The Laundromat. In: Norman, Marsha. Third and Oak, The
Laundromat. New York: Dramatists Play Service, 1980. Produced Louisville, Ky., 1979; off-Broadway, 1979.

Third and Oak. In: Norman, Marsha. Third and Oak, The Laundromat. New York: Dramatists Play Service, 1980. Produced
Louisville, Ky., 1979.

Biography

New York Times Biographical Service, 10, 5 (May 1979), 673-5.

Criticism

Gussow, Mel. "Women Playwrights Show New Strength. " New York Times, Feb. 15, 1981, p. 4+.

Reviews

Commonweal, 106 (Oct. 12, 1979), 559-60. [Getting Out.]

Ms. , 6 (June 1978), 26+. [Getting Out.]

Nation, 227 (Nov. 18, 1978), 26+. [Getting Out.]

New Yorker, 54 (Nov. 6, 1978), 557+. [Getting Out.]

New Yorker, 55 (Dec. 24, 1979), 73+. [The Laundromat.]

OATES, JOYCE CAROL (1938-   )

Plays

Miracle Play. Los Angeles: Black Sparrow, 1974. Produced off-Broadway, 1974.

Ontological Proof of My Existence. In: Partisan Review, 37, 4 (1970), 471-97. Produced off-Broadway, 1972.

Sunday Dinner. Unpublished. Produced off-Broadway, 1970.

Sweet Enemy. Unpublished. Produced off-Broadway, 1965.

Biography

Contemporary Authors; A Bio-bibliographical Guide to Current Authors and Their Works. Barbara Harte and Carolyn Riley, eds. Vol. 5-8, first revision. Detroit: Gale, 1969.

Current Biography Yearbook 1970. New York: H. W. Wilson, 1971.

Criticism

Creighton, Joanne V. Joyce Carol Oates. Boston: Twayne, 1979.

Friedman, Ellen G. Joyce Carol Oates. New York: Ungar, 1980.

Reviews

New York Times, Jan. 1, 1974, 12:1. [Miracle Play.]

Newsweek, 79 (Feb. 21, 1972), 99. [Ontological Proof....]

Nation, 211 (Nov. 16, 1970), 508. [Sunday Dinner.]

New York Times, Nov. 3, 1970, 28:1. [Sunday Dinner.]

New York Times, Nov. 8, 1970, sec. II, 1:1. [Sunday Dinner.]

Commonweal, 81 (March 12, 1965), 764. [Sweet Enemy.]

New York Times, Feb. 16, 1965, 39:1. [Sweet Enemy.]

ORR, MARY (1918-)

Plays

Be Your Age. Written with R. Denham. New York: Dramatists
Play Service, 1953. Produced Broadway, 1953.

Dark Hammock; A Play in Three Acts. Written with R. Denham.
New York: Dramatists Play Service, 1946. Produced Broadway,
1944.

Grass Widows. New York: Dramatists Play Service, 1976. Never
produced on the professional stage.

Minor Murder. Written with R. Denham. New York: Dramatists
Play Service, 1967. Produced London, 1967.

Platinum Set. Written with R. Denham. Unpublished. Produced
London, 1950.

Round Trip. Written with R. Denham. Unpublished. Produced
Broadway, 1945.

Sweet Peril. Written with R. Denham. Unpublished. Produced
London, 1952.

Wallflower; A Comedy in Three Acts. Written with R. Denham.
New York: Dramatists Play Service, 1944. Produced Broadway,
1944.

Wisdom of Eve. Written with R. Denham. New York: Dramatists
Play Service, 1964. Adapted from the story of the same name
by Mary Orr. The film All About Eve was based on this play,
which was never produced on the professional stage.

Women Must Work; Women Must Weep. New York: Dramatists
Play Service, 1963. Never produced on the professional stage.

Wonderful to Us. Written with R. Denham. Unpublished. Never
produced on the professional stage.

Biography

Contemporary Authors; A Bio-bibliographical Guide to Current Authors and Their Works. James M. Ethridge and Barbara Kopala,
eds. Vol. 1-4, first revision. Detroit: Gale, 1967. (See under
"Denham.")

Notable Names in the American Theatre. Clifton, N. J. : James T.
White, 1966.

Reviews

New York Times, Jan. 15, 1953, 24:2. [Be Your Age.]

New Yorker, 28 (Jan. 24, 1953), 56. [Be Your Age.]

Theatre Arts, 37 (March 1953), 69. [Be Your Age.]

New York Times, Dec. 12, 1944, 27:8. [Dark Hammock.]

Theatre Arts, 29 (February 1945), 76. [Dark Hammock.]

The Times (London), June 9, 1967, p. 8, col. D. [Minor Murder.]

The Times (London), March 31, 1950, p. 9, col. B. [Platinum Set.]

New York Times, May 30, 1945, 16:4. [Round Trip.]

The Times (London), Dec. 4, 1952, p. 4, col. G. [Sweet Peril.]

New York Times, Jan. 27, 1944, 14:2. [Wallflower.]

Theatre Arts, 28 (April 1944), 207. [Wallflower.]

OWENS, ROCHELLE (1936-   )

Plays

Beclch. In: Owens, Rochelle. Futz and What Came After. New
York: Random House, 1968. Produced Philadelphia and off-
Broadway, 1968.

Coconut Folk Singer. In: Owens, Rochelle. The Karl Marx Play
and Others. New York: Dutton, 1974. Never produced on the
professional stage.

Emma Instigated Me. In: Performance Arts Journal, 1 (Spring
1976), 71-94. Never produced on the professional stage.

Farmer's Almanac; A Ritual. In: Owens, Rochelle. The Karl Marx
Play and Others. New York: Dutton, 1974. Never produced on
the professional stage.

Futz. New York: Hawk's Well, 1961. Revised version in: Owens,
Rochelle. Futz and What Came After. New York: Random House,
1968. Also in: Poland, Albert, ed. The Off Off Broadway Book.
Indianapolis: Bobbs-Merrill, 1972. Produced Minneapolis, 1965;
off-Broadway, 1967.

He Wants Shih. In: Owens, Rochelle. The Karl Marx Play and
Others. New York: Dutton, 1974. Never produced on the professional stage.

Homo. In: Owens, Rochelle. Futz and What Came After. New
York: Random House, 1968. Produced off-Broadway, 1966.

Istanboul. In: Owens, Rochelle. Futz and What Came After.
New York: Random House, 1968. Produced off-Broadway, 1965.

The Karl Marx Play. Book and lyrics by Rochelle Owens. Music
by Galt MacDermot. In: Owens, Rochelle. The Karl Marx Play
and Others. New York: Dutton, 1974. Also in: Richards,
Stanley, ed. Best Short Plays 1971. Radnor, Pa.: Chilton,
1972. Produced off-Broadway, 1973.

Kontraption. In: Owens, Rochelle. The Karl Marx Play and Others.
New York: Dutton, 1974. Never produced on the professional
stage.

O. K. Certaldo. In: Owens, Rochelle. The Karl Marx Play and
Others. New York: Dutton, 1974. Never produced on the professional stage.

The Queen of Greece. Unpublished. Produced off-Broadway, 1969.

The String Game. In: Owens, Rochelle. Futz and What Came
After. New York: Random House, 1968. Produced off-Broadway,
1965.

The Widow and the Colonel. New York: Dramatists Play Service,
1977. Also in: Richards, Stanley, ed. Best Short Plays. New
York: Crown, 1977. Never produced on the professional stage.

Biography

Contemporary Authors; A Bio-bibliographical Guide to Current Authors and Their Works. Clare D. Kinsman, ed. Vol. 17-20,
first revision. Detroit: Gale, 1977.

Contemporary Dramatists. James Vinson, ed. 2nd ed. New York:
St. Martin, 1977.

Reviews

New York Times, Dec. 17, 1968, 59:1. [Beclch.]

Saturday Review, 50 (Jan. 7, 1967), 111. [Beclch.]

Time, 89 (Feb. 10, 1967), 58. [Beclch.]

New Republic, 159 (July 13, 1968), 31-2. [Futz.]

New York Times, June 14, 1968, 39:1. [Futz.]

New York Times, June 30, 1968, sec. II, 1:1. [Futz.]

New Yorker, 43 (Feb. 10, 1968), 88+. [Futz.]

New York Times, April 12, 1969, 40:2. [Homo.]

New Yorker, 49 (April 7, 1973), 58. [The Karl Marx Play.]

Newsweek, 81 (April 16, 1973), 117-8. [The Karl Marx Play.]

New York Times, April 12, 1969, 40:2. [The Queen of Greece.]

PARKER, DOROTHY (1893-1967)

Plays

After Such Pleasures. Written by Edward F. Gardner. Based on
Dorothy Parker's novel of the same name. Unpublished. Produced Broadway, 1934.

Candide. Book by Lillian Hellman. Music by Leonard Bernstein.
Lyrics by Dorothy Parker and others. Based on Voltaire's Candide. New York: Random House, 1957. Also in: Hellman,
Lillian. Collected Plays. Boston: Little, Brown, 1972. Produced Broadway, 1956.

Close Harmony: or, The Lady Next Door, A Play in Three Acts.
Written with Elmer L. Rice. New York: French, 1924. Produced Broadway, 1924.

The Coast of Illyria. Written with Ross Evans. Unpublished. Produced Dallas, 1949.

The 49ers, A Revue. Parker was one of a dozen contributors. Unpublished. Produced Broadway, 1922.

Here We Are. In: Ferris, Mack, ed. 24 Favorite One-Act Plays.
Garden City, N.Y.: Doubleday, 1958. Never produced on the
professional stage.

Ladies of the Corridor; A Drama in Two Acts. Written with Arnaud
D'Usseau. New York: French, 1954. Produced Broadway, 1953.

Shoot the Works, A Revue. Dorothy Parker was one of many contributors. Unpublished. Produced Broadway, 1931.

Biography

Contemporary Authors; A Bio-bibliographical Guide to Current Authors and Their Works. Christine Nasso, ed. Vol. 2. Perm.
series. Detroit: Gale, 1978.

Kinney, Author F. Dorothy Parker. Twayne U.S. Author Series.
Boston: Hall, 1978.

Oxford Companion to American Literature. James D. Hart, ed.
4th ed. New York: Oxford University Press, 1965.

Criticism

Kinney, Arthur F. Dorothy Parker. Twayne U.S. Author Series.
Boston: Hall, 1978.

Reviews

New York Times, Jan. 6, 1934, 18:6. [After Such Pleasures.]

Time, 23 (Feb. 19, 1934), 32. [After Such Pleasures.]

Commonweal, 65 (Dec. 28, 1956), 333-4. [Candide.]

New Republic, 135 (Dec. 17, 1956), 30-1. [Candide.]

New York Times, Dec. 3, 1956, 40:2. [Candide.]

Nation, 119 (Dec. 17, 1924), 686-7. [Close Harmony.]

New York Times, Dec. 2, 1924, 23:1. [Close Harmony.]

New York Times, April 5, 1949, 37:4. [The Coast of Illyria.]

Time, 53 (April 18, 1949), 78. [The Coast of Illyria.]

New York Times, Nov. 7, 1922, 14:1. [The 49ers.]

New York Times, Nov. 12, 1922, sec. VIII, 1:1. [The 49ers.]

Commonweal, 59 (Nov. 27, 1953), 197-8. [Ladies of the Corridor.]

New York Times, Oct. 22, 1953, 33:5. [Ladies of the Corridor.]

New Yorker, 29 (Oct. 31, 1953), 58-6. [Ladies of the Corridor.]

New Republic, 67 (Aug. 5, 1931), 317-8. [Shoot the Works.]

New York Times, July 22, 1931, 19:5. [Shoot the Works.]

PEABODY, JOSEPHINE (1874-1922)

Plays

The Chameleon. New York: French, 1917. Never produced on the
professional stage.

Fortune and Men's Eyes. New York: French, 1917. Also in: Peabody, Josephine. The Collected Plays of Josephine Preston Peabody. Boston and New York: Houghton Mifflin, 1927. Never produced on the professional stage.

Marlowe, A Drama in Five Acts. Boston: Houghton Mifflin, 1901. Also in: Peabody, Josephine. The Collected Plays of Josephine Preston Peabody. Boston and New York: Houghton Mifflin, 1927. Produced Radcliffe, N. Y. , 1900.

Pan; A Choric Idyl. Book and lyrics by Josephine Peabody. Music by Charles Harriss. London: Novello, 1904. Produced Ottawa, 1904.

The Piper, A Play in Four Acts. Boston and New York: Houghton Mifflin, 1909. Also in: Peabody, Josephine. The Collected Plays of Josephine Preston Peabody. Boston and New York: Houghton Mifflin, 1927. Also in: Moses, Montrose J. , and Joseph W. Krutch, eds. Representative American Dramas, National and Local. Boston: Little, Brown, 1941. Produced Stratford-on-Avon, 1910; London, 1911; New York, 1911.

Portrait of Mrs. W.; A Play in Three Acts with an Epilogue. Boston and New York: Houghton Mifflin, 1922. Never produced on the professional stage.

The Wings, A Drama in One Act. New York: French, 1917. In: Harper's, 110 (May 1905), 947-56. Never produced on the professional stage.

The Wolf of Gubbio, A Comedy in Three Acts. New York: Houghton Mifflin, 1913. In: Peabody, Josephine. The Collected Plays of Josephine Preston Peabody. Boston and New York: Houghton Mifflin, 1927. Never produced on the professional stage.

Biography

Biographical Cyclopaedia of American Women. Erma Conklin Lee, comp. Vol. II. New York: Franklin W. Lee, 1925, pp. 369-73.

Notable American Women 1607-1950; A Biographical Dictionary. Edward T. James, ed. Cambridge, Mass. : Belknap Press of Harvard University Press, 1971.

Criticism

French, J. L. "The Younger Poets of New England." New England, n. s. 33 (December 1905), 424-8.

Stimpson, M. S. "Josephine Preston Peabody: America's Dramatic Poet." New England, n. s. 42 (May 1910), 271-7.

Reviews

Bookman, 23 (March 1911), 29-30. [The Piper.]

Life, 57 (Feb. 16, 1911), 352-3. [The Piper.]

New York Times, March 20, 1920, 14:2. [The Piper.]

Theatre, 13 (January 1911), 72+. [The Piper.]

PRINTZLAU, OLGA

Plays

Back Here. Unpublished. Produced Broadway, 1928.

Jay Walker. Unpublished. Produced Broadway, 1926.

The Ostrich. Typescript at the New York Public Library. Produced Hollywood, Calif., 1930.

Window Panes; A Drama in Three Acts. New York: French, 1932.
Produced Broadway, 1927.

Reviews

New York Times, Nov. 27, 1928, 36:3. [Back Here.]

New York Times, Feb. 9, 1926, 33:1. [Jay Walker.]

New York Times, Feb. 22, 1927, 22:2. [Window Panes.]

PURCELL, GERTRUDE (189?-1963)

Plays

Just Fancy, A Musical Comedy. Written with J. Santley. Unpublished. Produced Broadway, 1927.

Luckee Girl, A Musical Comedy in Three Acts. Adapted from the French, Un Bon Garçon, by A. Barde and M. Yvain. Produced Broadway, 1928.

The Madcap. Written with Gladys Unger. Music by Maurie Rubens. Unpublished. Produced Broadway, 1927.

Tangletoes; A Modern American Play in Three Acts. New York: Co-national Plays, 1925. Produced Broadway, 1925.

Three Little Girls, A Musical Comedy. Adapted by Gertrude Purcell and Marie A. Hecht from an original script by H. Feiner and B. Hardt-Warden. Music by W. Rolls. Unpublished. Produced Broadway, 1930.

Voltaire. Written with L. Taylor. Unpublished. Produced Broadway, 1922.

Wolf! Wolf! Unpublished. Produced at Scarborough-on-Hudson, 1925.

Biography

"Curtain Call for the Author." Metropolitan Magazine, 55 (June 1922), 42-3.

DeCasseres, B. "Shy Girl Authors." New York Times, March 26, 1922, sec. VII, 8:1.

Reviews

Life, 90 (Nov. 3, 1927), 23. [Just Fancy.]

New York Times, Oct. 12, 1927, 30:2. [Just Fancy.]

Theatre, 47 (January 1928), 38. [Just Fancy.]

New York Times, Sept. 17, 1928, 28:6. [Luckee Girl.]

New York Times, Feb. 1, 1928, 31:2. [The Madcap.]

Theatre, 47 (May 1927), 41. [The Madcap.]

New York Times, Feb. 18, 1925, 17:1. [Tangletoes.]

Life, 95 (May 2, 1930), 18. [Three Little Girls.]

New York Times, March 30, 1930, sec. VIII, 2:7. [Three Little Girls.]

New York Times, April 15, 1930, 29:1. [Three Little Girls.]

Theatre, 51 (June 1930), 17+. [Three Little Girls.]

Nation, 114 (April 5, 1922), 403. [Voltaire.]

New York Times, March 21, 1922, 17:1. [Voltaire.]

New York Times, Oct. 30, 1925, 21:1. [Wolf! Wolf!]

REGAN, SYLVIA (1908-)

Plays

Fifth Season; A New Comedy in Three Acts. New York: French,
    1953. Also in: Theatre Arts, 38 (July 1954), 34-63. Produced
    Broadway, 1953.

Golden Door. Unpublished. Produced London, 1949.

Great to Be Alive! Unpublished. Produced Broadway, 1950.

Morning Star, A Play in Three Acts. New York: Dramatists Play
    Service, 1940. Produced Broadway, 1940.

Zelda. New York: Dramatists Play Service, 1969. Produced Broad-
    way, 1969.

Biography

Biographical Encyclopaedia and Who's Who of the American Theatre.
    Walter Rigdon, ed. New York: Heineman, 1966.

Notable Names in the American Theatre. Clifton, N.J.: James T.
    White, 1976.

Reviews

New York Times, Jan. 24, 1953, 13:2. [Fifth Season.]

New York Times, Feb. 25, 1954, 24:5. [Fifth Season.]

London News, 215 (Oct. 8, 1949), 552. [Golden Door.]

Theatre World, 45 (November 1949), 6. [Golden Door.]

New York Times, March 24, 1950, 28:2. [Great to Be Alive!]

New York Times, April 17, 1940, 26:4. [Morning Star.]

Time, 35 (April 29, 1940), 64. [Morning Star.]

New York Times, March 6, 1969, 38:1. [Zelda.]

RESNIK, MURIEL

Plays

Any Wednesday, A Comedy. New York: Stein and Day, 1964.
   Produced Broadway, 1964.

Biography

Notable Names in the American Theatre. Clifton, N.J.: James T.
   White, 1976.

Poirier, N. "Miracle on Broadway." Saturday Evening Post, 237
   (April 25, 1964), 83-6.

Reviews

Look, 28 (June 16, 1964), 100-4. [Any Wednesday.]

New York Times, Feb. 19, 1964, 34:1. [Any Wednesday.]

New Yorker, 40 (Feb. 29, 1964), 106. [Any Wednesday.]

Time, 83 (Feb. 28, 1964), 61. [Any Wednesday.]

RICARDEL, MOLLY (1907?-1963)

Plays

Clap Hands. Written with Gilbert Gabriel. Unpublished. Produced
   Broadway, 1934.

I Loved You Wednesday. Written with William DuBois. Typescript at the New York Public Library. Produced Broadway, 1932.

Biography

New York Times, April 3, 1963, 47:3. (Obituary.)

Reviews

Literary Digest, 118 (Sept. 1, 1934), 21. [Clap Hands.]

New York Times, Aug. 21, 1934, 12:7. [Clap Hands.]

New York Times, Oct. 12, 1932, 27:1. [I Loved You Wednesday.]

Stage, 10 (November 1932), 32-3. [I Loved You Wednesday.]

Theatre Arts, 16 (December 1932), 959. [I Loved You Wednesday.]

RINEHART, MARY ROBERTS (1876-1958)

Plays

The Bat, A Play of Mystery in Three Acts. Written with Avery Hopwood. New York: French, 1932. Also in: Cartmell, van H. , and Bennett A. Cerf, comps. Famous Plays of Crime and Detection. Philadelphia: Blakiston, 1946. Produced Broadway, 1920.

Breaking Point. New York: Doran, 1932. Produced Broadway, 1923.

Cheer Up. Unpublished. Produced Broadway, 1913.

Seven Days, A Farce in Three Acts. Written with Avery Hopwood. New York: French, 1931. Produced Broadway, 1909.

Spanish Love. Written with Avery Hopwood. Unpublished. Produced Broadway, 1920.

A Thief in the Night. Written with Avery Hopwood. Unpublished. Produced Broadway, 1920.

Biography

Cohn, Jan. Improbable Fiction: The Life of Mary Roberts Rinehart. Pittsburgh: University of Pittsburgh Press, 1980.

Hellman, G. T. "Mary Roberts Rinehart." Life, 20 (Feb. 25, 1946), 55-6+.

New York Times, Sept. 23, 1958, 1:6. (Obituary.)

Rinehart, Mary Roberts. My Story; A New Edition and Seventeen New Years. New York: Rinehart, 1948.

Who Was Who in the Theatre: 1912-1976. Detroit: Gale, 1978.

Reviews

Dramatist, 12 (April 1921), 1053. [The Bat.]

New York Times, Aug. 24, 1920, 6:1. [The Bat.]

New York Times, Nov. 14, 1920, sec. VI, 1:1. [The Bat.]

New York Times, July 1, 1923, sec. VI, 1:4. [Breaking Point.]

New York Times, Aug. 17, 1923, 8:4. [Breaking Point.]

Theatre, 38 (October 1923), 16. [Breaking Point.]

New York Dramatic News, 57 (Jan. 4, 1913), 23. [Cheer Up.]

New York Times, Dec. 31, 1912, 7:4. [Cheer Up.]

Dramatist, 1 (January 1910), 15. [Seven Days.]

Forum, 43 (February 1910), 183-4. [Seven Days.]

New York Times, Nov. 11, 1909, 9:1. [Seven Days.]

Life, 76 (Sept. 2, 1920), 408. [Spanish Love.]

New York Times, Aug. 18, 1920, 6:1. [Spanish Love.]

New York Clipper, 68 (June 23, 1920), 18. [A Thief in the Night.]

RIVES, AMELIE (TROUBETZKOY) (1863-1945)

Plays

Allegiance. Written with Prince Troubetzkoy. Unpublished. Produced Broadway, 1918.

Athelwold, A Drama in Five Acts and in Verse. New York: Harper,
1893. Also in: Harper's, 84 (February 1892), 394-424. Never
produced on the professional stage.

Augustine the Man. London: Lane, 1906.

Blackmail. Variant title of The Fear Market.

The Fear Market. Unpublished. Produced Broadway, 1916.

Herod and Marianne, A Tragedy. In: Lippincott's Monthly Magazine,
September 1888, pp. 305-89. Never produced on the professional
stage.

Love in a Mist; A Comedy in Three Acts. Written with Gilbert
Emery. New York: French, 1927. Produced Broadway, 1926.

November Eve. In: Troubetzkoy, Amelie. The Sea Woman's Cloak
and November Eve. Cincinnati: Kidd, 1923. Never produced on
the professional stage.

Out of the Midst of Hatred. In: Virginia Quarterly Review, 2
(April 1926), 226-37. Never produced on the professional stage.

The Prince and the Pauper. Based on Abby S. Richardson's dramatization of Mark Twain's story. Unpublished. Produced Broadway,
1920.

Say When. Unpublished. Produced Broadway, 1928.

The Sea Woman's Cloak. In: Troubetzkoy, Amelie. The Sea
Woman's Cloak and November Eve. Cincinnati: Kidd, 1923.
Produced off-Broadway, 1925.

Biography

Clark, Emily. Innocence Abroad. New York: Knopf, 1931, pp. 73-
84.

Kunitz, Stanley J., and Howard Haycraft, eds. Twentieth Century

Authors; A Biographical Dictionary of Modern Literature. New York: H. W. Wilson, 1942.

New York Times, June 17, 1945, 26:3. (Obituary.)

Notable American Women 1607-1950. Edward T. James, ed. Cambridge, Mass.: Belknap Press of Harvard University Press, 1971.

Reviews

Forum, 60 (September 1918), 362. [Allegiance.]

Green Book, 20 (October 1918), 588-92. [Allegiance.]

Life, 67 (Feb. 10, 1916), 252. [The Fear Market.]

Theatre, 23 (March 1916), 123+. [The Fear Market.]

Life, 87 (April 29, 1926), 21. [Love in a Mist.]

Nation, 122 (April 28, 1926), 484. [Love in a Mist.]

New York Times, April 13, 1926, 28:3. [Love in a Mist.]

New York Times, Nov. 2, 1920, 15:1. [The Prince and the Pauper.]

Theatre, 33 (January 1921), 5+. [The Prince and the Pauper.]

Weekly Review, 3 (Nov. 24, 1920), 510-11. [The Prince and the Pauper.]

New York Times, June 27, 1928, 29:3. [Say When.]

Outlook, 149 (July 11, 1928), 425. [Say When.]

New York Times, Nov. 5, 1925, 28:1. [The Sea Woman's Cloak.]

ROUVEROL, AURANIA (1885-1955)

Plays

All in Marriage. Published under the title Love Isn't Everything. New York: French, 1937. Produced London, 1936.

Andy Hardy; A Comedy in Three Acts. New York: French, 1953.
Play never produced but basis of film of same name.

The Great American Family; A Comedy. Adapted from the novel by
Lee Shippey. New York: French, 1947. Never produced on the
professional stage.

Growing Pains; A Comedy of Adolescence in Three Acts. New York:
French, 1934. Produced Broadway, 1933.

It Never Rains; A Comedy of Young Love in Three Acts. New York:
French, 1930. Produced Broadway, 1929.

Love Isn't Everything. Variant title of All in Marriage.

Places, Please. Unpublished. Produced Broadway, 1937.

Price of Love. In: Drama, 16 (March 1926), 219+. Never produced on the professional stage.

Skidding; A Comedy in Three Acts. New York: French, 1929. Produced Broadway, 1928.

When's Your Birthday? Based on the novel Paradise, by Alice
Brown. New York: French, 1927. Never produced on the professional stage.

Where the Heart Is. New York: French, 1941. Never produced on
the professional stage.

Young April. New York: French, 1940. Never produced on the professional stage.

Young Man of Today. New York: French, 1944. Never produced
on the professional stage.

Biography

Mantle, Robert B. Contemporary American Playwrights. New York:
Dodd, Mead, 1938, p. 323.

New York Times, June 25, 1955, 15:4. (Obituary.)

Reviews

London News, 189 (Nov. 7, 1936), 846. [All in Marriage.]

New York Times, Oct. 29, 1936, 31:3. [All in Marriage.]

New York Times, Nov. 24, 1933, 24:2. [Growing Pains.]

Time, 22 (Dec. 4, 1933), 49. [Growing Pains.]

Catholic World, 130 (February 1930), 592. [It Never Rains.]

New York Times, Nov. 20, 1929, 26:4. [It Never Rains.]

New York Times, Dec. 25, 1931, 29:3. [It Never Rains.]

New York Times, Nov. 13, 1937, 10:6. [Places, Please.]

New York Times, May 22, 1928, 18:5. [Skidding.]

Theatre, 48 (July 1928), 39+. [Skidding.]

RYERSON, FLORENCE (1892-1965)

Plays

Albuquerque Ten Minutes; A One Act Comedy. New York: French, 1951. Never produced on the professional stage.

All on a Summer's Day. Written with Colin Clements. In: Ryerson, Florence, and Colin Clements. All on a Summer's Day and Six Other Short Plays. New York: French, 1928. Never produced on the professional stage.

Angels Don't Marry. Written with Colin Clements. In: Ryerson, Florence, and Colin Clements. Angels Don't Marry and Other One Act Plays. New York: French, 1938. Never produced on the professional stage.

A Cup of Tea; A Farce in One Act. New York: French, 1927. Never produced on the professional stage.

The Devil on Stilts; A Comedy in One Act. Written with Colin Clements. New York: French, 1937. Never produced on the professional stage.

The Divine Flora, A Comedy. Written with Colin Clements. New York: French, 1947. Never produced on the professional stage.

Double Date; A Comedy in One Act. New York: French, 1951. Never produced on the professional stage.

Ever Since Eve, A Comedy in Three Acts. Written with Colin

Clements. New York: French, 1941. Never produced on the
professional stage.

Farewell to Love, A Comedy in One Act. New York: French, 1938.
In: One-Act Play Magazine, (November 1937), 579-96. Never
produced on the professional stage.

Fine Feathers; A Comedy in One Act. New York: French, 1937.
Never produced on the professional stage.

Follow the Dream; A Comedy. New York: French, 1951. Never
produced on the professional stage.

Gallant Lady; A Comedy Drama in One Act. Written with Colin
Clements. New York: French, 1938. Also in: Ryerson, Florence, and Colin Clements. Angels Don't Marry and Other One
Act Plays. New York: French, 1938. Never produced on the
professional stage.

Gay Ninety; A Play in One Act. Written with Colin Clements. New
York: French, 1934. Never produced on the professional stage.

Glamour Preferred; A Comedy in Three Acts. Written with Colin
Clements. New York: French, 1941. Produced Broadway, 1940.

Going! Going! Gone! A One Act Comedy. New York: French,
1951. Never produced on the professional stage.

Harriet; A Play in Three Acts. Written with Colin Clements. New
York: French, 1945. Produced Broadway, 1943.

Her Majesty the King; A Comedy in One Act. Written with Colin
Clements. New York: French, 1938. Also in: Ryerson, Florence, and Colin Clements. Angels Don't Marry and Other One
Act Plays. New York: French, 1938. Never produced on the
professional stage.

Hot Lemonade. Written with Colin Clements. In: One Act Plays
for Stage and Study. New York: French, 1929. Never produced
on the professional stage.

Jilted, A Satirical Comedy. Written with Colin Clements. Boston:
Baker, 1930. Never produced on the professional stage.

June Mad. Written with Colin Clements. New York: French, 1939.
Never produced on the professional stage.

Last Night, A Duologue. Written with Colin Clements. New York:
French, 1938. Also in: Emerson Quarterly, 19 (February 1939),
15-6. Never produced on the professional stage.

Letters. New York: French, 1934. Also in: Drama, 16 (April
1926), 253-4. Never produced on the professional stage.

Little Scandal; A Comedy. Written with Alice Miller. New York:
French, 1951.

The Loop. In: Emerson Quarterly, 10 (January 1930), 15-7. Never
produced on the professional stage.

Love Is Like That. Written with Colin Clements. New York:
French, 1928. Also in: Ryerson, Florence, and Colin Clements.
All on a Summer's Day and Six Other Short Plays. New York:
French, 1928. Produced Broadway, 1927.

Materia Medica; A Comedy in One Act. Written with Colin Clements.
New York: French, 1937. Never produced on the professional
stage.

Men Folk. Written with Colin Clements. New York: French, 1928.
Also in: Ryerson, Florence, and Colin Clements. All on a Sum-
mer's Day and Six Other Short Plays. New York: French, 1928.
Never produced on the professional stage.

Miss Sydney Carton; A Comedy in One Act. Written with Colin
Clements. New York: French, 1937. Never produced on the
professional stage.

Movie Mother; A Play in One Act. Written with Colin Clements.
In: Griffith, Francis J., and Joseph Mersaud, eds. One Act
Plays for Today. New York: Globe, 1945. Never produced on
the professional stage.

Needlework; A Comedy in One Act. New York: French, 1951.
Never produced on the professional stage.

Never Too Old; A Comedy in One Act. Written with Colin Clements.
New York: French, 1937. Never produced on the professional
stage.

Oh! Susanna; Musical Comedy. Written with Colin Clements. Music
and lyrics by Anne Ronell. Based on the songs of Stephen Foster.
New York: French, 1928. Never produced on the professional
stage.

On the Lot. Written with Colin Clements. In: Ryerson, Florence,
and Colin Clements. All on a Summer's Day and Six Other Short
Plays. New York: French, 1928. Never produced on the professional stage.

On the Other Side of the Wall; A Play for Armistice Day. Written
with Colin Clements. In: Sanford, A. P., comp. Peace Plays.
New York: Dodd, Mead, 1932. Never produced on the professional
stage.

Perfect Ending; A Play in One Act. Written with Colin Clements.
New York: French, 1924. Never produced on the professional
stage.

A Romantic Interval. Written with Colin Clements. New York: French, 1928. Also in: Ryerson, Florence, and Colin Clements. All on a Summer's Day and Six Other Short Plays. New York: French, 1928. Never produced on the professional stage.

Sky High, A Comedy. Written with Alice Miller. New York: French, 1950. Produced New York, 1925(?).

Spring Green, A Comedy in Three Acts. Written with Colin Clements. New York: French, 1944. Never produced on the professional stage.

Star-Struck, One Act Comedy. Written with Colin Clements. New York: French, 1937. Never produced on the professional stage.

Storm. Written with Colin Clements. In: Ryerson, Florence, and Colin Clements. All on a Summer's Day and Six Other Short Plays. New York: French, 1928.

Strange Bedfellows; A Comedy in Three Acts. Written with Colin Clements. New York: French, 1948. Produced Broadway, 1945.

Sugar and Spice; A Comedy in One Act. Written with Colin Clements. New York: French, 1938. Never produced on the professional stage.

The Tenth Word, A Comedy in One Act. Written with Colin Clements. New York: French, 1937. Never produced on the professional stage.

That's Hollywood; A Comedy in One Act. Written with Colin Clements. New York: French, 1940. Never produced on the professional stage.

The Third Angle; A Comedy in One Act. New York: French, 1928. Never produced on the professional stage.

Through the Night, A Mystery Play. Written with Colin Clements. New York: French, 1940. Never produced on the professional stage.

The Triumph of Job. New York: French, 1951. Never produced on the professional stage.

The Willow Plate. Written with Colin Clements. In: One Act Plays for Stage and Study. 6th series. New York: French, 1931. Never produced on the professional stage.

Write Me a Love Scene; A Comedy in One Act. Written with Colin Clements. New York: French, 1938. Also in: Ryerson, Florence, and Colin Clements. Angels Don't Marry and Other One

Act Plays. New York: French, 1938. Never produced on the
professional stage.

Years of the Locust; A Play in Three Acts. Written with Colin
Clements. New York: French, 1941. Never produced on the
professional stage.

Biography

Biographical Encyclopaedia and Who's Who of the American Theatre.
Walter Rigdon, ed. New York: Heineman, 1966.

Reviews

New York Times, Nov. 16, 1940, 13:2. [Glamour Preferred.]

Life, 14 (April 5, 1943), 37-8. [Harriet.]

New York Times, March 14, 1943, sec. V, 1:1. [Harriet.]

Theatre Arts, 27 (May 1943), 265-7. [Harriet.]

New York Times, April 19, 1927, 24:1. [Love Is Like That.]

New York Times, Jan. 15, 1948, 27:3. [Strange Bedfellows.]

Newsweek, 31 (Jan. 26, 1948), 82. [Strange Bedfellows.]

SEARS, ZELDA (1873-1935)

Plays

Broke. Variant title of A Lucky Break.

The Clinging Vine. Book and lyrics by Zelda Sears. Music by
Harold Levey. Unpublished. Produced Broadway, 1922.

Lady Billy. Book and lyrics by Zelda Sears. Music by Harold
Levey. Typescript at the New York Public Library. Produced
Broadway, 1920.

Lollipop. Book by Zelda Sears. Music by Zelda Sears and W.
DeLeon. Music by V. Youmans. Unpublished. Produced Broadway, 1924.

A Lucky Break; A Farce Comedy in Three Acts. Written with
  Harold Levey. New York: Longmans, Green, 1926. Produced
  Broadway, 1925.

Magic Ring. Book and lyrics by Zelda Sears. Music by Harold
  Levey. Unpublished. Produced Broadway, 1923.

Biography

Mullet, Mary B. "Zelda Sears." American Mercury, 100 (December
  1925), 18+.

New York Times, Feb. 20, 1935, 19:1. (Obituary.)

Who Was Who in the Theatre: 1912-1976. Detroit: Gale, 1978.

"A Woman Playwright's Secret." Theatre, 39 (September 1924), 24+.

Reviews

New York Times, Dec. 25, 1922, 20:2. [The Clinging Vine.]

New York Times, Dec. 31, 1922, sec. VII, 1:1. [The Clinging
  Vine.]

New York Times, Dec. 15, 1920, 18:2. [Lady Billy.]

Theatre, 33 (February 1921), 107. [Lady Billy.]

New York Times, Aug. 12, 1925, 16:2. [A Lucky Break.]

New York Times, Oct. 2, 1923, 10:1. [Magic Ring.]

Theatre, 38 (November 1923), 75. [Magic Ring.]

SHANGE, NTOZAKE (1948-)

Plays

Boogie Woogie Landscapes. In: Shange, Ntozake. Three Pieces.
  New York: St. Martin, 1981. Never produced on the professional
  stage.

For Colored Girls Who Have Considered Suicide When the Rainbow

Is Enuf. San Lorenzo, Calif. : Shameless Hussy, 1975. Also
New York: Macmillan, 1976. Produced off-Broadway, 1975;
Broadway, 1976.

Mother Courage and Her Children. Adapted by Ntozake Shange from
the play by Bertolt Brecht. Unpublished. Produced off-Broadway,
1980.

A Photograph: A Study of Cruelty. In: Shange, Ntozake. Three
Pieces. New York: St. Martin, 1981. Produced off-Broadway,
1977.

Spell #7. In: Shange, Ntozake. Three Pieces. New York: St.
Martin, 1981. Produced off-Broadway, 1979.

Where the Mississippi Meets the Amazon. Unpublished. Produced
off-Broadway, 1977.

Biography

Contemporary Authors; A Bio-bibliographical Guide to Current Authors and Their Works. Frances C. Locher, ed. Vol. 85-88.
Detroit: Gale, 1980.

"Ntozake Shange Interviews Herself." Ms. , 6 (December 1977),
34-5.

Page, James A. Selected Black American Authors: An Illustrated
Bio-bibliography. Boston: Hall, 1977.

Reviews

Dance, 51 (May 1977), 92. [For Colored Girls....]

Ms. , 5 (September 1976), 36+. [For Colored Girls....]

New Republic, 175 (July 3, 1976), 20-1. [For Colored Girls....]

Newsweek, 87 (June 14, 1976), 99. [For Colored Girls....]

Essence, 11 (August 1980), 21. [Mother Courage....]

New York, 13 (May 26, 1980), 80. [Mother Courage....]

New Yorker, 56 (May 26, 1980), 77. [Mother Courage....]

New York, 11 (Jan. 16, 1978), 58. [A Photograph.]

New Yorker, 53 (Jan. 2, 1978), 48-9. [A Photograph.]

Saturday Review, 5 (Feb. 18, 1978), 42. [A Photograph.]

New York, 12 (July 30, 1979), 57. [Spell #7.]

New Yorker, 55 (July 16, 1979), 73. [Spell #7.]

Newsweek, 94 (July 30, 1979), 65. [Spell #7.]

SHELLEY, ELSA (1905?-)

Plays

Background for the Defense. Unpublished.

Famished Eagle. Unpublished.

Female and Nest. Unpublished.

Fox Hole in the Parlor, A Play in Three Acts. New York: Dramatists Play Service, 1946. Produced Broadway, 1945.

The Game of Conquer. Unpublished.

My Missus Is a Saint. Unpublished.

No Sex for Susan. Unpublished.

Pick Up Girl; A Play in Three Acts. New York: Dramatists Play Service, 1946. Also in: Mantle, Robert B. , ed. Best Plays of 1943-1944. New York: Dodd, Mead, 1944. (Condensation.) Produced Broadway, 1944.

Tomorrow Is a Secret. Unpublished. Produced London, 1952.

VIP. Unpublished.

With a Silk Thread. Unpublished. Produced Broadway, 1950.

Biography

Who's Who in America. 38th ed., 1974-1975. Chicago: Marquis Who's Who, 1974.

Reviews

New Republic, 112 (June 11, 1945), 815+. [Fox Hole....]

New York Times, May 24, 1945, 15:4. [Fox Hole....]

Life, 16 (June 12, 1944), 68-70. [Pick Up Girl.]

New York Times, May 4, 1944, 25:2. [Pick Up Girl.]

New York Times, April 13, 1950, 34:3. [With a Silk Thread.]

New Yorker, 26 (April 22, 1950), 60+. [With a Silk Thread.]

SHORE, VIOLA BROTHERS (1891-1970)

Plays

Fools Rush In. Unpublished. Produced Broadway, 1934.

Is This a Zither? Written with J. Hayden. Prompt book at the
    New York Public Library. Produced White Plains, N.Y., 1935.

New Faces. Written with Nancy Hamilton. Unpublished.
    Produced Broadway, 1934.

Piper Paid. Unpublished. Produced Broadway, 1934.

Stage Struck. Written with John Golden. New York: French, 1930.
    Never produced on the professional stage.

Biography

New York Times, March 31, 1970, 41:3. (Obituary.)

Reviews

New York Times, Dec. 26, 1934, 19:2. [Fools Rush In.]

New York Times, June 11, 1935, 24:3. [Is This a Zither?]

New York Times, March 16, 1934, 24:5. [New Faces.]

Stage, 11 (May 1934), 10-11. [New Faces.]

Time, 23 (March 26, 1934), 36. [New Faces.]

New York Times, Dec. 26, 1934, 19:1. [Piper Paid.]

SKINNER, CORNELIA OTIS (1901-1979)

Plays

Captain Fury. Unpublished. Produced off-Broadway, 1925.

Edna His Wife. Adapted from the novel by Margaret A. Barnes. In: Mantle, Robert B., ed. Best Plays of 1937-1938. New York: Dodd, Mead, 1938. (Condensation.) Produced Broadway, 1938.

Mansion on the Hudson. Unpublished. Produced Broadway, 1935.

One Woman Show. Chicago: Dramatic Publishing, 1974. This is a collection of monologues written and performed by Skinner on tour.

Paris '90. Unpublished. Produced Broadway, 1952.

The Pleasure of His Company. Written with Samuel Taylor. New York: Random House, 1959. Also in: Kronenberger, Louis, ed. Best Plays of 1958-1959. New York: Dodd, Mead, 1959. (Condensation.) Produced Broadway, 1958.

Biography

Contemporary Authors; A Bio-bibliographical Guide to Current Authors and Their Works. Clare D. Kinsman, ed. Vol. 17-20, first revision. Detroit: Gale, 1976.

Current Biography Yearbook 1964. New York: H. W. Wilson, 1965.

Reviews

New York Times, Dec. 8, 1937, 30:3. [Edna His Wife.]

Time, 30 (Dec. 20, 1937), 33-4. [Edna His Wife.]

New York Times, April 3, 1935, 20:4. [Mansion on the Hudson.]

Commonweal, 55 (March 21, 1952), 592. [Paris '90.]

New York Times, March 5, 1952, 33:2. [Paris '90.]

New Yorker, 28 (March 15, 1952), 48. [Paris '90.]

New York Times, Oct. 23, 1958, 36:1. [The Pleasure of His Company.]

New Yorker, 34 (Nov. 1, 1958), 97-8. [The Pleasure of His Company.]

Time, 72 (Nov. 3, 1958), 48+. [The Pleasure of His Company.]

SPEWACK, BELLA (1899-)

Plays

Boy Meets Girl. Written with Sam Spewack. New York: Random House, 1936. Also in: Cerf, Bennett A. Sixteen Famous American Plays. New York: Garden City Publishing, 1941. Produced Broadway, 1935.

Clear All Wires! Written with Sam Spewack. New York: French, 1932. Produced Broadway, 1932.

Festival. Written with Sam Spewack. New York: Dramatists Play Service, 1955. Produced Broadway, 1955.

Golden State. Written with Sam Spewack. New York: Dramatists Play Service, 1951. Produced Broadway, 1950.

Kiss Me Kate. Book by Bella and Sam Spewack. Music and lyrics by Cole Porter. New York: Knopf, 1953. Produced Broadway, 1949.

Leave It to Me. Written with Sam Spewack. Adapted from their plays Clear All Wires. Typescript at the New York Public Library. Produced Broadway, 1938.

Miss Swan Expects. Written with Sam Spewack. Prompt book at the New York Public Library. Produced Broadway, 1939.

My Three Angels. Written with Sam Spewack. Based on La Cuisine des Anges, by Albert Husson. New York: Random House, 1953. Also in: Gassner, John, ed. Twenty Best European Plays on the American Stage. New York: Crown, 1957. Produced Broadway, 1953.

Out West It's Different. Written with Sam Spewack. Unpublished. Produced Princeton, N.J., 1940.

Poppa; A Comedy in Three Acts. Written with Sam Spewack. New York: French, 1929. Produced Broadway, 1928.

Solitaire Man; A Melodrama in Three Acts. Written with Sam Spewack. New York: French, 1934. Never produced on the professional stage.

Spring Song. Written with Sam Spewack. Typescript at the New
York Public Library. Produced Broadway, 1934.

Trousers to Match. Variant title of Miss Swan Expects.

Woman Bites Dog, A Comedy in Three Acts. Written with Sam
Spewack. New York: Dramatists Play Service, 1947. Produced
Broadway, 1946.

Biography

Gould, Jean. Modern American Playwrights. New York: Dodd,
Mead, 1966, pp. 135-40.

Kunitz, Stanley J., and Howard Haycraft, eds. Twentieth
Century Authors; A Biographical Dictionary of Modern
Literature. New York: H. W. Wilson, 1942.

New York Times Biographic Service, 7, 4 (April 1976), 605.

Reviews

New York Times, Nov. 19, 1935, 27:2. [Boy Meets Girl.]

Stage, 13 (January 1936), 2+. [Boy Meets Girl.]

Nation, 135 (Sept. 28, 1932), 290-1. [Clear All Wires!]

New York Times, Sept. 15, 1932, 19:1. [Clear All Wires!]

Theatre Arts, 16 (November 1932), 865+. [Clear All Wires!]

New York Times, Jan. 19, 1955, 22:1. [Festival.]

New Yorker, 30 (Jan. 29, 1955), 46-7. [Festival.]

Time, 65 (Jan. 31, 1955), 71. [Festival.]

New York Times, Nov. 27, 1950, 29:3. [Golden State.]

New Yorker, 26 (Dec. 2, 1950), 82. [Golden State.]

Time, 56 (Dec. 4, 1950), 65. [Golden State.]

Life, 26 (Feb. 7, 1949), 99-100. [Kiss Me Kate.]

New York Times, Jan. 16, 1949, sec. II, 1:1. [Kiss Me Kate.]

Saturday Review, 32 (Jan. 22, 1949), 34-5. [Kiss Me Kate.]

Time, 53 (Jan. 10, 1949), 36+. [Kiss Me Kate.]

Nation, 147 (Nov. 26, 1938), 572-3. [Leave It to Me.]

New York Times, Oct. 23, 1938, sec. IX, 3:5. [Leave It to Me.]

Newsweek, 12 (Nov. 21, 1938), 24. [Leave It to Me.]

New York Times, Feb. 21, 1939, 15:2. [Miss Swan Expects.]

Newsweek, 13 (March 6, 1939), 28. [Miss Swan Expects.]

Life, 34 (May 11, 1953), 101-2. [My Three Angels.]

New Yorker, 29 (March 21, 1953), 64+. [My Three Angels.]

New York Times, Dec. 25, 1928, 31:1. [Poppa.]

Theatre, 49 (April 1929), 46. [Poppa.]

New York Times, Oct. 2, 1934, 18:2. [Spring Song.]

New York Times, April 18, 1946, 21:2. [Woman Bites Dog.]

STANLEY, MARTHA (1879-?)

Plays

The First Mrs. Chiverick; A Comedy in Three Acts. Written with
Adelaide Matthews. New York: French, 1930.

Innocent Anne; A Light Comedy in Four Acts. Written with Adelaide
Matthews. New York: French, 1930.

Let and Sub-Let, A Farce Comedy of Youth. New York: French,
1930. Produced Broadway, 1930.

My Son, A Play in Three Acts. New York: French, 1929. Produced Broadway, 1924.

Nightie Night; A Farce in a Prologue and Three Acts. Written with
Adelaide Matthews. New York: French, 1929. Produced Broadway, 1919.

Puppy Love; A Farcical Comedy in Three Acts.   Written with Adelaide Matthews.   New York: French, 1927.   Produced Broadway,
1925.

Scrambled Wives.   Written with Adelaide Matthews.   Unpublished.
Produced Broadway, 1920.

The Teaser.   Written with Adelaide Matthews.   Unpublished.   Produced Broadway, 1921.

The Wasp's Nest; A Mystery Comedy in Three Acts.   Written with
Adelaide Matthews.   New York: French, 1929.   Produced Broadway, 1927.

Where Innocence Is Bliss, A Light Comedy in Four Acts.   Written
with Adelaide Matthews.   New York: French, 1929.

Biography

Mantle, Robert B.   American Playwrights of Today.   New York:
Dodd, Mead, 1929, pp. 307-8.

Who Was Who in the Theatre: 1912-1976.   Detroit: Gale, 1978.

Reviews

New York Times, May 20, 1930, 32:2.   [Let and Sub-Let.]

Theatre, 52 (July 1930), 42.   [Let and Sub-Let.]

Dramatist, 16 (January 1925), 1244-5.   [My Son.]

New York Times, Sept. 18, 1924, 18:2.   [My Son.]

Forum, 62 (October/November 1919), 500.   [Nightie Night.]

Life, 74 (Sept. 25, 1919), 548.   [Nightie Night.]

New York Times, Sept. 10, 1919, 16:1.   [Nightie Night.]

New York Times, Oct. 4, 1925, sec. IX, 2:1.   [Puppy Love.]

Vogue, 67 (April 1, 1926), 95+.   [Puppy Love.]

New York Times, Aug. 6, 1920, 16:1.   [Scrambled Wives.]

Theatre, 32 (October 1920), 165+.   [Scrambled Wives.]

Nation, 113 (Sept. 3, 1921), 215.   [The Teaser.]

New York Times, July 28, 1921, 8:3.   [The Teaser.]

New York Times, Oct. 26, 1927, 26:3. [The Wasp's Nest.]

STEIN, GERTRUDE (1874-1946)

Plays

Byron a Play. In: Stein, Gertrude. Last Operas and Plays. New
York: Rinehart, 1949. Never produced on the professional stage.

A Circular Play. In: Stein, Gertrude. Selected Operas and Plays
of Gertrude Stein. John M. Brinnin, ed. Pittsburgh: University
of Pittsburgh Press, 1970. Never produced on the professional
stage.

Doctor Faustus Lights the Lights. In: Best One Act Plays of 1949-
1950. M. G. Mayorga, ed. New York: Dodd, Mead, 1950.
Produced off-Broadway, 1951.

An Exercise in Analysis. In: Stein, Gertrude. Last Operas and
Plays. New York: Rinehart, 1949. Never produced on the professional stage.

For the Country Entirely. In: Stein, Gertrude. Selected Operas
and Plays of Gertrude Stein. John M. Brinnin, ed. Pittsburgh:
University of Pittsburgh Press, 1970. Never produced on the
professional stage.

Four Saints in Three Acts; An Opera to Be Sung. Libretto by Ger-
trude Stein. Music by Virgil Thomson. New York: Random
House, 1934. Also in: Stein, Gertrude. Selected Operas and
Plays of Gertrude Stein. John M. Brinnin, ed. Pittsburgh:
University of Pittsburgh Press, 1970. Produced Broadway, 1934.

An Historic Drama in the Memory of Winnie Elliot. In: Stein,
Gertrude. Last Operas and Plays. New York: Rinehart, 1949.
Never produced on the professional stage.

In a Garden. Libretto by Gertrude Stein. Music by M. Kupferman.
In: Stein, Gertrude. The Gertrude Stein First Reader and Three
Other Plays. Dublin: Fridberg, 1946. Produced off-Broadway,
1950.

In Circles. Unpublished. Produced off-Broadway, 1967.

In Savoy; or, Yes Is for a Very Young Man, A Play of the Resist-
ance in France. London: Pushkin, 1946. Produced off-Broadway,
1949.

Ladies Voices. In: Stein, Gertrude. Selected Operas and Plays of Gertrude Stein. John M. Brinnin, ed. Pittsburgh: University of Pittsburgh Press, 1970. Never produced on the professional stage.

Listen to Me. In: Stein, Gertrude. Last Operas and Plays. New York: Rinehart, 1949. Never produced on the professional stage.

Look and Long. In: Stein, Gertrude. The Gertrude Stein First Reader and Three Other Plays. Dublin: Fridberg, 1946. Produced off-Broadway, 1955.

The Maids. In: Stein, Gertrude. The Gertrude Stein First Reader and Three Other Plays. Dublin: Fridberg, 1946. Produced off-Broadway, 1955.

A Manoir. In: Stein, Gertrude. Last Operas and Plays. New York: Rinehart, 1949. Never produced on the professional stage.

The Mother of Us All, An Opera. Libretto by Gertrude Stein. Music by Virgil Thomson. Scenario by Maurice Grosser. New York: Music Press, 1947. Also in: Stein, Gertrude. Last Operas and Plays. New York: Rinehart, 1949. Produced off-Broadway, 1947.

Paisieu. In: Stein, Gertrude. Last Operas and Plays. New York: Rinehart, 1949. Never produced on the professional stage.

Photograph. In: Stein, Gertrude. Last Operas and Plays. New York: Rinehart, 1949. Never produced on the professional stage.

Play. In: Stein, Gertrude. Last Operas and Plays. New York: Rinehart, 1949. Never produced on the professional stage.

A Play Called Not and Now. In: Stein, Gertrude. Last Operas and Plays. New York: Rinehart, 1949. Never produced on the professional stage.

A Play of Pounds. In: Stein, Gertrude. Last Operas and Plays. New York: Rinehart, 1949. Never produced on the professional stage.

Say It with Flowers. In: Stein, Gertrude. Selected Operas and Plays of Gertrude Stein. John M. Brinnin, ed. Pittsburgh: University of Pittsburgh Press, 1970. Never produced on the professional stage.

Short Sentences. In: Stein, Gertrude. Last Operas and Plays. New York: Rinehart, 1949. Never produced on the professional stage.

The Tavern. Unpublished. Produced off-Broadway, 1920.

They Must Be Wedded. To Their Wife. In: Stein, Gertrude. Selected Operas and Plays of Gertrude Stein. John M. Brinnin, ed.
Pittsburgh: University of Pittsburgh Press, 1970. Never produced
on the professional stage.

Third Historic Drama. In: Stein, Gertrude. Last Operas and Plays.
New York: Rinehart, 1949. Never produced on the professional
stage.

Three Sisters Who Are Not Sisters. In: Stein, Gertrude. The Gertrude Stein First Reader and Three Other Plays. Dublin: Fridberg, 1946. Produced off-Broadway, 1955.

Turkey and Bones and Eating and We Liked It. In: Stein, Gertrude.
Selected Operas and Plays of Gertrude Stein. John M. Brinnin,
ed. Pittsburgh: University of Pittsburgh Press, 1970. Never
produced on the professional stage.

What Happened. In: Stein, Gertrude. Selected Operas and Plays
of Gertrude Stein. John M. Brinnin, ed. Pittsburgh: University
of Pittsburgh Press, 1970. Never produced on the professional
stage.

Will He Come Back Better, Second Historic Drama, In the Country.
In: Stein, Gertrude. Last Operas and Plays. New York: Rinehart, 1949. Never produced on the professional stage.

Biography

American Writers: A Collection of Literary Biographies. New York:
Scribner, 1974.

Greenfeld, Howard. Gertrude Stein. New York: Crown, 1973.

Hobhouse, Janet. Everybody Who Was Anybody. New York: Put-
nam, 1975.

Criticism

American Writers: A Collection of Literary Biographies. New York:
Scribner, 1974.

Brinnin, John M. "Introduction." Selected Operas and Plays of
Gertrude Stein. John M. Brinnin, ed. Pittsburgh: University
of Pittsburgh Press, 1970, pp. xi-xviii.

Encyclopedia of World Literature in the 20th Century. New York:
Ungar, 1971.

Hoffman, Michael J. Gertrude Stein. Boston: Twayne, 1976.

Reviews

New York Times, Dec. 3, 1951, 23:4. [Doctor Faustus....]

Nation, 138 (Feb. 28, 1934), 256-7. [Four Saints....]

Theatre Arts, 18 (May 1934), 354-7. [Four Saints....]

Time, 23 (Feb. 19, 1934), 35. [Four Saints....]

New York Times, June 15, 1950, 41:7. [In a Garden.]

Time, 55 (June 26, 1950), 76+. [In a Garden.]

New York Times, Oct. 14, 1967, 12:1. [In Circles.]

New York Times, Nov. 5, 1967, sec. II, 1:7. [In Circles.]

Commonweal, 50 (June 24, 1949), 271. [In Savoy.]

New York Times, June 7, 1949, 27:2. [In Savoy.]

Theatre Arts, 31 (July 1947), 17-8. [The Mother of Us All.]

Time, 49 (May 19, 1947), 47. [The Mother of Us All.]

New York Times, Oct. 10, 1920, sec. VI, 1:1. [The Tavern.]

Outlook, 126 (Dec. 8, 1920), 633. [The Tavern.]

SWADOS, ELIZABETH (1951-)

Plays

Agamemnon. Adapted by Elizabeth Swados and Andrei Serban from the play by Aeschylus. Music by Elizabeth Swados. Unpublished. Produced off-Broadway, 1977.

Alice in Concert. Unpublished. Produced off-Broadway, 1981.

Dispatches. A rock-war musical based on the novel by Michael Herr. Adapted and composed by Elizabeth Swados. Unpublished. Produced off-Broadway, 1979.

Fragments of a Trilogy. Unpublished. Produced at LaMama, New York, 1976.

The Good Woman of Setzuan. Adapted by Elizabeth Swados from the
  play by Bertolt Brecht. Music by Elizabeth Swados. Unpublished.
  Produced at LaMama, New York, 1975.

Haggadah. Unpublished. Produced by the New York Shakespeare
  Festival at the Public Theater, 1980.

Medea. Adapted by Elizabeth Swados and Andrei Serban from the
  play by Euripides. Unpublished. Produced at LaMama, New
  York, 1972.

Nightclub Cantata. A musical revue. Unpublished. Produced at
  Top of the Gate, New York, 1977.

Runaways. New York: Bantam, 1979. Produced Broadway, 1978.

The Sea Gull. Adapted by Jean-Claude van Itallie from the play by
  Chekhov. Music by Elizabeth Swados. Unpublished. Produced
  off-Broadway, 1980.

The Trojan Women. Adapted by Andrei Serban from the play by
  Euripides. Music by Elizabeth Swados. Unpublished. Produced
  at LaMama, New York, 1974.

Wonderland in Concert. Unpublished. Produced off-Broadway, 1979.

Biography

Current Biography Yearbook 1979. New York: H. W. Wilson, 1979.

Gussow, Mel. "Elizabeth Swados--A Runaway Talent." New York
  Times Magazine, March 5, 1978, 18-20+.

New York Times Biographical Edition, 8, 1 (January 1977), 158.

"People Are Talking About...." Vogue, 168 (July 1978), 140-5.

Reviews

Nation, 224 (June 4, 1977), 701. [Agamemnon.]

New York, 14 (Jan. 19, 1981), 38. [Alice in Concert.]

New Yorker, 56 (Jan. 19, 1981), 90. [Alice in Concert.]

Newsweek, 97 (Jan. 19, 1981), 81. [Alice in Concert.]

Nation, 228 (May 12, 1979), 549. [Dispatches.]

New York, 12 (May 7, 1979), 85. [Dispatches.]

New Yorker, 55 (April 30, 1979), 95. [Dispatches.]

New Republic, 180 (May 12, 1979), 25. [Fragments....]

New York Times, Jan. 18, 1976, sec. II, 5:1. [Fragments....]

Nation, 222 (Feb. 14, 1976), 189. [The Good Woman....]

New Republic, 174 (March 13, 1976), 28. [The Good Woman....]

New York Times, Jan. 27, 1976, 28:1. [The Good Woman....]

Nation, 230 (May 3, 1980), 540. [Haggadah.]

New York Times, April 2, 1980, sec. III, 22:4. [Haggadah.]

Saturday Review, 7 (May 1980), 56. [Haggadah.]

Nation, 214 (March 27, 1972), 411. [Medea.]

New Yorker, 47 (Feb. 12, 1972), 69. [Medea.]

Saturday Review, 55 (March 11, 1973), 12-3. [Medea.]

Ms., 5 (June 1977), 18+. [Nightclub Cantata.]

Nation, 224 (Jan. 29, 1977), 124-5. [Nightclub Cantata.]

New Republic, 176 (Feb. 5, 1977), 24+. [Nightclub Cantata.]

Nation, 226 (April 1, 1978), 379. [Runaways.]

New York, 11 (March 27, 1978), 70-1. [Runaways.]

New Yorker, 54 (March 20, 1978), 88. [Runaways.]

Newsweek, 91 (March 27, 1978), 74-5. [Runaways.]

New Republic, 183 (Dec. 6, 1980), 28-9. [The Sea Gull.]

Newsweek, 96 (Nov. 24, 1980), 131. [The Sea Gull.]

Time, 116 (Nov. 24, 1980), 64-5. [The Sea Gull.]

New York Times, Oct. 20, 1974, 64:3. [The Trojan Women.]

Encore, 8 (Feb. 5, 1979), 41. [Wonderland in Concert.]

New Yorker, 54 (Jan. 15, 1979), 89. [Wonderland in Concert.]

TAYLOR, RENEE (193?-)

Plays

Acts of Love and Other Comedies. Written with Joseph Bologna.
Television play produced 1973. Unpublished.

It Had to Be You. Unpublished. Produced Broadway, 1981.

Lovers and Other Strangers. Written with Joseph Bologna. New
York: French, 1969. Also in: Richards, Stanley, ed. Modern
Short Comedies from Broadway and London. New York: Random
House, 1970. Produced Broadway, 1968.

Paradise. Television play produced 1974. Unpublished.

Three for Two. Television play produced 1975. Unpublished.

Biography

Notable Names in the American Theatre. Clifton, N.J.: James T.
White, 1976.

Reviews

New York, 14 (May 25, 1981), 96-7. [It Had to Be You.]

New York Times, May 11, 1981, sec. III, 13:1. [It Had to Be You.]

New Yorker, 57 (May 18, 1981), 143. [It Had to Be You.]

Nation, 207 (Oct. 21, 1968), 412. [Lovers....]

New York Times, Sept. 19, 1968, 63:1. [Lovers....]

New Yorker, 44 (Sept. 28, 1968), 89. [Lovers....]

Time, 92 (Sept. 27, 1968), 66+. [Lovers....]

TERRY, MEGAN (1932-   )

Plays

All Them Women.   Unpublished.   Produced off-Broadway, 1974.

American King's English for Queens.   Unpublished.   Produced Omaha, 1978.

American Wedding Ritual Monitored/Transmitted By the Planet Jupiter.   In: Places: A Journal of the Theatre, 1 (1973).   Never produced on the professional stage.

Approaching Simone.   In: Kriegel, Harriet, ed.   Women in Drama: An Anthology.   New York: New American Library, 1975.   Never produced on the professional stage.

Babes in the Big House.   Unpublished.   Produced Omaha, 1974.

Beach Grass.   Unpublished.   Produced Seattle, 1955.

Brazil Fado.   Unpublished.   Produced Omaha, 1977.

Calm Down Mother.   New York: French, 1966.   Also in: Hatch, James, and V. Sullivan, eds.   Plays By and About Women.   New York: Vintage, 1974.   Produced off-Broadway, 1965.

Changes.   Unpublished.   Produced at LaMama, New York, 1968.

Comings and Goings.   In: Terry, Megan.   Viet Rock; Comings and Goings; Keep Tightly Closed in a Cool Dry Place; The Gloaming, Oh My Darling: Four Plays.   New York: Simon & Schuster, 1967.   Produced off-Broadway, 1966.

Couplings and Groupings.   New York: Pantheon, 1973.   Never produced on the professional stage.

The Dirt Boat.   Television play produced 1955.   Unpublished.

Eat at Joe's.   Unpublished.   Produced off-Broadway, 1963.

Ex-Miss Copper Queen on a Set of Pills.   New York: French, 1970. Also in: Ballet, Arthur H., ed.   Playwrights for Tomorrow. Vol. 1.   Minneapolis: University of Minnesota Press, 1966. Never produced on the professional stage.

The Gloaming, Oh My Darling.   In: The Norton Introduction to Literature.   Carl E. Bain, ed.   New York: Norton, 1973.   Produced Minneapolis, 1965.

Go Out and Move the Car. Unpublished. Produced Seattle, 1955.

Grooving. Unpublished. Produced off-Broadway, 1972.

Hothouse. New York: French, 1975. Produced off-Broadway, 1975.

Jack-Jack. Unpublished. Produced Minneapolis, 1968.

Keep Tightly Closed in a Cool Dry Place. In: Tulane Drama Review, 10 (Summer 1966), 177-200. Produced off-Broadway, 1965.

The Key Is on the Bottom. Unpublished. Produced Los Angeles, 1968.

Lady Rose's Brazil Hide Out. Unpublished. Produced Omaha, 1977.

Magic Realists. In: Richards, Stanley, ed. Best One Act Plays of 1968. Radnor, Pa.: Chilton, 1969. Produced off-Broadway, 1966.

Massachusetts Trust. In: Poland, Albert, and Bruce Mailman, eds. The Off Off Broadway Book. Indianapolis: Bobbs-Merrill, 1972. Produced Waltham, Mass., 1968.

Megan Terry's Home: or Future Soap. New York: French, 1974. Television play produced 1968. Produced London under the title As Theatre, 1974.

Narco Linguini Bust. Unpublished. Produced Omaha, 1974.

New York Comedy: Two. Unpublished. Produced Saratoga, N.Y., 1961.

Nightwalk. Indianapolis: Bobbs-Merrill, 1975. Produced off-Broadway, 1973.

100,001 Horror Stories of the Plains. Unpublished. Produced Omaha, 1976.

One More Little Drinkie. Television play produced 1969. In: Terry, Megan. Three One-Act Plays. New York: French, 1971.

People vs. Ranchman. In: Terry, Megan. The People vs. Ranchman and Ex-Miss Copper Queen on a Set of Pills: Two Plays. New York: Dramatists Play Service, 1968. Produced Minneapolis, 1967.

Pioneer. In: Terry, Megan. Pioneer and Pro-Game. New York: Ragnarok, 1975. Produced off-Broadway, 1974.

Pro-Game. In: Terry, Megan. Pioneer and Pro-Game. New York: Ragnarok, 1975. Produced off-Broadway, 1974.

St. Hydro Clemency. Unpublished. Never produced on the professional stage.

Sanibel and Captiva. In: Terry, Megan. Three One-Act Plays.
New York: French, 1971. Radio broadcast, 1968.

The Tommy Allen Show. In: Scripts, 2 (December 1971), 36-61.
Never produced on the professional stage.

Viet Rock. In: Tulane Drama Review, 11 (Fall 1966), 196-227.
Produced off-Broadway, 1966.

We Can Feed Everybody Here. Unpublished. Produced off-Broadway,
1974.

When My Girlfriend Was Still All Flowers. Unpublished. Produced
off-Broadway, 1963.

Willie-Willa-Bill's Dope Garden. New York: Ragnarok, 1977.
Never produced on the professional stage.

Biography

Contemporary Authors; A Bio-bibliographical Guide to Current Authors and Their Works. Frances C. Locher, ed. Vol. 77-80.
Detroit: Gale, 1979.

Contemporary Dramatists. James Vinson, ed. New York: St.
Martin, 1973.

Notable Names in the American Theatre. Clifton, N.J.: James T.
White, 1976.

Reviews

America, 122 (June 6, 1970), 612. [Approaching Simone.]

New York Times, March 9, 1970, 43:1. [Approaching Simone.]

Newsweek, 75 (March 16, 1970), 64. [Approaching Simone.]

New York Times, Oct. 24, 1974, 49:1. [Hothouse.]

Saturday Review, 1 (April 6, 1974), 48. [Hothouse.]

New York Times, June 23, 1968, 74:5. [Jack-Jack.]

New York Times, Sept. 1, 1968, sec. II, 1:1. [Massachusetts
Trust.]

New York Times, Oct. 28, 1968, 56:1. [People vs. Ranchman.]

New Yorker, 44 (Nov. 9, 1968), 116+. [People vs. Ranchman.]

Newsweek, 72 (Nov. 11, 1968), 121. [People vs. Ranchman.]

Time, 92 (Nov. 8, 1968), 94. [People vs. Ranchman.]

Nation, 203 (Nov. 28, 1966), 587+. [Viet Rock.]

New York Times, Oct. 12, 1966, 34:1. [Viet Rock.]

Newsweek, 68 (Nov. 21, 1966), 114. [Viet Rock.]

Time, 88 (Oct. 21, 1966), 61. [Viet Rock.]

TONKONOGY, GERTRUDE (1908-)

Plays

Three-Cornered Moon; A Comedy in Three Acts. New York: French, 1933. Produced Broadway, 1933.

Town House. Written with George Kaufman. Based on New Yorker stories by John Cheever. Unpublished. Produced Broadway, 1948.

Biography

Contemporary Authors; A Bio-bibliographical Guide to Current Authors and Their Works. Christine Nasso, ed. Vol. 21-24, first revision. Detroit: Gale, 1977.

Mantle, Robert B. Contemporary American Playwrights. New York: Dodd, Mead, 1938, p. 207.

"Two of the Authors." New York Times, March 26, 1933, sec. IX, 2:1.

Reviews

New York Times, March 17, 1933, 20:6. [Three-Cornered Moon.]

Time, 21 (March 27, 1933), 33. [Three-Cornered Moon.]

Vogue, 81 (May 15, 1933), 59+. [Three-Cornered Moon.]

New Republic, 119 (Oct. 11, 1948), 30. [Town House.]

New York Times, Sept. 24, 1948, 31:2. [Town House.]

Newsweek, 32 (Oct. 4, 1948), 77. [Town House.]

TREADWELL, SOPHIE (1890-1970)

Plays

Gringo. Unpublished. Produced Broadway, 1922.

Hope for a Harvest. New York: French, 1942. Also in: Mantle,
Robert B., ed. Best Plays of 1941-1942. New York: Dodd,
Mead, 1942. (Condensation.) Produced Broadway, 1941.

Intimations for Saxophone; A Play in Four Acts. Typescript at the
New York Public Library.

Ladies Leave. Unpublished. Produced Broadway, 1929.

The Last Are First. Typescript at the New York Public Library.

The Life Machine. Unpublished. Produced London, 1931.

Lone Valley. Unpublished. Produced Broadway, 1933.

Loney Lee. Unpublished. Produced Atlantic City, N.J., 1923.

Machinal. Typescript at the New York Public Library. In: Gass-
ner, John, ed. Twenty-Five Best Plays of the Modern American
Theatre: Early Series. New York: Crown, 1949. Produced
Broadway, 1928.

O Nightingale. Unpublished. Produced Broadway, 1925.

Plumes in the Dust. Typescript at the New York Public Library.
Produced Broadway, 1936.

Poe; a Play. Typescript at the New York Public Library.

Biography

Mantle, Robert B. Contemporary American Playwrights. New York:
Dodd, Mead, 1938, p. 326.

New York Times, March 14, 1970, 31:2. (Obituary.)

Ross, Ishbel. Ladies of the Press. New York: Harper, 1936, pp. 583-5.

Reviews

Bookman, 56 (February 1923), 749-50. [Gringo.]

New York Times, Dec. 15, 1922, 26:3. [Gringo.]

Nation, 153 (Dec. 13, 1941), 621. [Hope for a Harvest.]

New York Times, Nov. 27, 1941, 28:2. [Hope for a Harvest.]

Theatre Arts, 26 (January 1942), 5+. [Hope for a Harvest.]

New York Times, Oct. 2, 1929, 28:3. [Ladies Leave.]

Outlook, 153 (Oct. 16, 1929), 272. [Ladies Leave.]

Theatre, 50 (December 1929), 68. [Ladies Leave.]

London News, 179 (Aug. 15, 1931), 272. [The Life Machine.]

New Statesman, 2 (July 25, 1931), 110. [The Life Machine.]

New York Times, March 11, 1933, 18:6. [Lone Valley.]

New York Times, Nov. 11, 1923, sec. VIII, 2:6. [Loney Lee.]

American Mercury, 15 (November 1928), 376-7. [Machinal.]

New York Times, Sept. 16, 1928, sec. IX, 1:1. [Machinal.]

Theatre, 48 (November 1928), 46-7. [Machinal.]

New York Times, April 16, 1925, 25:2. [O Nightingale.]

New Republic, 89 (Nov. 25, 1936), 116. [Plumes in the Dust.]

New York Times, Nov. 7, 1936, 14:2. [Plumes in the Dust.]

Newsweek, 8 (Nov. 14, 1936), 58+. [Plumes in the Dust.]

UNGER, GLADYS BUCHANAN (1885-1940)

Plays

African Vineyard. Written with Walter Armitage. Typewritten
  prompt book at the New York Public Library. Produced New
  Orleans, 1940.

Beau Brummel; An Operetta in Two Acts. Libretto by Gladys Unger.
  Lyrics by Edward Elliescu. Based on Clyde Fitch's play. Type-
  script without music at the New York Public Library. Produced
  St. Louis, 1933.

Betty. Written with F. Lonsdale, A. Ross, P. Rubens. Unpublished. Produced Broadway, 1933.

The Business Widow; A Comedy in Three Acts. New York: Co-
  National Plays, 1923. Produced Broadway, 1923.

The Chenerys. Adapted by Gladys Unger from Les Fresnay, by F.
  Vandereni. Unpublished. Never produced on the professional
  stage.

Cross Your Heart; A Modern Comedy in Three Acts. Written with
  M. Burke. Typescript at the New York Public Library.

The Demi-Reps; A Play in Three Acts and Epilogue. Written
  Stuart Walker. Based on Harriette Wilson's memoirs. Typescript at the New York Public Library.

Double Exposures; An Original Comedy in Three Acts. New York:
  Rialto Bureau, 1928(?).

Edmund Kean. Written 1903. Unpublished. Never produced on the
  professional stage.

Experience Unnecessary. Unpublished. Produced Broadway, 1931.

The Fair Circassian. Unpublished. Produced Broadway, 1921.

The Goldfish; A Comedy of Many Manners in Three Acts. Freely
  adapted from the French of Armont and Gerbiden. New York:
  Co-National Plays, 1922(?). Produced Broadway, 1922.

In an Arab Garden. Written 1908. Unpublished. Never produced
  on the professional stage.

Inconstant George. Adapted by Gladys Unger from the French of
  R. de Flers and A. de Caillavet. Unpublished. Produced Broadway, 1909.

Ladies of Creation; A Modern Comedy in Three Acts. New York:
French, 1932. Produced Broadway, 1931.

Lemonade Boy. Written 1906. Unpublished. Produced New York,
1906(?).

London Pride. Written with A. Neil Lyons. Unpublished. Produced London, 1916.

Love Habit. Adapted by Gladys Unger from the farce by L. Verneuil. Unpublished. Produced Broadway, 1923.

Love Watches. Unpublished. Produced Broadway, 1908.

The Lovely Lady. Book by Gladys Unger and Cyrus Wood. Music
by D. Stamper and H. Levey. Lyrics by Cyrus Wood. Based
on the French Déjeuner de Soleil. Unpublished. Produced
Broadway, 1927.

The Madcap. Adapted by Gladys Unger and G. Purcell from the
French of R. Gignoux and J. Thery. Music by Maurice Rubens.
Unpublished. Produced Broadway, 1928.

The Marionettes. Play by P. Wolff. Adapted by Gladys Unger.
Unpublished. Produced Broadway, 1911.

The Marriage Market. Written by M. Brody and F. Martos.
Adapted for the English stage by Gladys Unger. Unpublished.
Produced Broadway and London, 1913.

The Merry Countess. Adapted by Gladys Unger from J. Strauss's
Die Fledermaus. Unpublished. Produced Broadway, 1912.

The Monkey Talks. Adapted by Gladys Unger from the work by R.
Fauchois. Unpublished. Produced Broadway, 1925.

A Night in Athens. Based on the French of André de Badet. Typescript at the New York Public Library.

Nightbirds. Variant title of The Merry Countess.

Nona. Unpublished. Produced Broadway, 1932.

Our Mr. Hepplewhite; A Comedy in Three Acts. New York: French,
1919. Produced London, 1919; Broadway, 1920.

The Refugee. Typescript at the New York Public Library.

Richard Brinsley Sheridan. Typescript at the New York Public Library. Produced London, 1904.

The Son and Heir; or, The English. New York: French, 1913.
Produced London, 1913.

Starlight. Typescript at the New York Public Library. Produced Broadway, 1925.

Stolen Fruit. Unpublished. Produced Broadway, 1925.

Striking. Written with P. Rubens. Unpublished. Produced London, 1915.

The Sultan Complex. Written with Walter Armitage. ©1930. Typescript at the New York Public Library.

Sunshine of the World. Operetta by Gladys Unger, K. K. Ardaschir, and C. Cuvillier. Unpublished. Produced London, 1920.

Top Hole. Book by E. Conrad and G. Dill; revised by Gladys Unger. Music by J. Gorney. Lyrics by O. Murphy. Unpublished. Produced Broadway, 1924.

Toto. Libretto by Gladys Unger. Music by A. Joyce and M. Morgan. Lyrics by A. Anderson. Piano-vocal score published, London: Ascherberg, Hopwood, 1916. Produced London, 1916.

$25 an Hour. Written with L. Georgie. Typewritten copy at the Library of Congress. Produced Broadway, 1933.

Two Girls Wanted; A Play in Three Acts. New York: French, 1926. Produced Broadway, 1926.

The Virgin of Bethulia. Unpublished. Produced Broadway, 1925.

The Werewolf. Translated by Gladys Unger from the play by R. Lother. Unpublished. Produced Broadway, 1924.

Biography

Mantle, Robert B. American Playwrights of Today. New York: Dodd, Mead, 1929, pp. 310-1.

New York Times, May 26, 1940, 35:3. (Obituary.)

Who Was Who in the Theatre: 1912-1976. Detroit: Gale, 1978.

Reviews

Green Book, 16 (December 1916), 976+. [Betty.]

Opera, 3 (November 1916), 26-7. [Betty.]

Theatre, 24 (November 1916), 284. [Betty.]

New York Times, Dec. 11, 1923, 27:1. [The Business Widow.]

Theatre, 39 (February 1924), 19+. [The Business Widow.]

New York Times, Dec. 31, 1931, 16:2. [Experience Unnecessary.]

New York Times, Dec. 7, 1921, 22:3. [The Fair Circassian.]

Bookman, 55 (June 1922), 390. [The Goldfish.]

Life, 79 (May 4, 1922), 18. [The Goldfish.]

New York Times, April 18, 1922, 15:3. [The Goldfish.]

Dramatist, 1 (April 1910), 49-50. [Inconstant George.]

Forum, 42 (November 1909), 439. [Inconstant George.]

New Republic, 68 (Sept. 23, 1931), 154-5. [Ladies of Creation.]

New York Times, Sept. 9, 1931, 25:1. [Ladies of Creation.]

London News, 149 (Dec. 16, 1916), 752. [London Pride.]

The Times (London), Dec. 7, 1916, p. 11, col. C. [London Pride.]

New York Times, March 15, 1923, 17:1. [Love Habit.]

Theatre, 37 (May 1923), 15. [Love Habit.]

New York Times, Oct. 4, 1908, pt. 6, 2:5. [Love Watches.]

New York Times, Dec. 30, 1927, 22:1. [The Lovely Lady.]

Theatre, 47 (March 1928), 56+. [The Lovely Lady.]

New York Times, Feb. 1, 1928, 31:2. [Madcap.]

Theatre, 47 (May 1927), 41. [Madcap.]

Dramatist, 3 (April 1912), 236-7. [Marionettes.]

Theatre, 15 (January 1912), 3+. [The Marionettes.]

Green Book, 10 (December 1913), 966-7. [The Marriage Market.]

New York Times, Sept. 23, 1913, p. 11. [The Marriage Market.]

Green Book, 8 (November 1912), 801-2. [The Merry Countess.]

Theatre, 16 (October 1912), 99+. [The Merry Countess.]

New York Times, Dec. 29, 1925, 20:1. [The Monkey Talks.]

Theatre, 43 (March 1926), 13+. [The Monkey Talks.]

New Outlook, 161 (November 1932), 46. [Nona.]

New York Times, Oct. 5, 1932, 26:4. [Nona.]

London News, 154 (April 12, 1919), 538. [Our Mr. Hepplewhite.]

The Times (London), April 4, 1919, p. 14, col. D. [Our Mr. Hepplewhite.]

British Review, 1 (March 1913), 246-53. [The Son and Heir.]

Saturday Review, 115 (Feb. 8, 1913), 170-1. [The Son and Heir.]

American Mercury, 5 (May 1925), 120. [Starlight.]

New York Times, March 4, 1925, 17:2. [Starlight.]

Dramatist, 17 (July 1926), 1309-10. [Stolen Fruit.]

New York Times, Oct. 8, 1925, 31:4. [Stolen Fruit.]

London News, 146 (May 15, 1915), 614. [Striking.]

The Times (London), May 6, 1915, p. 11, col. E. [Striking.]

London News, 156 (Feb. 28, 1920), 350. [Sunshine....]

The Times (London), Feb. 19, 1920, p. 12, col. B. [Sunshine....]

New York Times, Sept. 2, 1924, 22:3. [Top Hole.]

Theatre, 40 (November 1924), 72. [Top Hole.]

London News, 148 (April 29, 1916), 546. [Toto.]

New Outlook, 161 (June 1933), 49. [$25 an Hour.]

New York Times, May 11, 1933, 14:4. [$25 an Hour.]

Life, 89 (June 16, 1927), 19. [Two Girls....]

New York Times, Sept. 10, 1926, 25:3. [Two Girls....]

Theatre, 44 (November 1926), 68+. [Two Girls....]

New York Times, Feb. 24, 1925, 17:2. [The Virgin....]

American Mercury, 3 (October 1924), 247-8. [The Werewolf.]

Life, 84 (Sept. 11, 1924), 18. [The Werewolf.]

New York Times, Aug. 26, 1924, 6:1. [The Werewolf.]

VOLLMER, LULA (1898-1955)

Plays

Dearly Beloved. Typescript at the New York Public Library. Produced Newark, N. J. , 1946.

The Dunce Boy. Typescript at the New York Public Library. Produced Broadway, 1925.

Green Stones. Written with G. G. Dawson-Scott. Unpublished. Never produced on the professional stage.

The Hill Between. New York: Longmans, Green, 1939. Produced Broadway, 1938.

The Honor and the Glory. Typescript at the New York Public Library.

In a Nutshell. Typescript at the New York Public Library. Produced Baltimore, 1937.

Moonshine and Honeysuckle. New York: French, 1934. Produced Boston, 1933.

The Sentinels. Unpublished. Produced Broadway, 1931.

The Shame Woman. Typescript at the New York Public Library. Produced Greenwich Village, N. Y. , 1923.

She Put Out to Go. Typescript at the New York Public Library.

Sun-up. New York: Brentano, 1924. Also in: Quinn, Arthur H. , ed. Representative American Plays from 1767 to the Present Day. 7th ed. New York: Appleton-Century-Crofts, 1953. Produced Provincetown Playhouse, New York, 1923.

Trigger. Unpublished. Produced Broadway, 1927.

Troyka. Adapted from the Hungarian of I. Fazekas. Unpublished. Produced Broadway, 1930.

Biography

Mantle, Robert B. American Playwrights of Today. New York: Dodd, Mead, 1929, pp. 192-4.

New York Times, May 13, 1955, 31:2. (Obituary.)

Who Was Who in the Theatre: 1912-1976. Detroit: Gale, 1978.

Reviews

American Mercury, 5 (June 1925), 247. [The Dunce Boy.]

New York Times, April 4, 1925, 20:2. [The Dunce Boy.]

New York Times, March 12, 1938, 12:5. [Hill Between.]

One Act Play Magazine, 1 (April 1938), 1120. [The Hill Between.]

Time, 31 (March 21, 1938), 30. [The Hill Between.]

New York Times, Dec. 26, 1931, 15:1. [The Sentinels.]

Outlook, 160 (Jan. 6, 1932), 22. [The Sentinels.]

Nation, 117 (Nov. 21, 1923), 587-8. [The Shame Woman.]

New York Times, Oct. 17, 1923, 14:1. [The Shame Woman.]

Current Opinion, 75 (December 1923), 701+. [Sun-up.]

New York Times, Aug. 14, 1925, 13:4. [Sun-up.]

New York Times, Sept. 18, 1928, 34:6. [Sun-up.]

Theatre, 38 (July 1923), 16. [Sun-up.]

Life, 90 (Dec. 22, 1927), 19. [Trigger.]

New York Times, Dec. 7, 1927, 32:1. [Trigger.]

Theatre, 47 (February 1928), 39-40. [Trigger.]

Life, 95 (April 18, 1930), 18. [Troyka.]

New York Times, April 2, 1930, 32:6. [Troyka.]

Theatre, 51 (May 1930), 70+. [Troyka.]

WASSERSTEIN, WENDY (1950-   )

Plays

Any Woman Can't.   Written 1971.   Unpublished.   Never produced on
the professional stage.

Isn't It Romantic?   Unpublished.   Produced off-Broadway, 1981.

Uncommon Women and Others.   New York: Dramatists Play Service,
1978.   Produced off-Broadway, 1977.

Biography

New York Times Biographical Service, 12, 5 (May 1981), 759.

Reviews

New York, 14 (June 29, 1981), 36.   [Isn't It Romantic?]

New Yorker, 57 (June 22, 1981), 87.   [Isn't It Romantic?]

Nation, 225 (Dec. 17, 1977), 667-8.   [Uncommon Women.]

New York, 10 (Dec. 12, 1977), 103.   [Uncommon Women....]

New Yorker, 53 (Dec. 5, 1977), 115.   [Uncommon Women....]

WATKINS, MAURINE DALLAS (1900-1968)

Plays

Chicago.   New York: Knopf, 1927.   Also in: Mantle, Robert B.,
ed.   Best Plays of 1926-1927.   New York: Dodd, Mead, 1927.
(Condensation.)   Produced Broadway, 1926.

Gesture in Three Acts.   ©1926.   Typewritten copy at the Library
of Congress.   Never produced on the professional stage.

Revelry.   Based on the novel by S. H. Adams.   Unpublished.   Produced Broadway, 1927.

Biography

Mantle, Robert B. American Playwrights of Today. New York: Dodd, Mead, 1929, pp. 201-4.

Reviews

American Mercury, 10 (March 1927), 375-6. [Chicago.]

Dramatist, 18 (January 1927), 1329-30. [Chicago.]

Life, 89 (Jan. 20, 1927), 19. [Chicago.]

New York Times, Dec. 31, 1926, 11:1. [Chicago.]

American Mercury, 12 (November 1927), 376-8. [Revelry.]

Life, 90 (Sept. 29, 1927), 19. [Revelry.]

New York Times, Sept. 13, 1927, 37:1. [Revelry.]

WEST, MAE (1892-1980)

Plays

Babe Gordon. Variant title of Constant Sinner.

Catherine Was Great. Unpublished. Produced Broadway, 1944.

Constant Sinner. Based on her novel published in 1931 by Macauley; (reprinted New York: Sheridan House, 1949). Produced Broadway, 1931.

Diamond Lil. Play unpublished. Novel published by Macauley, 1932. Produced Broadway, 1928.

Pleasure Man. Play unpublished. Novel published by Dell, 1975. Produced Broadway, 1928.

Wicked Age. Unpublished. Produced Broadway, 1927.

Biography

Biographical Encyclopedia and Who's Who of the American Theatre. Walter Rigdon, ed. New York: Heineman, 1966.

Clarke, G. "She Was What She Was." Time, 116 (Dec. 1, 1980), 80. (Obituary.)

Current Biography Yearbook 1967. New York: H. W. Wilson, 1967.

West, Mae. Goodness Had Nothing to Do with It; An Autobiography. New York: Prentice-Hall, 1959.

Reviews

Life, 17 (Aug. 21, 1944), 71-2. [Catherine Was Great.]

New York Times, Aug. 3, 1944, 16:1. [Catherine Was Great.]

Theatre Arts, 28 (October 1944), 575. [Catherine Was Great.]

Nation, 133 (Sept. 30, 1931), 344. [Constant Sinner.]

New York Times, Aug. 30, 1931, sec. VIII, 1:6. [Constant Sinner.]

New Republic, 55 (June 27, 1928), 145-6. [Diamond Lil.]

New York Times, April 10, 1928, 32:1. [Diamond Lil.]

Theatre Arts, 12 (June 1928), 394. [Diamond Lil.]

Life, 92 (Oct. 19, 1928), 19. [Pleasure Man.]

New York Times, Oct. 2, 1928, 34:7. [Pleasure Man.]

Dial, 84 (January 1928), 82-3. [Wicked Age.]

New York Times, Nov. 5, 1927, 16:6. [Wicked Age.]

YANKOWITZ, SUSAN (1941-)

Plays

Acts of Love. Unpublished. Produced Atlanta, 1973.

The American Piece. Unpublished. Produced Los Angeles.

Basics. Unpublished. Produced Brooklyn Academy of Music, New York.

Boxes. In: Ballet, Arthur H. , ed. Playwrights for Tomorrow. Vol. II. Minneapolis: University of Minnesota Press, 1973-75. Produced Berkeley, Calif. , 1972.

The Cage. Unpublished. Produced off-Broadway.

Ha-Ha Play. In: Scripts, 1 (October 1972), 81-92. Produced off-Broadway, 1970.

The Lamb. Unpublished. Produced off-Broadway, 1970.

Nightmare. Unpublished. Produced by the Yale University Theatre, 1967.

Positions. Unpublished. Produced off-Broadway, 1972.

Qui Est Anna Marks? Unpublished. Produced Paris, 1979.

Sideshow. Unpublished. Produced by the National Theater of the Deaf on tour.

Slaughterhouse Play. In: Hoffman, William M. , ed. New American Plays. Vol. 4. New York: Hill & Wang, 1971. Produced off-Broadway, 1971.

Still Life. Unpublished. Produced off-Broadway, 1976.

Terminal. In: Scripts, 1 (November 1971), 17-45. Also in: Open Theatre: Three Works. New York: Drama Book Specialists, 1974. Produced off-Broadway, 1970.

That Old Rock-A-Bye. Unpublished. Produced off-Broadway, 1968.

Transplant. Unpublished. Produced Omaha, 1971.

True Romance. Unpublished. Produced Los Angeles, 1978.

Who Done It. Written 1979. Unpublished.

Wooden Nickels. Unpublished. Produced off-Broadway, 1973.

Biography

Contemporary Authors; A Bio-bibliographical Guide to Current Writers. Ann Evory, ed. New revision series. Vol. 1. Detroit: Gale, 1981.

Contemporary Dramatists. James Vinson, ed. New York: St. Martin, 1977.

Reviews

Nation, 210 (June 22, 1970), 765-6. [Terminal.]

New York Times, May 24, 1970, sec. II, 3:1. [Terminal.]

Newsweek, 75 (May 4, 1970), 89. [Terminal.]

Saturday Review, 53 (May 2, 1970), 12. [Terminal.]

YOUNG, RIDA JOHNSON (1876-1926)

Plays

Barbara's Dilemma, A Monolog Sketch. New York: Witmark, 1906.
    Never produced on the professional stage.

Barry of Ballymore. Unpublished. Produced Academy of Music,
    New York, 1911.

Boys of Company B. New York: Rosenfield, 1907. Produced
    Broadway, 1907.

Brown of Harvard. New York: French, 1909. Produced Broadway,
    1906.

Buried Treasure. Variant title of Captain Kidd, Jr.

Captain Kidd, Jr. New York: French, 1920. Produced Broadway,
    1916.

Chatterton, A Dramatic Monolog. New York, 1906. Never produced
    on the professional stage.

Cock o' the Roost. Unpublished. Produced Broadway, 1924.

Dream Girl. Written with H. Atteridge. Music by Victor Herbert.
    New York: Harms, 1924. Produced Broadway, 1924.

The Front Seat. Unpublished. Produced Washington, D. C., 1921.

The Girl and the Pennant; A Baseball Comedy in Three Acts. New
    York: French, 1917. Produced Broadway, 1913.

Glorious Betsy. Unpublished. Produced Broadway, 1908.

Her Soldier Boy. Adapted from a play by V. Leon. Music by E. Kalman and S. Romberg. New York: Schirmer, 1916. (Selections.) Produced Broadway, 1916.

His Little Widows. Written with W. C. Duncan and W. Schroeder. Unpublished. Produced Broadway, 1917.

Isle o' Dreams. Unpublished. Produced Grand Opera House, New York, 1913.

John Clayton, Actor; A Play in One Act. New York: Witmark, 1906. Never produced on the professional stage.

Lady Luxury. Written with W. Schroeder. Unpublished. Produced Broadway, 1914.

Lancers. Unpublished. Produced Broadway, 1907.

Little Old New York; A Comedy in Four Acts. New York: French, 1828. Produced Broadway, 1920.

Little Simplicity. Written with A. Barratt. Unpublished. Produced Broadway, 1918.

Lot 79. Unpublished. Produced London, 1918.

Lottery Man; A Comedy in Three Acts. New York: French, 1924. Produced Broadway, 1909.

Macushla. Typescript at the New York Public Library. Produced Grand Opera House, New York, 1912; Broadway, 1920.

Maytime. Written with Sigmund Romberg. Piano-vocal score. New York: Schirmer, 1917. Produced Broadway, 1917.

Naughty Marietta; A Comic Opera. Written with Victor Herbert. New York: Witmark, 1910. Produced Broadway, 1910.

Next! Typescript at the New York Public Library. Produced Broadway, 1911.

The Rabbit's Foot. Unpublished. Produced Broadway, 1924.

Ragged Robin. Written with R. Olcott. Unpublished. Produced Academy of Music, New York, 1910.

The Red Petticoat. Written with P. West and J. D. Kern. Unpublished. Produced Broadway, 1912.

Shameen Dhu. Unpublished. Produced Grand Opera House, New York, 1914.

Soldier Boy. Written with E. Wallace and F. Chappelle. Music by S. Romberg. Unpublished. Produced Broadway, 1918.

Some Time; A Musical Romance in Two Acts.   Written with R.
   Friml. New York: Schirmer, 1946. Produced Broadway, 1918.

A Wise Child; A Play in Three Acts.   Typescript at the New York
   Public Library.

Biography

Bennett, H. C. "The Woman Who Wrote Mother Machree." American Magazine, 90 (December 1920), 34-5.

Pierce, Lucy F. "Rida Johnson Young." Green Book, 7 (May
   1912), 1062-3.

Who Was Who in the Theatre: 1912-1976. Detroit: Gale, 1978.

Reviews

New York Dramatic Mirror, 65 (Feb. 1, 1911), 7. [Barry of Ballymore.]

New York Times, Jan. 31, 1911, 10:2. [Barry of Ballymore.]

Theatre, 7 (May 1907), 115-6. [Boys of Company B.]

New York Times, Feb. 27, 1906, 9:1. [Brown of Harvard.]

Theatre, 6 (April 1906), 87+. [Brown of Harvard.]

Dramatist, 8 (October 1916), 735-6. [Captain Kidd, Jr.]

Green Book, 17 (February 1917), 203-5. [Captain Kidd, Jr.]

New York Times, Nov. 14, 1916, 8:4. [Captain Kidd, Jr.]

New York Times, Oct. 14, 1924, 23:1. [Cock o' the Roost.]

New York Times, Aug. 21, 1924, 12:2. [Dream Girl.]

Theatre, 39 (October 1924), 16. [Dream Girl.]

New York Times, May 22, 1921, sec. VI, 1:6. [The Front Seat.]

Life, 62 (Nov. 6, 1913), 791. [Girl and the Pennant.]

New York Times, Sept. 8, 1908, 9:1. [Glorious Betsy.]

Theatre, 25 (January 1917), 24. [Her Soldier Boy.]

Green Book, 18 (July 1917), 4&. [His Little Widows.]

New York Times, May 1, 1917, 11:1. [His Little Widows.]

Theatre, 25 (June 1917), 340+. [His Little Widows.]

Green Book, 13 (March 1915), 574. [Lady Luxury.]

Nation, 99 (Dec. 31, 1914), 783. [Lady Luxury.]

New York Times, Dec. 26, 1914, 7:3. [Lady Luxury.]

Life, 76 (Sept. 30, 1920), 583. [Little Old New York.]

New York Times, Sept. 9, 1920, 9:2. [Little Old New York.]

New York Times, Nov. 5, 1918, 11:3. [Little Simplicity.]

Theatre, 28 (December 1918), 347. [Little Simplicity.]

London News, 152 (April 27, 1928), 504. [Lot 79.]

Forum, 43 (February 1920), 184-5. [Lottery Man.]

New York Times, Dec. 7, 1909, 7:2. [Lottery Man.]

New York Times, May 18, 1920, 9:3. [Macushla.]

Theatre, 31 (June 1920), 527. [Macushla.]

Green Book, 20 (August 1918), 202+. [Maytime.]

Life, 70 (Sept. 6, 1917), 283. [Maytime.]

New York Times, Aug. 17, 1917, 7:1. [Maytime.]

Munsey, 44 (February 1911), 707. [Naughty Marietta.]

New York Times, Oct. 22, 1929, 26:2. [Naughty Marietta.]

Theatre, 12 (December 1910), 265-6. [Naughty Marietta.]

New York Dramatic Mirror, 66 (Oct. 4, 1911), 10. [Next!]

New York Times, Oct. 1, 1911, 13:1. [Next!]

New York Times, April 27, 1924, sec. VIII, 2:3. [The Rabbit's Foot.]

New York Dramatic Mirror, 63 (Feb. 5, 1910), 7. [Ragged Robin.]

Green Book, 9 (January 1913), 183-4. [The Red Petticoat.]

Munsey, 48 (January 1913), 683-4. [The Red Petticoat.]

New York Dramatic Mirror, 71 (Feb. 4, 1914), 7. [Shameen Dhu.]

New York Times, Feb. 3 1914, 11:4. [Shameen Dhu.]

New York Times, Oct. 5, 1918, 11:1. [Some Time.]

Theatre, 28 (December 1918), 346. [Some Time.]